The Books of Light

The Books of Light
Angelic Peace and Healing

Anita Colussi-Zanon

ISBN (book) – 978-1-7753704-0-6

ISBN (electronic book) – 978-1-7753704-1-3

ISBN (audiobook) – 978-1-7753704-2-0

Some characters and events in this book are fictitious. Any similarity to real persons, living or dead, is coincidental and not intended by the author.

Neither the publisher nor the author are engaged in rendering professional advice or services to the individual reader. The ideas, procedures, and suggestions contained in this book are not intended as a substitute for consulting with your physician. All matters regarding your health require medical supervision. Neither the author nor the publisher shall be liable or responsible for any loss or damage allegedly arising from any information or suggestion in this book.

Cover Design by Anita Colussi-Zanon

Printed in the United States of America

Published by Horizon Design Studio

10660 Yonge Street, P.O. Box 30575

Richmond Hill, ON, Canada   L4C 0C7

Visit <u>www.AngelsandInsights.com</u>

Dedication

To all Angel types and to all who listen.

For Steve, Tyler, Jamie and Haley with love.

And with a special thank you to Paul.

Table of Contents

Contents

Acknowledgements

I want to acknowledge the help of a lot of people in helping to make this book possible.

My family first of all – Steve, Tyler, Jamie, and Haley who provide lots of love and support always. Also my mom and dad Claudia and Alceste and my sister Crystal who have always created a nurturing environment.

My friend and mentor Paul Greblick who started me off on the Angelic journey and who developed Inner Influencing, the breakthrough technique I use.

My editor Susan for helping to whip my manuscript into shape. My business coach Jeannette Hay for helping to keep me on track.

My clients for teaching me how to help them and for participating with me in an Angelic journey just by letting me help them.

Also everyone who has helped with reviewing the book and with getting the word out. I humbly thank the following:

Crystal Hunt, Louise Lee, Lisa, Natalie Ligato, Veronica Martin, Sabrina Romeo, Josie Kirk, Emily Sposato, Teresa Farro Romeo, Karen Beam, Anna Morrone, Rita Amendola, Diane Alexander, Anna Maria DiBartolo, Daniela Hoffman, Jeannette Hay, Paul Greblick, Kathy Alimi, Larry Chapman, Nancy Holton, Ray Giusto, Kim Luu, Nancy McRae, Stephen and Allena Coleman, Sandy McNeil, Shzone Ali, Lena Mascerin, Josie Durante, Miranda Wong, Amanda Borys, and Stefanie Roemer.

Forward

Archangel Gabriel speaks

This book is called *The Books of Light* because it is meant to usher Light into the world, to welcome Angels back into the world, and to allow God to exist in the world in ways that are more present and more real.

The Angels have always been here in your world, in the background. We have always been able to help but never to initiate. You have had to call upon us. We have given you hints, messages, and clues as to how you might ask us for assistance. We have sent messengers and continue to send them to you. Some of you have listened. Some of you have asked the Angels for help and been rewarded. We have assisted you when you really needed help. Sometimes we jump in and help you without having been asked. But those cases are very rare. Instead, we assist you in big and small ways when you call upon us. We are your helpers. We are your Divine helpers.

God has been here on earth too. God exists quietly in the background, omniscient, ever-present, and all-seeing. Because He has granted free will, He will not always take action in your lives. You have to ask for Divine Help. You have always had to ask.

Help has been available to you but remotely and at a distance from you. The whys and wherefores will be explained to you here.

Enjoy this work. By reading it, you are participating in bringing the Angels to your life and to the earth.

This book contains Divine energy. It is written with the guidance and the direction of the Angels. Some sections, such as this one, are written completely by the Angels. Simply by reading and thinking about these things, you are bringing Angel and Divine energy into your life. This is a good thing. Allow yourself to be blessed. Allow for some magic in your life, and for something Divine. The world does not have to be as cold as some of you see it. Allow yourself the ability to see beyond, to see the beauty of all things, and to feel what you feel. Do not close yourself off to things. Do not be afraid.

There is beauty within you, and beauty outside of you. If you can look at this beauty, if you can see it, then more magic and blessings will come to you. It is our wish that you live a wonderful and a glorious life. It is our wish that you have a life that far exceeds anything that you have imagined. Begin this journey with us, and follow the calling that your heart can hear. Can you hear us speaking to you? Can you receive messages from us directly? By the end of this book, you may have more connection with us than you thought possible.

Go now about your day. Put this book down for a while. Pick it up again when you feel the time is right. You will know when that is. You will feel the energy of the words calling you. You will know when you need to read it again.

This book will be read by you in its own time. You, the Universal you, know what you need from these pages. You will know when you need to consult this book, read further, or think about the things that it is saying. You will know when you want to refer to the pages briefly, or spend more time with them. Remember that this book contains special energy, so don't be surprised if you approach it differently than other things.

This book was written with Divine Energy, Grace and Presence.

We encourage you to surround yourself with the possibilities of healing. Consider too and contemplate the ailments that you have, and ask that they be lifted from you. We encourage you to heal in ways that are familiar to you too. Seek out medical help, including the experts you need, that you are blessed with. Do not neglect this. This book is not a replacement for medical advice or help.

The Angels want you to pick up this book whenever you feel guided to do so. They offer it as a respite for your soul and spirit, a source of healing, and a source of information.

You will feel more complete after you read it. You will feel more whole. And it will heal you in and of itself.

May peace be with you.

Introduction

Welcome to the Books of Light.

This is a book of healing and a book of joy. Stop for a moment and see if you can feel anything. If you don't, that's okay. You can be skeptical and still read the book. You can be skeptical and still gain something meaningful from what is written here. This book does not seek to convince you. This book asks that you be open to experiencing the words on the page and seeing how they match up or don't match up with what you already know, and what your experience of the world is.

It's okay if this book changes you. It's okay if it does not change you. It's okay if you are a silent observer, an unwilling participant. Allow the book to draw you in or not. Read the whole thing or only parts. It is a choice that you make with all the other aspects of your life, so why not with this?

All the writing in this book is guided by the Angels. As I write these words to you, I am hearing them in my head, as if I were reading aloud. I listen to what the Angels say and I write it down for you. Sometimes the words and direction are similar to what I would write or choose. And sometimes they are different. But I know that they are true. I know that the words are given to me by the Angels. I can hear what they are telling me to write. And I can feel the Divine energy as I am writing this.

For those of you who are wondering what this energy feels like, it is a cool energy enveloping me although I don't feel cold. I actually am somewhat warm. Strange to feel two temperatures at once, I know. I also experience energy shifts in my head – I have 'head cracking' – so imagine the sound that knuckles make when they crack. I have a quieter version of that in my head when I am connected to the Angels, which is most of the time.

There are several types of writing in this book. One is a mystical writing, where the Angels relate some aspects of the Divine story that you might find interesting or add to your understanding. Because there has been so much suffering, the Angels believe this kind of writing will help all of us to understand the human story better and ease the pain that so many people have. The Angels want people to be healed and whole and to be able to have their divinity back too. They want them to reclaim their universal selves and to understand that they are a part of Divine, that they are a part of God, one of His many strands of light.

Pause for a moment and consider that. Consider that you are a strand of Divine light. Honour the light within you.

Elements of the story will be presented in an episodic fashion, woven throughout the book. They will arrive when needed. They will arrive when they serve a purpose, to fill a gap, mend a misunderstanding or erase confusion. They might even create confusion. It may be that you will enjoy these parts of the book. You might enjoy the narrative, enjoy the information. It might fill holes in your understanding and these will suddenly be not a problem anymore. The information, the story will be sustaining and nourishing in some way.

There is a fair bit of jumping around that goes on in terms of the voice used. Sometimes I am writing as myself and other times I am writing with the voice of the Angels. This should be fairly evident when you read.

Another kind of writing is something the Angels want to call The Declarations. These are sections that expound on different aspects of existence, or Divine, or life as we know it. These don't really deal with the everyday aspects of existence as we might think about them. Rather they deal with things like light and shadow, good and evil. The Angels have a lot to say on these topics. They want to add light to the world by doing so, and they want to add the light of understanding. This is the main purpose.

The Declarations portion of this book is a different kind of writing…something to dip into now and again perhaps. They are bite size pieces, small bits of information or things that the Angels want me to tell you. Indeed they are arranged this way, often in numbered paragraphs. You will know how to read these sections based on how you feel when you look at them. If you are strongly pushed away from any of these sections, then leave them for another time. They are not for you now. They might be for you at another time, a different time. It might be that more life has to be lived before they can be read. It doesn't have to do with experience necessarily, as much as perspective. At certain times in our lives we are able to hear certain things, and at other times we are not. Sometimes we have a very fixed reality and viewpoint, and fixed ideas about who we are and what life is. Sometimes our notions are more fluid. And sometimes we change and life changes too. All this affects your taking in of this book. Indeed, all this affects your taking in of everything in your life. Allow yourself to understand the you that is approaching this book, the you that you are, and also the viewpoint that you bring to it. Allow these thoughts to inform your reading of this book. Read it openly. Welcome it. And as for the parts you don't quite like or can't cotton to, leave them for when you might be more willing to look at them. Read only what you want to read. Full participation is not required.

Also included in this book are the Incantations and Prayers that are within. The word Incantations has been used to offer a wider notion of what is presented rather than simply using the word Prayer. The word Prayer can have a lot of associations that link it to religion. Incantations have other kinds of associations – perhaps of magic, pagan rituals. The point of using both is to offer a space where everyone can find something that they can use. The usual recommendation is to pray to your own God. We do not dispute this. We want to ask that you call upon the Angels for help in your own way, be it a prayer or an incantation or something in between. We offer words to help you call us and call for our help. And we ask that you do.

Enjoy the book and consider it a journey and an adventure. Consider it a journey taking you to the heart of the story of the Angels here on earth, and an adventure in that what you discover here might change you. It might change your perspective about how you see things. It might change how you feel. And it could change your life too.

When we talk about Angels, we often wonder about their presence here on earth. Are they here on earth? Can they help us? These are just some of the questions that might arise if your thoughts lean in this direction. If you have thought about Angels, you might wonder if you are able to get their help in your life, or where they fit in. Is it possible to have their help? The answer is yes.

It is possible to get their help in all ways. You need to ask them for help. If you do, you will start to see the possibilities. You will start to see that things open up for you. Ways that you were blocked are blocked no longer. The Angels can see more than you can. They have an unlimited perspective, so when you ask them for help, you can receive it in bigger ways than you might have imagined. They also know what is in your heart and in your mind. They know what you want and where you want to go. They also know the reasons for all of this. And often they know what you would prefer.

So have faith that asking the Angels is a good thing for you to do and that it will bring good things to your life. Have faith that being connected to Divine or seeking out connection is also a good thing for you. Ask yourself, how can you make your life better, and more valuable to you? And then ask the Angels to help you make this a reality. The Angels will help you. They will help you to have a better life. They will help you to have more meaning, more joy, more abundance, and more happiness. They want you to have a good life and they want you to want this for yourself too. Allow them a chance to help you. Ask them. Take a moment right now and ask them for help. Do this with whatever words feel right to you. The right words will come. All words will be heard.

The Angels want to be present in your life so that they can make it better. They want to be present in the world too. They are a tonic for a troubled time. Imagine the possibilities of having the Angels here on earth. Imagine living in a world where there can finally be peace, with no strife or struggle. Imagine living in a world where effort is rewarded always, and where not much effort is required to begin with. Imagine a world where you only have to think and dream and you can begin to make your dreams a reality. Would this not be Heaven on earth? The Angels would like to help you achieve this.

Ask the Angels into your life. Ask them to help here on earth too. They can provide a salve for the ills of the world and they can benefit all of us. They can allow all of us to do everything that we want and need with a great sense of ease, with a complete understanding of our purpose. When we ask the Angels for help, we will get a hand to guide us through the disparate vagaries, the disparate issues and problems that all of us face. We will be well guided, and the path will become easy and clear.

Find peace and sustenance in these pages. Find solace and happiness too. Read as you will, read as you are guided. Ask the Angels for help. Ask us for help. We are able to help you and we will help you in all ways.

The Woman on the Hill

A Divine History

Who is the woman on the hill and why do we speak of her?

The woman on the hill is on a hill in Heaven, or more precisely a hill in the Realm. She is important because she brought the knowledge of the Realm and of the Divine story to those who would bring it to you.

The woman was a grandmother in this lifetime. But in other lives she also had other roles that were very significant from a Divine perspective. The grandmother had passed away a long time ago. She had a name that meant sorrow, but you can simply think of her as Nonna, which means grandmother. She was a good woman, in the best sense of the word. As if her goodness was woven into her.

For many years, Nonna waited on the hill for her granddaughter and for the granddaughter's colleague to find her. She stood on the hill waiting to communicate truth about the Realm, truth about Divine, truth about our existence here on earth, and about what it meant and could mean to be human.

It is interesting that her name meant sorrow because she was there, on the hill, to let it be known that sorrow would soon be at an end, and that suffering would be over. This is what she was about to say.

Nonna had appeared to the granddaughter in dreams long ago, when her granddaughter was a child. In the dreams, Nonna appeared in the same location, in a garden room located in the middle of a laneway that the child knew. When the little girl would check this location, there was nothing there. But in her dreams, when the girl went into this room, there was her beloved grandmother. Her grandmother radiated joy at her like the sun. She was so happy to see her! The granddaughter missed her grandmother very much. She missed the way she had felt so cherished and treasured by her grandmother, like a wonderful gift.

As a grownup, the grandmother was not always in the woman's mind. Life took over…life, growing up, and normal challenges. The grandmother was not forgotten but not uppermost in her mind. The grandmother continued to watch her granddaughter, and wait for the time to be right, for the time when she would appear to her granddaughter again.

Who was this granddaughter? And who was this colleague who were to receive this information? And why was this important?

It was important because it was they who had been tasked with bringing it to the world. It was they who needed to receive this information because they needed to bring it to others. They needed to bring it to others, and the time was coming when they would deliver this information. But before they could, there were things to do, things to finish, matters to see to and attend to.

The time was almost right when the grandmother decided to contact her granddaughter and the partner. The wheels needed to be set in motion. They needed to do all the things that they would do in order to come to this point. They needed to understand the story, they needed to understand why things were stuck, and why so many things were so wrong. And it was time that they began on their journey, a journey of understanding.

The granddaughter was already walking on the path towards the Divine, towards the light. She was seeking to learn, and to connect to something greater than herself. She was seeking to understand the greater world, and the world of the Divine. This brought her into contact with the partner. He was a herald of these things too. He talked of Angels and he spoke with Angels. And after a while, he taught her to connect with the Angels too. The Angels began speaking to her, giving her information.

The Angels gave her information just as she had sometimes received when she was a child. They had given her information then but she did not know this. She didn't know how she knew the things that she did. Many times it felt natural, but sometimes it felt strange, so she turned away from this information slightly so that the depth of this knowledge did not shock her. Knowing was always part of her life. She preferred to think it came from study and hard work. But looking back, there was a deeper source at the root of all of it, an innate connection to the Divine.

The partner came to his own understanding through hardship and a very particular journey. Some would have called it a journey of awakening. But it was a difficult journey, fraught with undesirable things and with pain. He was moving away from that and gaining peace and beginning to feel more resilient, more himself. Now he was on a mission to bring Angels and understanding of them to the world. He was committed to this and helping people improve their lives and alleviate their suffering through a method that the Angels themselves had given him. This method was a tool to help with emotional pain and it could help to heal people. This method is called Inner Influencing. It is an important tool and it is helpful to learn and apply to your life. His name is Paul Greblick, and I encourage you to visit his website for more information about this.

I am the granddaughter and the writer of this book. My grandmother, or Nonna, appeared to me in dreams as a child. The connection I had as a child to something more didn't necessarily frighten me, but wasn't entirely comfortable either. Nonna reconnected to me and to this partner, Paul, that I speak of. Paul began as a mentor and a teacher and taught me to reconnect with the gift of the Angels and also taught me Inner Influencing, of which I am a practitioner. We began to think of ourselves as partners because of the many hours we have worked together and because of our mutual commitment in doing this work and of bringing it to the world. We continue to work together in this shared goal and part of the vision of doing this work is to bring peace and understanding to a world that is sometimes lacking both.

This is the point at which we are now. But the woman on the hill, Nonna, appeared to us a few years ago now. She appeared to us in a shared vision, a vision we both could see. She wore a skirt and sweater, a light jacket, and a head kerchief that covered brown curls. She had brown eyes, a wide smile, smiling eyes, and a medium frame and wore kindness in every aspect of her person. She appeared to us in a waking vision, as I sat in my office near Toronto and as Paul sat a long distance away in Florida. She appeared to both of us and she spoke to me about the way that the world was, and about the pain and the suffering.

This is a summary of what she said –

We have suffered greatly. The world has suffered. For too many years the world has suffered, and the people of the earth have suffered. They have suffered in their own darkness. They have suffered because of the darkness of others. They have suffered because of hardship and misery. And they have suffered because they were not understood and could not understand either. They sought solace. They sought healing. But it was not always available to them. Comfort was not available.

This suffering represented and was felt by millions upon millions of individual lives through time. Millions upon millions. It is time now for the suffering to end. It is time now for all that suffering and striving to have been worth something. The Angels will return to the earth to help people and to alleviate this suffering. But first there are a few things to do. The Angels will tell you. And once these things are accomplished, then the Angels can return. The Light will be held back no longer.

The woman said she would be more present in their lives. She would help them. She would relay information and show them what they had to do, and where they should focus their attention. And so a journey began. Sometimes frustrating, sometimes tiring, but a journey that was always undeniably important.

The Angels want to interject directly here and comment on this:

They say that Paul and I are instruments in the story, instruments in bringing the story to life and in bringing the Angels to the world. It may not be that you yet see evidence of the Angels presence in your life or in the world. But you will. As you progress through the pages of this book, this evidence will be more apparent to you.

The Angels also want to say that Nonna was right, and that there has been too much suffering and sorrow. That all of this happened. And that in the best world, the most ideal form of the world, that this would not have happened at all. Was this a test or a challenge? It was, of a kind. And now the test is over and we can be released from our difficulties and from the darkness.

The darkness is leaving. In these pages you will learn more about the ascent of the darkness and how it was vanquished. You will learn the tale of another place and how this place affected all of us.

Some of this history is scattered throughout the book. You are meant to fill in something of the story for yourself. The pieces will come to you. They will come to your mind. We ask that you open yourself to this information. You can even ask the Angels to tell you something about all of this now. You can ask Nonna to tell you directly too if you like.

The Angels also say that they know many things are confusing in your life. Things don't always makes sense, and life itself doesn't entirely make sense. The sense that you are seeking is coming to you, and it will soothe you. The Angels want you to accept this soothing. They want you to recognize it and to watch it work upon you as it mends you. Information itself can be healing.

The Angels will continue to speak to you through this book and in other pages of this book. They are mainly writing the entire book and I am putting it down on paper. For now though, they want to turn your attention to something else or Someone Else. It appears that God would like to add something here also.

God speaks

You are not used to being addressed by Me, I recognize that. But it is important that you listen and hear these words.

It has been difficult these many many years for all of you. There has been too much trouble, too much injury, too much damage, too much hate. The time of darkness can now be over. Allow the darkness to leave you, allow any darkness that is inside you or that is affecting you to leave you. You do not have to entertain it anymore. You do not have to welcome it or give it a home in any way. Banish the darkness. Consecrate it to the light. Send it to Me. And I will dispel it in all ways.

The darkness is going. It is important that you know this. It is important to know that the Light and the Angels are returning. I am returning too. You did not know I was gone. I was never gone. But I have been weakened. I am not weakened any more. Strength is here. And My strength is your strength. With My strength all will be well. All will be better than before.

We know that you are asking now how is it that God was weakened? How is it that He was not strong? We know that you are asking these questions. You will have answers. You will know what you need to complete your understanding but we need to start from another vantage point. We need to begin our explanations in another location – Heaven.

Heaven – the seat of all things

What is Heaven? Heaven is the beginning of all things – the start of it all. Heaven is the home of God and the Angels. Heaven is the home of the Divine. The place where the sanctified can reign and be at home.

First was God and then Heaven was created. Because even God needs a home. And then God created the Angels. And many other things, and people too.

About the story: both stories are true. The Biblical one and the scientific story too. The Biblical one in the metaphorical sense and the scientific one in the logistical sense. Both can coexist. In the Divine Realm, everything is possible.

Heaven continues to this day. It is the place where the Angels and God reside. It is the place where departed souls go. It is the place that looks upon us and our earthly doings and it seeks to nudge us this way and that, through the hints of the Angels. It is home for everyone, and for every soul.

The soul of all things, of every last thing and person, can find rest in Heaven. It is the place of ultimate respite and belonging.

And yes, Heaven does contain majestic buildings and wonderful landscapes, including the Divine hill that is spoken of. It contains the masters and the saints and all of their wonderful creations. Heaven is full of creation and creativity. Divinity thrives on creativity. And creation and creativity bloom when they are in touch with the Divine.

When new souls reach Heaven, they are welcomed and healed and allowed to rest from their journey. The journey is not a difficult one, but there is a sense of deep and profound change. The soul returning to its former knowledge of all things Divine, and remembering its time on earth. The review of the soul, the examination of the lessons. All this takes place. The new soul finds its way and finds its home again, its place in Heaven. The adjustment takes place. The soul becomes one with all Divine but retains itself too. It is an I and an All, all at the same time.

All healing that is needed occurs. This can occur over time or it can occur instantly. It depends on what the soul wants and needs. Some souls prefer a longer rest period. When the adjustment is made, when the soul is ready and again used to the feeling and idea of not being mortal, of not having a physical self, then it becomes integrated and a full part of Heaven.

There is more, but we want to leave the space for you to fill in your own ideas about Heaven. Doing this will give you peace and healing. Reading about Heaven from other sources will give you peace and healing too.

There is another place we want to talk about too, a place called the Realm.

What is the Realm?

You heard us speak about this earlier, when we were speaking about the woman on a hill in the Realm.

The Realm is much like Heaven. It is sister to Heaven and sits beside it geographically. Of course the better word to use would be energetically because Heaven doesn't exist anywhere that we can actually travel to.

The Realm is a place where things are governed and decided upon. It is, in a sense, the administrative centre for both Heaven and earth. Heaven is the location where Divine government, if you like, exists. And the Realm is the place where the logistical things are taken care of. They are not the same logistical things that we might be accustomed to on earth. They are more overarching and conceptual concerns covering the balancing of energy and making sure that the right things are happening at the right times. If you skeptically remark that not a lot of this has necessarily been happening through human history, you would be right.

The capacity of the Realm and of Heaven to govern or to do anything at all has been significantly curtailed for many years because of the restraints that have been put upon the Angels and even on God. Let this not shock you. Have you not wondered why things have been so bad in certain cases? Do you think that a Divine and all-powerful God would have let this happen?

The answer, actually, is not necessarily. A Divine and all-powerful God would not let this happen. However, upon the creation of His peoples and of earth, it came to pass that not all was Light, there was darkness too. How this darkness came to the world can be debated. But the short answer for our purposes is that having created everything, God did indeed create Everything. And that included the dark.

The darkness existed, and it had to be hunted out and vanquished. Then the Realm could be restored, and Heaven too, and God and the Angels could return to earth. This is actually a summation of the contents of much of this book. The other factor is that the darkness would not willingly show itself, willingly bring itself to the light. It would only come out if it were safe to do so. Hence the willing self-restraint of all Divine, the willing self-weakness. Without weakness, the dark/the evil could never have been routed.

And what of Lucifer? What of the tale of the fallen angel who brought evil into the world? The Angels want you to be careful to think that evil is just the creation of one Divine entity. The darkness surfaced through different factors, different manifestations of this concept of the fallen one. We have had in our history many figures, sadly, that represented evil quite well here upon the earth. They did not need any Divine power to do so. Consider that the fallen angel did indeed play his part, as did everyone else who has ever committed an act of evil.

It is important to know is that the Realm is the centre of activity, the glue that holds things together. And now it can return to working well and the way it should. As can all of Divine.

The Realm offers a bridge between thinking of Heaven and thinking about earth. It offers a less intimidating idea of what the afterlife could be. It is, the Angels say, a place that resembles the nicer parts of earth without the attendant problems that we have, and without the needs that we humans have. It is, like Heaven, a perfect place.

The Gates Are Open Now

The gates to both Heaven and to the Realm are open now. They are open and we may pass through them. Not in a physical sense, rather, in an energetic sense.

Energetically, we now have more access to everything. We have more access to our own knowledge, to our own selves, to the knowledge of the universe, to the knowledge of what lies before us and between us. The understanding between us will grow too.

We have been segmented and polarized in the past. There have been deep divisions between us, between different peoples, different nations, different cultures and societies. We have all desired to be identified and to be separate. We have all desired to articulate fully who or what we are, and so often, that was in contrast to the other. We might still partake of these definitions and identifications. The Angels are not asking us to throw away our identities, to throw way our self-definitions and ideas about ourselves and our histories. But they are asking us to consider a wider definition of ourselves, one that includes these markers of separation and identity, and a further definition that looks beyond all the things that could divide us. Another kind of definition where we can all consider ourselves part of a greater whole, part of the Divine. This is how we are to be, separate and united too. This is how we are to be, self-identified and infused with the Divine. We will not lose our identities, our self-determination and ideas about ourselves. But we will gain a new understanding, the idea that we are deeply connected, and that we are embraced and held by the Divine.

And so our story begins.

The Light and the Shadow

The Light was always the Light, and the Shadow also existed. Most of the time the Shadow had to bow to the Light. The Shadow had to keep well-hidden if it wanted to preserve itself, if it wanted to last, and to exist even.

The Shadow had emerged during a time of darkness, close to the Beginning when all was being thought through, decided, and created. The question was asked: was there room for a shadow? Was there room for some kind of opposite to good, and to Light?

The Light itself had imagined the shadow. The Light itself had caused its opposite into being. Not to cast a gloom on anything. Not to create anything at all bad. The shadow was seen instead as a respite from the light, a turning down of the intensity of all that is. The Light was breathtaking and wild and beautiful and intense and focused. The shadow was there to show the depth of things, to show the cooler tones that could exist, the other textures. It was all meant to be a good thing. It was all meant to be a celebration of possibilities -- an idea that more than one kind of truth could exist. An idea that the Light, in its fullness and full realization, did not have to be and exist in only a single way all the time.

So to this end we now have not just the Light, but we have the dappled sunlight, the noon day sun, the hot equator, the cool mountains, the icy lakes, the dark woods, the hidden pockets of shade and shadow. We have full measure of all expression of light and darkness, light and shadow in the world, in the physical geography of the place where we live.

And so we have full expression of the Light and the Dark, of the Light and the Shadow in all other ways. We have full expression of Good and Evil, we have full variety of expression of all of this in all the ways it can be. We allow this to exist, we condone and permit it.

So how have we called all this into being? How have we created the negative and can we only create the positive? The answer is that we did not call it into being. The Light called the Dark into being, called the Shadow into being. But now it is time for the shadow and the dark to recede, to go, in ourselves and in the world, and in the universe. There is no more room for the darkness. The time of the shadow is at an end. The Light has had its fill of the dark. And for this we can be glad.

Dispersing the Darkness

The darkness was to be dispersed, although it had not been dispersed yet. It had agreed to go. Everybody hoped it would go soon like an unwelcome visitor. The dispersal was commanded, but the fragments of authority were in pieces. No one could know, not even the Darkness, what was to be done. But finally, in consultation with itself and others, including shadow and misfortune, and at the behest of Light, the Darkness concluded that perhaps it was best for it to go.

So the Dispersal was at hand now and ready to begin at any time.

What would it take for this to truly happen? What would be the necessary push? How could this begin?

It was necessary that some kind of ceremony be held…an initiation for the end of the Darkness.

The Darkness did not want to go quietly or slink or slide away. It did not want to simply disappear. It was not seeking revenge or commitment to itself. It somewhat sadly wanted some recognition, some honouring of its service to humanity, to mankind. It wanted some recognition that it had been the foil for the Light, that it had been the basis of so many actions that mankind had taken.

The Light replied that it needed no foil and no companion. Light also said that the dark could claim no merit for these actions. The actions were dark too and had no value.

Still, if the darkness were to be dispersed peacefully, it wanted its due measure. So something was quickly arranged and with a few words, and then the darkness was ready to go, some several millennia after God had said "Let there be Light."

Now, finally, the Light did not have to co-exist with anything other than Truth and Goodness.

And all was good.

The Light

1   - The Light – Magnificence All Around You

The Light was all around you and its magnificence was all around
you. You could not see it. Not because it was not there. You could
sense its great power and you could feel that it was there. But you
could not see the Light because you were covered in darkness, and
because you were shielded and made blind. You who had been
waiting for the Light, and who wait still, you cannot see. The veil
has not been lifted from you. The coverings are upon your eyes, and
they have been there for centuries. Is it possible that they are to be
lifted now? No, but they will be lifted soon. Read on, and continue
the journey of how the Light relates to you. Read on, and let the
Light seep into you so that it becomes a part of you, and gently
encourages or even forces an awakening. The Light is of benefit to
you. You need to be blind to it no longer.

2 – The Light as Sustenance

The Light is sustenance and it sustains you. Do not say that you
want no part of the light and that the light is not part of you. The
light that is in you will not be denied. The glimmer that exists in
you, that exists in all of you will not be denied. It wants to grow and
expand and create and be in the world. It wants you to rejoin with
the Divine, and with your Universal Self. It wants all this for you.
Sometimes you feel the stirrings of the Light within you, and you
might call it Spirit, or Soul. Then you might say yes, that is what I

am and that is what I am made of. But sometimes you are afraid. Sometimes you are afraid of life, and of your own power too. This is why you need the Light. You need the Light to sustain you, to build you up, and to help you grow. You need the light to make you more of what you are, to help you recognize the inner strength that is waiting to grow, develop, and rise inside you. It merely needs you to recognize it and it will come alive. Come alive in the Light. Come alive. Let not the world diminish you. Allow the Light that burns within you to come forth. It is a force for good in the world, ready to do good, and ready to do you good too. Allow it to come to the forefront of your life and of your awareness and allow it to sustain you as indeed it can. Look for the Light. You will not be disappointed.

3 – The Light Chases Away the Darkness

The Light chases away the darkness. The light chases away all that is dark because of its very nature. The light is stronger than the dark. The light had been held back too, like the Angels. Or rather, it had held itself back. Because this is the only way that the light could have been held back. How do you tell something more powerful than the sun to shutter itself? And yet this is what happened. The Light contained itself for many years because this was necessary, and because it was asked to do this. There was sadness involved, and it could not be helped. The darkness had to be allowed to come out and play for a time, for a long time. The darkness had to come out and see what it could do and what it could ruin. Everyone had to see all of this, all of it. It had to be painted, portrayed, and experienced. The misery had to be felt. And then finally after all these ravages, after everything was done, the darkness could go.

The darkness never had any interest in staying really. It had no interest in building, or in creating. That was the providence of its near cousin the Light. No, the darkness had no interest in doing anything other than cutting a wide path on its way to wherever. Finally it was time for it to go, and the Light could be said to have chased it away. It was more complicated than that, of course. But for now, that was enough.

4 – The Light Is Your Light

The Light is your Light. It is your birthright and has always been your birthright, waiting to come alive and waiting to rejoice with you in the Everything of Everything. The Light within you is what makes all possible. What will you do with your light? What can you create and build? What can you contribute? Do not fear the power of your own person. For in and of yourself, you have the power to move the world, and you have the power to change things. It is possible for you to be a light in the world. You already are in many ways. It is up to you how bright that light is, how much you shine and how much you illuminate. Shine a light on your own life and when you are ready, expand and shine your light outward to everything and everyone around you.

5 – What Kind of Light Do You Have?

What kind of light do you have? Is it a shallow glimmer? Is it strong and steadfast, never extinguishing? It is up to you to understand the light that you have within. You have strength of character. You have defining characteristics that you describe yourself with. Let these understandings of yourself give you an understanding of your light also. Paint yourself in the light and let the light paint you. Let yourself be described by the light and let yourself be included in the light. All of the light within you is strong and willing to emerge and to help you in your life. You need this light to emerge in order for you to grow and prosper. You need this light in order to help you see how valued you are, how important you are, and how good you are. You need this light in order to connect to all things, in order to connect to the Divine, to the Angels, to God, and even to the Tree. Your light is your powerful connection to all of that. It is your magnifier, your ticket to all of creation. It is your realization that the universe is within you contained in this Light. It is your realization that you are a part of Divine just as you are, and that you are a strand of God's light. So with God, so with you. What a powerful realization to make. Connect to the Light within you. It will connect you to everything and the great Everything too.

6 – What is the Nature of your Light?

Is your light strong? Is it weak? Does it have much in the way of understanding? What kind of light do you bring to the world? How do you shine? Do you glitter or glimmer? Do you reveal? Do you clearly illuminate? There are many ways that our Light affects the world and affects the Light of the world too. What is your contribution? Can your light shine more brightly or differently?

These choices belong to all of us. The Light will manifest itself through whatever vessel you provide it, through whatever shape you create. All of it is possible. All of it can change and be a changing agent in your life and in the life of the world too. Allow the light to shine cleanly and brightly within you. It will still reflect the real you. You will not be lost in this, not at all. Instead you will be more clearly the you that you have always known, and the you that you have always wondered about under the surface. The longed for you is here, just beneath somewhere. Allow it to emerge. Allow the true light that is you to emerge.

7 – The Light of the Day

The Light of the day is the fierce light of everything. The light of the day shines brightly over everything, revealing all. It reveals how things are. It reveals their strength and their wholeness. It reveals everything put together in all ways. It reveals the cracks and the broken parts. It reveals what we have done and what we still need to do. It reveals our thoughts and our prayers. It reveals our worries and what we keep hidden. The light of day reveals all. It is a supreme source of information. It reveals all to those who look. It reveals some to those who would not look.

We may wonder about the light of day, what it will tell to us, what it will not tell to us. We may wonder about the expression of the light of day. Will its communication to us be what we want, will it help us? Will its revelations bring us joy? Will they instead cast us down? Will the nature of the revelation be soothing to us, will it be completing or nourishing? The communication, this communication of light allows all to see with their own eyes, but only sometimes with their hearts. Is this communication valid? Does it stand the test of time? It is the only real communication of all. It is the only truly deeply revealing communication that we have. What does the light of day bring to you? What has it brought to you today? The honesty of the light of day is its blessing. What honesty is it bringing you now? What blessing is it bringing you now? Be happy with this light of day. It does you good and it means you well.

8 – The Light of the Sun

The Light of the Sun is the maker of all things. It bakes our bread. It raises our children. It teaches the birds to sing and allows the crops to grow. It allows us to grow and to be nourished too. Of course, it allows us to live. Life could not be possible without the sun. We give it its due. We give it its deference. Where would we be without this fiery ball in the sky to sustain us? But we are reminded that the sun is also our emblem of beauty and strength. We that have a light within us, we can model the sun. We can be that bright and that strong. We can be that important. Do not cast yourself down. Do not feel that you have no light, that you are not worthy. You are as worthy and as valuable as the sun. Connect to your inner light, to the light within you that represents the Divine and the Sun. This Light within you can heal you. It can heal you of your feelings of lack of worth, of inadequacy. All of this is true, must be true. You that were born under the sun and have grown under the sun, be inspired to look within yourself and to find your own sun, to find your own strength and beauty and to bring that to the world.

9 – The Light of God

The Light of God is the Light of the World. The Light of God is the light of Heaven and the Angelic Realms shining down upon us. The Light of God is God Himself and this belongs to all of humanity. The Light of God is God Himself and yet the Light is its own entity too. Just as God Is, so to Light Is. Do we recognize the Light of God? The Light is the most visible part of God. We are strands of Light. We are strands of Light that belong to God and we are strands of God too. We are Divine Essence made manifest in Light. The Light is ours, and it is ours to claim. This is how we create. We create in the Light and with the Light. This is why darkness seems so strange to us, it is not our true nature. Our true nature is light and we do not need to struggle to accept this. We need only to see. When we see this, then everything is revealed to us. When we see this, then all the deep layers of meaning become understandable.

10 – The Light of Heaven

The Light of Heaven is the Light of Creation and is the oldest of Light. It originates from God, near the beginning. The Light of Heaven is pure and beautiful, made up of many swirls of colours and crystals and shines down upon us, though we don't always see this. The Light of Heaven is the light that bathes us every day, and every night too. It is the light of the chakras and the auras. It is the light of the dawn and that of the twilight. It is the light by which the Angels can see you and the measure of you and how much you need their help, were you to ask. The light of heaven forms a silhouette in our lives and we do not see it but it colours our world and our lives. Ask the Angels to help you see the Light of Heaven. Ask them to help you see this very oldest of Light that bathes our world. For the Light of Heaven is the sepia tone of the sunset, the crisp light of the fall, the haze of the dawn, and the sunlit evenings. Bathe in this light and let it fill and nourish you. Let it inspire you.

11 – The Light of the Angels

The Light of the Angels is happiness itself. It blesses us and we are blessed by the presence of the Angels in our lives. This light brings us joy. Many do not feel joyful, however, and many do not see the Angels or feel that they can be in our lives. I ask you to open

yourself to the possibility of having Angels in your life. You may
not be able to see the Angels. But I believe that many of you will
sense them. Many of you will feel the presence of the Angels in
your life if you ask them to be there. You will feel an unseen force
beside you. Ask the Angels to be present in your life and ask them
to help you. You will be surprised by what this can bring. Also the
presence of the Angels in your life and how you will feel may be
surprising to you. You may not have allowed yourself to feel deeply
and you may not have allowed your emotions to expand and grow
to their full potential. You may find that the light of the Angels, and
having the Angels in your life, illuminates you and changes you in
an important way. There may be new emotions, new feelings, and a
new depth to your experience of life and the way you are living it.

12 – The Light of Your Soul and Spirit

The Light of your soul and your spirit shines through the world. No
matter who you are, your soul and spirit go with you, and go before
you and announce your presence. You have a light within you and
this can shine brightly or dimly. It is not entirely about your free
will. It is also about what has happened to you and how you have
been treated and how you have treated others. Yet your spirit and
soul can still be developed. The light in your soul and spirit can
shine more brightly than it has up to this point. In many ways your
soul's journey is just beginning. You can keep the things that have
shaped you, or you can let them go. You can be free of the many
things that have impeded you and you can free yourself of any
damage that you have. After all, you are Light and you come from
Light. And Light, above all other things, can remake itself in the
most whole and perfect way. Be that Light and let your soul and

spirit bathe in the light. Once you have allowed this to be possible, then you can allow yourself to heal fully. Allow yourself to heal fully in all dimensions and in every aspect of your being. Look at the damage and the things that you have suffered. Look at them and remark how they have changed you, how they have shaped you the way an artist would draw a portrait. Remark how this line or that came from this sorrow or this trauma, and then let all of this float away. Let all of it be erased. Allow your Light, and the Angels and God to take away everything and to leave you whole. Allow the Light of your soul and spirit to be free and shine brightly. You will be a beacon to the world and you will be brilliant and whole.

13 – The Light of All There Is

The Light of All there is is the light of the world and of heaven and God too. The Light of all there is is the running of things, the cosmic operation of the universe and how all the billions upon billions of interactions take place. It allows for multiple things to exist in multiple places, different explorations and events to simultaneously fire off at once all over the world, all over the earth, and all over the cosmos. The light of all there is is creation made manifest, and the energy of it all at the same time. It is the light of heaven too where everything is overseen also. It is the light of creation, the light that fuels everything happening everywhere. Without it we are shadows of ourselves. Without it we might exist practically but just barely so. Without it we are inanimate shells. The Light of all there is is what imbues us with ourselves, and with personality and possibility and spirit. We are all dwellers in this light, we are all bringers of this light and we reside within this light.

14 – The Light of the Word

First God spoke and then the Word took hold. First God spoke and then there was Light and the Earth and Heaven and the Angels. All of it began with the Word. It is the Word that lights our way. It is words that create everything, good or bad. The word made manifest creation. Even the light came from Word, from the Speech of God. But the word has its own light. It has always had its own light. There is the Word and this has Light, the Light of creation, the Light of God, the Light of All that Is. There are also words and they too have light. They have the light which can light a path to God, and to freedom. They can light the path of a journey or of a downward spiral.

Words have power and meaning because they have context and implication. They can suggest and they can allude. They can be direct or not. They can be resonant and import other things. And they can be used. They can be used for reasons for which they should not be used. Words have power to do good and bad. Choose your words well and good things will follow. Do not use your words for ill. Do not use words in any way that deviates from the light. The words have light but they can have power too that is not light. Make sure your words are chosen well and are aligned with light. Words that have Light can bring Light to the world, and can bring possibilities and potential that we cannot dream of or fathom. What can the Light of the Word bring to you? What word will you speak today? What Word will you speak today? What Light will you bring forth?

The Light of God, and the Light of Angels are included in the best words that you utter and write. Make your words have meaning above all things. Envelop your words with light and make sure that this light is inspiring and truth seeking. This is all you need to do. It is not difficult. It is about you expressing the most pure light that you have to the world. This expression only needs to come forth through your words, your thoughts, your actions, and even your prayers. When God said let there be light, He was referring to the Light within you too. Be that Light and show the world the Light that is within your words. Harbour not darkness in your heart or in your words, and let not your light be clouded. Let it be clear and magnificent, let it reflect the divine in you, and let it expand the divine to all things that you encounter. Be a container for the Light. Let if fill you and let it emanate from you too. In this way there is Light in the world. There is light in the world because it comes from you, it comes from you, your words, and your heart. Let your light shine upon the world. Be not afraid of it.

15 – The Light that you see before you

The Light that you see before you is the light of the other, of the one that crosses your path as you go about your day. You have light and others around you have light too. The light is in all living things, including animals and plants, and even objects around you. The light that you see before you is the very collection of objects and people that make up the world, as well as the energy between those things. This is all energy and all of this is light too. The light that you see before you comes forward to meet you. It comes forward to meet you and you meet it with all that you are, but sometimes you hide parts of yourself. You do this because you are not ready, and you do not want to cast all of yourself out in the world to meet the other light. And often, the light that comes out to meet you is also partial, is also not fully emerged. How do we deal with this? How do we interact with only part of our light? We cannot be fully emerged always. And others also cannot be fully emerged. Sometimes we must rest within ourselves. We must rest and nourish our light. Sometimes we feel, and rightfully so, that our light will not be appreciated. And sometimes we do not fully like or appreciate that which others brings to us. This is our real experience of everything. We are all Light, and somewhat shielded, meeting others who are all Light too and also shielded. Let us respect these necessary protections, and let us meet the light that is there to meet us. Let us put forth the light that we want others to meet too. In time, the Light that is within us will grow more brightly and emerge into the world and expand and find the light that is in others too.

16 – The Light that you have within you

The Light that you have within you shines brightly. Whether it be dim or the fiercest of fires it shines as brightly as it can. Do you feel this light within you? Do you feel the fire, the spirit, the soul that is yours and yours alone? Are you fully aware of yourself and your possibilities? Are you fully aware of who you are and of how you might shine your light into the world? All of this is real for you. All of us have a light. In each of us it shines differently. How can you make the most of this light that you have within you? How powerful can this light be? How strong? Take some time to work on the strength of your light. Take some time to work on its purity and clarity and its strength and its shine. How will you do this? Simply by thinking about it. Simply by thinking upon it. You can call it meditation if you want. But really you have only to think about this and it will be true. You have to think that you want to make your light stronger, brighter, clearer and all this will be possible for you. Do this and then take some time to let your light strengthen you too. Let it mend you and repair you. Let it make the necessary changes to you so that you can be whole. Feel the light within you. Feel the light grow strong and emanate from you also.

17 – Moments where Light Prevails

When does the Light prevail? When is it necessary for it to prevail? The Light often does prevail, often has prevailed, even in times that were dark, and even in times where it felt like all hope, all goodness was held back. There were moments when there was light. There were moments when there was a glimmer of sanctity and of peace. Those who chose to follow the Light, who made a commitment to follow it, could see this most clearly. They could view its appearance and take small moments of hope and goodness as a sign that yes there was Light in the world, and that there was goodness in the world. Sometimes following the light was a struggle. Sometimes following it was a conscious choice that was not been easy. Complicated emotions rose to the surface, there were feelings that we were not sure about. Sometimes the light had difficulty coming through. Sometimes it was hidden from view, and it could not emerge from within a person's heart where it was sheltering. All this was difficult. The light could not simply broadcast happiness all the time and everywhere. The light only shone through in these simple, single moments when it was unchallenged, and when there was no reason for it not to be. Still these restraints were coming to an end. These restraints were coming to an end and soon the Light would prevail more fully, and all the time.

18 – Let the Light prevail

Let the Light prevail now then, We say to you, so speak the Angels and God. We are commanding the Light to be and now commanding it to come back, to bring back all of itself. The full glory of the light can exist now. The full glory of the light can shine now everywhere and upon everything. The Light is here and can be here at last. Darkness is gone. Shadow and doubt are gone. It need not glimmer faintly. It need not subsist and hide. It can shine brightly now and it can cast truth upon everything. The light was bright. It was beautiful and brilliant and it appeared to all mankind, renewed and effervescent. It appeared in our minds and in our hearts and in our world. It appeared in the things around us and was prevalent everywhere. Things of darkness could not hide themselves from the light. They could not hide themselves and so the light shone upon them and prevailed. All was well because the light prevailed. The light rose forth and shone over a new day. The light shone everywhere, bathing everything. Much like the sun but brighter, more divine. It shone over you and over me and everyone. It heralded the coming of the Angels. The time was at hand. It forecast the coming of the Angels. The light was the bearer of witness. The light would announce the Angels. It was emerging in and from the heart of every person and emerging, radiating from each of us to say yes, we are ready, yes we are ready for the Light. And the Light then made us whole. The light then made us whole in preparation for the Angels. And it is making you whole now, as you read these words. It is making you whole and perfect in every way. Let the Light then take hold and let it prevail in you too.

19 – Be Open to the Light

Be open to the light. Let it fall upon you and fall into you in every way. Let it bathe you in its magnificence. Let it bathe you and let it honour you with its presence. Let it make you whole and complete in all ways. The light comes into you and creates a feast within you. It nourishes you and makes you complete. It builds a resource in you. It builds light and energy and strength. And it takes away the things you have no need of. It takes away your fears, and sorrows, and difficulties. It builds you in strength and it removes your weaknesses. It shapes you inside and out. It gives you something to hold on to and it gives you something to shape yourself with. It lets you see the world in new ways. In all ways you are blessed when you are open to the light. In all ways you are blessed when you look with the light and look upon the light. The light allows you to see more clearly and it allows you to see into your own heart and into the heart of others. This light can fill you so that you are complete and so that you want for nothing. You are fulfilled and whole in all ways. You are fortunate when you see with the light and when you are part of the light. When you are filled with the Light, all the good of the world can come to you. All the good and the abundance and the friendship and the love can come to you. When you fill yourself with light, you fill yourself with love. Where else would light dwell but within love? And even when you think that the light offers you cold clarity, and offers you something that you don't want to see, be open to this anyway. Be open to the idea that not all things can dwell in the light, only good things. And that all that is revealed in light must have a good ending, must be good in and of itself. Be open to the light, for it can do you no harm, it can do you only good. Be open to the light, and let the light fill you. For this is the only destiny you seek. This is the light of the truth. Let truth and light be your guide always.

20 – The Dawning of the Light

Are you skeptical? Are you skeptical that the dawning of the light is
here? Can the light be upon us now? Can the light come and bring
us joy and peace now. We must not doubt that this is possible. For if
you doubt this, then you bring yourself only misery. You cast
yourself down and may fall into despair. But if you believe in the
coming of the light, then you are glad, then you are filled with joy.
Let yourself choose the option of joy. Choose to be joyful and glad.
Choose to be abundant and generous in your belief. Choose to
consider that the dawning of the light is upon you now, just as if
you were watching the sun rise. The sun is rising for you. The light
is coming to your heart and to your world, to your mind, to your
spirit, and to the minds and spirits of those around you. You can be
at peace. You can be at peace for the light is coming to you now.
Allow the light to come to you. Allow the light to embrace you. The
light is dawning. And it is dawning in your own heart.

21- The Sun Rising

The sun is rising now in your heart and in all ways. It is rising in all
the ways that you need it to rise. It is rising for you and for the earth
and for everything upon the earth. It is rising for everyone you
know. It is rising and it will lift you as it does. It will lift everything.
It is rising and you can heed this call. You can heed the call to be
alive and to be vibrant and shine just like the sun. You can be
vibrant and intense too. The sun is rising. Let it rise within you. Let
it shape you and let it shape your destiny. And let it give you
strength and support too.

22 – The Sun and the Light

The Sun is not the light. The sun does not take the place of the light. The sun is a fraction of the light and a part of the greater Magnificence that we call Light. For how could the Light of God be contained in a single fiery orb? How could the light of God not be bigger and more magnificent than the sun? The sun is breathtaking and beautiful and significant and meaningful. But it is not the light. It is the visual representation of a part of the light. The light surrounds us and engulfs us should we choose to look, and should we choose to see. Often we do not because we are afraid. The sun and the light are two separate and distinct things.

23 – The Son and the Light

The Son and the light were all things to each other. How could they not be? The Son was the rising of the Light. The Light held the son within it. All were held by the light. But the son himself had brought the light. The son had brought the light of the human soul back to humanity. And for this the light was grateful. It was grateful to be able to come back, and to be able to touch the world again.

24 – The Light of Human History

The light of human history had been dimly lit for a long time. But perhaps the light could shine more brightly now. Perhaps the light could shine more brightly and all could be awakened to the light. All could be awakened and have a chance to shine themselves.

Perhaps this could be true. Perhaps the future of human history could be brighter than it had been.

25 – The Light of the Soul

The light of the human soul had not shone brightly. It was time for it to shine more brightly than it had done. The soul could be brighter. It could shine more brightly and it had to reveal itself to the light. It had to allow the light to help it grow in all ways and it had to be nourished by the light too. Then it would shine more. Then, the soul would prosper and the spirit too.

26 – The Light of the Spirit

Where the soul went, the spirit followed. The spirit too needed light, needs light. What spirit does not need to grow in the light? What spirit requires to be housed in the darkness? The spirit needed light. The spirit needed a chance to flourish and to be magnificent. All this was possible. Magnificence and greatness were possible for the spirit but only in the light. Without the light it would be cast down and would not be able to see the way forward. The light would nourish the spirit and nurture it. The light would propel it forward in all ways.

27 – The Light of the Holy Spirit

Where went the soul of man, so went the Holy Spirit. It too resided in the light. The Holy Spirit knew the light and was the light just as it knew God and was God. All things were possible because the

Holy Spirit was made in and of the light. So too would all things be possible for man if he would just realize this very same idea. The Holy Spirit could bring light to mankind. The Holy Spirit could bring light to all of humanity. This was possible. The Holy Spirit had to be invited in, just as the light had to be invited in. The Holy Spirit was a part of God and a part of divine. It would not simply act upon man. It had to be asked and invited. It was not the same as God the father or God the son. It was separate. It had an affinity for the light and the angels. It believed that man could not be forced to take the course of best action. When the Holy Spirit entered someone, when the Holy Spirit was invited in, then the course of action became apparent, and undeniable. This was why it had to be invited in. This is why the invitation of the light was key.

28 – The Light of Faith

The light of faith was important in order to bring light to mankind. Man needed the light of faith in order to carry on in the world. The light of faith kept man in balance and in all ways. Without faith, man could not have light. Without faith, man could not feel safe in the world. Faith was the light. Faith illuminated his path. Faith kept man travelling in the right direction and in the light. Faith and the light of faith were essential. They are essential to you too.

29 – The Light We Bring to Each Other

We bring light to each other. This light soothes us and keeps us. It offers us kindness and warmth and lights us up. We all need this light. We need to have our own light and to give it to others too. For in giving our light and in receiving light from others we are enriched. Our lights are different because we ourselves are different. In sharing our light, we explore new ways of being, and we consider new perspectives. These add to us and we add to the light of other people. In participating with each other, we bring each other closer to a higher source, closer to the Divine itself.

30 – The Light We Shine Upon the World

We shine light upon the world. We shine light from our very beings. We give this light to the world and we give this light to other people too. Can you feel your light? Can you feel how you give light to the world? You do this whether you mean to or not. The quality of the light you give is under your control. But the fact that you give light is not in question, it is not up to you to decide whether to turn it off or not. It is yours to give and you were born and so you give it. It emanates from you always. It emanates from you and shines out no matter what. You can see as you go about your day. You can see how your light emerges from you. You can see how your light affects the people you encounter and how their light affects you. You can see and you can experience how the light that you shine upon the world has a very real effect on you and on everyone else. Stop and notice this. Don't pretend it does not happen. Don't pretend that you have no impact. You always have an impact with every single thing you do. Let your light be a benefit to the world and to yourself. Let it shine as brightly as it can.

31 – Light in the Time of Darkness

Where was the light in the time of darkness? Some would say that we are still in the time of darkness. I believe we are emerging. I believe that the dark is going now, finally having been encouraged and allowed and told to leave. As for previously, the light was present. It was present in the time of darkness but it was not as visible as it could have been. The light in the time of darkness was held back, allowing the darkness to exist. It was allowing the darkness to do more than creep at the periphery. For a time the light was on the sidelines. From now on the light will be central. From now on the darkness will be no longer. And we do not have to keep the light at bay. None of us, now, have to keep the light at bay any longer. The time for the light to shine strongly and brightly is at hand now as we write and read these words. Gather the forces of light within you. Gather the forces of light and ask the darkness to leave. It can leave now. It can leave now because it must. And you can let it leave now too. You do not have to allow it to stay.

32 – Removing the Darkness; replacing it with Light

How will you remove the darkness within you? How will you replace it with the light? It is simple to do. Ask the darkness to leave. Ask it to leave from your soul and your spirit. Ask for this now. You can feel the melancholy energy leaving you. You can feel all that has been making you sad and sick within yourself leaving you. Try this now. Do not be afraid to let the darkness go. You have no need of this crutch. And then once this is done, ask the light to come into you. Ask it to come into you and to shine within you brightly. Ask it to fill you and heal you and mend all parts of you. The light wants to come into you. It wants to come into you and heal you and fix you and repair you. You do not need to be broken any longer. You do not have to wonder about the state of your soul and your spirit. Be at peace. You can be whole in the Light and continue to be whole. Allow the light to shine and to heal and fix you. Allow it to work its magic upon you and be at peace.

33 – The Light of the Divine

The light of the Divine is a soft light, soft and strong. It is the light of God, strong as God. It is soft, softer than anything, softer than the softest flower, softer than you might imagine the clouds to be. This Light being both soft and immeasurably strong, can illuminate you, it can shine a light into the darkest corner of your life and bring it healing. You have only to open yourself up to this light. You have only to open yourself up to it and let it heal you now.

34 – The Light of the Realm

The light of the Realm is a soft sweet light too. It is a healing energy that allows you to be free and to free your spirit. In the light of the realm you can be yourself. In the light of the realm you can be yourself in all your faults and weaknesses. These do not matter. It is easy for you to be healed with the soft forgiving light of the realm. It is ready to bathe you in its energy and to heal you perfectly. It is ready to bring joy and lightness to your spirit. Ask for this light to fill you and heal you whenever you need your spirit to be lighter and more whole.

35 – The Light of Life

The light of life is the light of irrepressible joy. This is the light that you call upon when you need more in your life – when you need more peace, more joy, and more wisdom even. It is the light that you can call upon when you need guidance. The light of life fills you with joy and with life too. If joy is missing from your life, if joy is missing from your spirit, call upon the light of life, and ask the Angels and God to bring this light to you so that you may be more illuminated, more joyful, and so that you may be filled with light and so that this light may shine from you too.

36 – The Light of Joy

The light of joy smiles upon you. The light of joy makes you joyful, and brings joy to your life. It brings light to your soul and to your life. The light of joy gives us the best experience of life that we could possibly have. Allow joy and the light of joy to fill you and to enter into your life. Allow it to bring you peace.

37 – The Light of Laughter

The light of laughter is a salve and a balm to your soul. It is a balm for you in all ways. It reaches the deepest corners of you and heals you in the best way possible. It lifts you out of the misery and dread of darkness. It fills your heart and spirit with light. It is impossible to know how much good the light of laughter will do you, it is impossible to know how much light it will fill you with. The light of laughter has infinite effects upon you. The light that laughter brings enters freely into the corners of your spirit that you think are beyond repair. Everything can be repaired. And this laughter provides a deep healing that other energies do not always approach. Allow laughter, and the light it brings, to be a part of your life. Do not shut yourself off from this.

38 – The Light of Forgiveness

Forgiveness brings the light of peace both to the one who forgives and to the one who is forgiven. The light of forgiveness is the light of new beginnings, of new possibilities, and of a slate wiped clean. The light of forgiveness is meaningful, it brings substance and meaning to our lives. We have meaning in our lives already. We are meaning and our lives have meaning. But it is forgiveness and the act of forgiving that brings a different character to our lives. We are redeemed and we redeem also. How nourishing this is for us. It builds value in us and in the other. Allow the light of forgiveness to be a part of your life. Allow it to make your life lighter.

39 – Light and Shadow

The light and the shadow are always near each other. They are always somewhat side by side, one foiling the other. The shadow covers the light. The light evaporates the shadow. One falling into the other. One changing the other. The light and the shadow. Are they always to remain? Only the kinder parts of the shadow are to stay. Not the difficult darkness. Not the surly sinister qualities of it. Only the shadow that brings a comfort when shade is wanted and the light is blazing brightly. Only when a respite from its bright brilliance is needed. But never the darkness. Never the true darkness ever again.

40 – The Revelation of the Light

The light reveals everything to all. The revelations of the light are many. Truth does not hide from the light. Truth is plain, plainly in view. The light is not kind but it is not unwise. It reveals. It lets all be seen. If things are hidden from the light, then they are hidden. But if they are revealed in the light, then they can be brought about properly. There can be encouragement and scrutiny, goodwill and evaluation. Everything can be made right in the light, as long as those who look upon this are also themselves in the light. If they are not, if they are corrupt or worse, then the truth can be subject to manipulation. Things can be made to seem a certain way that they are not. All of this is revealed by the light, the things that are judged and those who judge. The attitudes of those who judge must be looked at too. Their attitudes are also in the light and they are also in the light. What do you want to reveal in the light? Is there anything that you know of that should be brought to light?

41 – Where Did the Light Come From?

The light came from God just as all of us did. But instead of a strand of light shaped into a new form, this strand gathered more strands to it and became the light. Shards of light, dapples of light, crystals of light, skies of light. In all the manifestations, this light was created. All this light was created to shine light onto our worlds, into our lives, and to illuminate our spirits. Our light came from this light. This light illuminates all and moves closely with God. This light illuminates all and we can light our lives by it. The Angels can help us to do this.

42 – Grow with the Light

Grow with the light and let your light come from God. Grow with the light and let it illuminate you, let it fuel your life, mend your spirit and nourish your soul. Grow with the light and ask the Angels to help you with your light. Ask them to help you grow this light and to grow your spirit. Ask that your light be able to shine everywhere and in all ways. Allow your light to shape you and bless you and to shape your life. Allow it to make you holy even if you think this cannot be. Allow it to make you Divine even though you think it cannot be. Allow the light to instruct you and inform you and help you do magnificent things in the world. For in the light, you are of the light and you can grow into your power. You can grow profoundly and grandly. You can grow and you can be a light to the world too.

43 – Be Well with the Light

Be well with the light and let it serve you well, let it instruct you in all things. Let it instruct you in life. Let it instruct your spirit and inform your heart. Let your thoughts and actions be formed with the ideas that are brought to you by the light. It will bring you good thoughts and recommend good actions. The light is the light of your spirit and your soul. The light is the light of all. It covers you and illuminates you. Do well with the light. Act in keeping with the ways of the light. For though you are made of light, you are separate from the light too. And you can choose a path away from the light. But you should always choose the light. The light is of benefit to you. It is of service to you. It is meaningful and it constructs you. Choose the light always then. And let not the temporal distractions of our times lead you away from it. Always seek the higher way and always choose the higher path. For the light will seek you out and bless you when you choose this.

44 – Be Healed with the Light

The light can heal you. You may not think that healing is available to you or that it is possible. But healing is possible for you and for everyone. It is possible even if you don't believe it is. The light can bring you healing. It is your own light and the light of God. Why should it not heal you and bless you? Why should it not take away your infirmities, and your weaknesses? Why should it not take away all the ways that you have been wronged, and all the things that have been done to you? Why should it not also heal the things that you have done? All these things are possible. You can have this healing. Allow your mind to have a glimmer of this possibility. Allow your mind to connect to this. You walk in the light and you are made by the light. Allow it to cleanse and clear you and allow it to fix that which needs fixing. Ask for this healing by the light in your own words. The Angels will help you.

45 – The Light Shows the Truth

The light shows the truth and shows the apparent rightness of things. The light shows the truth though sometimes the truth is hidden. Sometimes the truth evades the light but sometimes it can be pulled forward, pushed forward into the light. The light shows the truth and all should benefit from this revelation. If the truth be used to hurt then it is not light filled, it is stained and maligned, and it is made unwhole and impure. Be sure to examine the truth. Be sure to examine the light that it is presented in. Be sure that all is as it should be. It is not easy when there are truths hidden from view. Perhaps they need to stay hidden. Perhaps there is reason that they are hidden. But the light should not be used to manipulate the truth. It should not be though sometimes it is. Because those who shine the light may not be light filled themselves, or they may be hiding, or they may not have all the information they need. The truth can be shaped and sculpted but this is not truth. Let the light show the truth in fullness so that all may more fully understand the right course of action.

46 – The Light Shows Nuance

The light shows nuance. The light shows tiny intricacies. The light shows the relationship of one thing to another, of one person to another. Sometimes these relationships are not made plain. Ask the Angels to allow you to have all the understanding that you need. Ask to understand the complexities and the deeper connections between things. The light shows the nuance of all things. But you must look for it too. It will not be obvious to you. Nuance is restrained. The light reveals it simply. And you must look for it. It will not be pointed out for you unless you ask, unless you ask for the light of understanding to come to you. Unless you yourself ask to be illuminated.

47 – The Light as Revelation

The light is revelatory. The light reveals what it can and what it must. The light reveals but does not always connect things for you. It is up to you to do your own work. You must be a full participant with the light and with your life. You must be engaged. The light reveals what is there to see. The question is what are you able to see? What are you willing to see? The light reveals nothing to those who are blind. Revelation is meaningless to those who do not want to understand. If you want to stay at the surface of things then that is where you will remain. Revelation will do you no good. The light will not show you what you don't want to see. Not because it is not there but because you do not have the capacity to see.

48 – The Light as Truth

The light is the truth of things and reveals the truth. Yet the light and the truth can be ignored, they can be put to the side. Do not be the one who chooses to put the truth to the side. Do not be the one who will not shine the light properly. For it is your responsibility to use the light in the spirit of the truth. It is your responsibility to see that the light is used wisely. Do you shine the light properly in your own life? Do you shine it properly on your understanding of the world around you? Do not be misled by those who have no intention of dealing truthfully with you. Do not be misled by those who are not truthful or who want to manipulate things to their own ends. There will come a time when even they will not matter. But for now you must safeguard the truth. You must make sure the truth is accurately and fairly seen and not obscured. When you do this, you will be rewarded in and of yourself. You will feel whole and balanced. You will feel that you are on the side of right and the light. You will be nourished and at ease.

49 – The Light as Source

The light is the source of all things. All things grow in the light and are rooted in the light. Good things take hold in the light. The source and the light feed you and supply you with all that you need all your life. You may nourish yourself well with the light and the source. You may also be a light and a source to others and to the world. How will you be a light and a source? How will you feed yourself with the light so that you can be a light too? How brightly will you be able to shine? Feed yourself well and replenish the source and the light that are at the root of you, at the heart of you. Nourish yourself that you may be complete and that you might add to the world. Do not deplete yourself. Do not let the strand of light that you are be affected. You are important and it is important that you nourish yourself well. For as you do this then you nourish the Source that you are too. As you do this you also nourish the Light that you are. The Light and the Source that you are require and demand this nourishment. You are entraining yourself to the Divine. You must do this. It is not a selfish act. It is as necessary as eating and sleeping. Look upon your relationship with Divine and with Source and Light and build upon this in all ways.

50 – The Light as Energy

The light is energy. The light energizes and renews and makes whole. The light is everything and illuminates everything. It is light, pure light that brings light and life to our souls. It brings energy to our beings. When we falter and struggle, it is this light that we need. We need this light to remove the things that weigh us down and we need it to fill us with light and peace and joy. This gives us the means to do what we need to do. It propels us forward.

51 – The Energy of the Light

The light has its own energy, its own powerful source. The light is magnificent. It is powerful and can travel where it will. The energy and strength of the light stay in the background quietly. They stay in the background but they are there. This strength illuminates everything. This strength carries the light and is given to us too. We are the light and the energy of the light is in us too. Drink in this energy. Let it sustain and fuel you. Let it be a good source for you.

52 – Welcome the Light

Welcome the light in all ways. Welcome the light in all the ways it helps you. Welcome the light in all the ways it shines on you and carries you. The light is the source of life and of all things. Welcome the light and let it soothe you. The light is irrepressible and illuminating. The light will fill you with the joy of all things. Welcome the light and let it embrace you. Welcome the light and let its strength help you in your power too.

53 – The Beauty of the Light

The light is beautiful in all ways. It shines in an effervescent manner. It sparkles and imparts a glow on everything. It shares the light of Divine with everything it shines upon. The light is beautiful and it brings out the beauty of all it shines upon. If you choose to partake in the light, it will make you beautiful too. It will make you beautiful and you will not be lost. You will not be lost and you will stop wondering if you have meaning. You will be beautiful in the light and your meaning will be known to you. Your value will be known to you. You are cherished in the light. You are valued. The light brings you value and it mends your soul.

54 – The Reflection of the Light

The light shines upon all and then it is coloured by all that it shines upon. It is coloured briefly before regaining its majestic strength. But it is coloured by all it shines upon – by you and me and everyone we know, by the objects around us, by everything everywhere. All this is bound up in the light. The things that are reflected back into the light are made pure by it. They do not tarnish the light. They rather bring to the light that which needs to be purified, so that we will be a strong reflection, a pure reflection of light in and of ourselves. So that we will only reflect and emanate the most joyful and honest rendition of ourselves, the very best things about ourselves. This is the reflection of the light. We can let it add to us and add to our lives.

55 – The Light Creates Happiness

The light creates happiness in you and about you. It shines on you like sunshine and creates happiness within you. It is capable of bringing joy to you. Allow yourself to partake in this happiness. Allow the light to bless you. Accept the light and accept the lightening of your burdens. Ask that your burdens be taken away and ask that you be filled with light and happiness instead. Ask that the light make you happy in all ways.

56 - The Light Radiates

The light radiates. It radiates from you and into the world and allows the world to see you. You are of the light and you bring light to the world. The light is visible within you and it radiates outward.

This brings light to everyone and everything. Allow this light to radiate. Allow this light to come forward in the world and not be diminished. Allow it to be beautiful in all ways and to make you beautiful and whole. The radiance of the light will nourish you and the radiance of the light will heal you in all ways.

57 – The Light Quells the Darkness

The light quells the darkness. The light stills it in all ways. The light takes the measure of the darkness and is not afraid. It stops the darkness and renders it useless. The light does not allow the darkness to continue. The light absorbs the darkness and banishes it. The light says to the darkness, let there be light. And then the dark too must become light. This cannot be stopped. The dark must turn into light. The dark becomes absent. The light brings its own magic and the darkness cannot fight it. It is not strong enough. The darkness must go.

58 – The Light Illuminates

The light illuminates all in its path. It illuminates all that it shines upon. It illuminates the whole world, bathing it in a mystical substance. The light is pure and it shines into all corners. No darkness will remain. It illuminates everything. Everything is lit perfectly and the light cannot be still. The light must take over. The light must illuminate everything and shine upon everything.

59 – The Light Symbolizes

The light symbolizes the truth and the light is the truth. The light is the torch of truth. It reveals what needs to be seen. When the light is shone then the truth must be told. The light is the symbol of truth. It is the symbol of wholeness and purity. The light exists in many forms. The light exists and is symbolic. It symbolizes your spirit too. It symbolizes your spirit and the ways that you are made glad. Take hold of this powerful symbol and let it make you powerful too.

60 – The Light of Art

The light of art illuminates the world and gives us a new perspective on the world. It changes our view of things both literally and figuratively. It explains and reveals, and it does not explain and it mystifies. The eyes of the artist become our eyes. We may wonder at the message, trying to decipher it. It brings us beauty and hope. It shows what is there to be shown and gives us a different truth than maybe we had considered. We can think with the mind of the artist too. We can evaluate the colour and the truth of things. We can reduce or expand the world to be less and more than what it is. Challenge yourself to see the world and yourself differently and in a different light than you ordinarily do. Challenge yourself and you may paint a new picture, different than what you expected, and come to new realizations and understandings.

61 – The Light of Thought

The light of thought is spirit alive within our own minds. The light of thought is the light of day as it breaks over the horizon. It is the ability to see clearly and to elucidate. The light of thought allows you to break free of old fears and beliefs and it brings relief to your senses and peace and calm to all of you. The light of thought is yours to grab hold of and it gives you the tools that you need to take on the challenges that you come across. Seek to come to an understanding larger and greater than the one that you began with. The light of thought helps to root out that which came in the way before. It helps to clear the way forward for your mind to understand new concepts and ideas. The light of thought clears you for adventure. Be brave. Allow your thoughts to consider new and compelling ideas. Allow your thoughts to be illuminated by generosity and compassion and allow the light of your mind to venture out into the world and become enriched. When your mind and your thoughts are alive with light and spirit, then your heart and your whole life will be too.

62 – The Light of Virtue

The light of virtue is the blessing of God upon the universe. Virtue and those who practice virtue give to the world by their actions. Virtue in this case is purity of mind and spirit and action. This is not a constraint or an old notion of chastity. This is about a pure mind and spirit and heart acting and being alive in the world. The simple act of being, in a pure and virtuous state, brings light to the world and light to all those who are around this person. The light of virtue sets you free. It sets you free to enliven virtue in the world too, and virtue in those that are around you. All can be peaceful when virtue is called into being. All can be peaceful within you when you choose the path of virtue. Seek this out and it will enrich your life.

63 – The Light of Love

The light of love is a balm to the soul and to the spirit. It serves us and heals us. It gives us nourishment and joy. It builds us and it builds our lives. The light of love and love itself make us free. We are free to love and we are free to bring the light that this love creates to the world. Let us bring joy to the world with the light of this love and let us bring joy to the world with the light of our spirits. Light and love can weave their energy throughout the universe, to bind the universe and all within it unto each other. Light and the light of love can bring fruitfulness and grace to your purpose, character to your words, and capability to your person. When the light of love gives you a direction, then you are no longer lost. When light and love give clarity to your mind, then you see all things with a great understanding. This light brings your spirit healing and it brings your spirit joy.

64 – Meditate On the Light

Meditate on the light and let it soothe you. Meditate on the light and let it come into your spirit, and make you peaceful and happy. Let it give you joy. You who are joyful may be made still more joyful by the light. You who have peace will gain still greater peace with the light. You who are troubled will find relief with the light. The light is beautiful to you. Meditate on the light and let it become one with you. Let your spirit be mended. Let your soul no longer be damaged in any way. The light will heal you. The light will soothe you completely.

65 – The Light Shines

The light shines upon you. The light of God and of the Angels and of Divine shines upon you. It shines upon you and makes you whole and makes you light and it gives you possibility. All things are made light and all things are illuminated. You become illuminated through the work of the light. The light will not stifle you. It will not hurt you and it brings you great joy. The light brings you triumph of spirit as it shines upon you, and as it shines upon your heart and your light. You are made ever-present by the light. You are made whole and ageless and eternal. The light is beautiful in you as it shines upon you and makes you radiant and perfect. The light perfects you and renders you complete and beautiful. It illuminates you as the precious being that you are. You become again the strand formed from God's light. You are one with the light as it shines upon you. You are one and perfect.

66 – Bring Forth the Light

Bring forth the light that it may shine on you. Bring forth the light that it may shine on the world, and that it may render the world beautiful. Let the light, the sunlight, and all the light shine upon you. Let all the light shine and bring it forth. Bring it forth for truth-telling, bring it forth for the illumination of all. Bring it forth for proper elucidation and for clarity and joy. Bring it forth that others may know of it too, who may still be in darkness. Bring it forth so that it may shine brightly and perfectly among and upon all things.

67 – The Light of the World

The light of the world is its majesty and its splendour. The light of the world is magnificent. It shows us the vast creation that the world is, and the vast achievement. The light of the world also shows us the worlds' darkness too. The light of the world does not hide this. It shows us where the shadows are, and where the light has not yet done all the work that is needed. The light of the world shines on everything and everything is illuminated. The creations and the achievements of the world have their own light too. This light replicates and creates still more things, and these too have their own light. The growth of light in the world continues. The darkness that we have ignored will not be ignored any longer. The light shines upon it. The light shines upon the incongruities and we can always tell where there is failure, error, and lack of alignment. The light of the world is growing and growing. We follow it and learn from it. Now there is no hiding in darkness, and there is no hiding in ignorance. Now more than ever, the light of the world reveals all.

68 – The Substance of Light

The light is substance. The light is substance itself, made from the finest of things, made from the gossamer strands of God. The light is pure and light and stealthy. It survives among all things and it thrives despite all things. The light makes its own way. It strikes out on its own journey and brings substance wherever it goes. It brings meaning and understanding and joy and significance. The significance of the light, and of the things it shows, and of the things it brings cannot be underestimated. By the glimmer of the light, you will understand all. The light will show all things and substance above all. It will light your way and give you more substance and add to you. The journey of the light is the journey of the soul. The light, the source, is the substance upon which you may nourish yourself. It fills you wholly and completely and adds substance to your substance, and light to your light. The light illuminates you. It lifts you up and it gives you meaning. It adds to your understanding where you did not fully comprehend. It paints the picture more fully and gives you what you need.

69 – The Creation of Light

The light was created by God and given forth by God and emanated from God. The light is many strands of God woven together. It is many strands of magnificence and of soul, of spirit, and of gentleness, and of humility. The light professes everything and declares nothing. Yet the light shows and reveals, all that is needed to be known and understood. Open your eyes and understand with all your senses the knowledge that is put before you. Do not let the words transfix you, do not let the words trap you with their meaning. Look beyond the words to the Divine energy that is contained within them. Understand now that you can know more than what you read upon the page. Your heart and mind are yearning for you to understand that the Divine can transmit instantly to you. The light can create a bridge to the Divine as can the Angels. Look beyond what is matter-of-fact and mechanical. Look beyond what you know and accept to be true. Accept the journey that the light and the energy of Divine would bring you, and you will connect far more deeply than you thought possible. The depth of the light is your depth. The creation of light is your creation too. For you are a facsimile of God, you are a representation. And so the light must dwell within you, and must emanate from you. You who are Divine and not Divine. Accept the limitless. Accept the boundaries too. But then know how you can traverse them. Know how you can be a part of the light by your simple breath, by your simple presence. Will this in yourself. Allow this and you will find that the creation of light speaks new meaning to your mind and your heart.

70 – Light in its Own Space

The light keeps its own space and its own time. It is not owned, nor is it owner. The light floats in and out of the day, the moment, the hour, and yourself. The light keeps its peace and would keep yours too. The light is your caregiver and it is your freedom. The light is effervescent and non-retiring. The light will keep you. The light honours the light and spirit within you and looks at how you keep your own space. It looks at how you make your own space in the world and what creations you bring to the world too. The light is fluid and ever-changing. The light is real and perfect. The light is safe and it harbours you. It shelters you and protects you from the jagged darkness, the deceptive night. The mystics speak of the light, but we are all mystic. The light is mystical and you are mystical too. You are not ordinary. You are important and you can keep your own space and time too.

71 – The Light Speaks

The light speaks to you and it tells you to honour everything about yourself. The light tells you not to tarnish yourself through self-diminishment. It asks you to govern yourself so that the most light can emanate from you. The light is in pieces within you. The light asks that you repair your soul and spirit, mending that which is broken, making whole all that is damaged. You do not need to be damaged anymore. You can be whole and blessed. Ask the light for this wholeness now. Ask the Angels for this blessing now. Be at peace now and always.

72 – The Path of Light

The journey of light is never done. The journey of the light is vast and unending, reaching from the outskirts of the universe to the centre of the earth. This journey is not easy to undertake. We are mortal. We cannot take this journey. But our universal selves can take this path of light. And in our mortal state we can travel the path to the centre of ourselves and become illuminated, and become more in all ways. The clarity of the light is the path that we have to follow. The clarity of light is perfect and it shows us the journey and the path. We need the light to show this path to us – perfectly and without delay. We need to be measured in our journey. We need to be responsible and sure. We are sure in our path of the light. We walk in energy and we walk with the light. We walk with our spirit front facing, beautiful and secure in all ways. We walk easily and without reservation. We are guided by the light and are secure in its trueness, its sage and wise discourse, and its complete illumination.

73 – The Journey of the Light

The journey of the light is true. The journey of the light is forthwith. The journey of the light is yours to take.

74 – Where the Light Leads You

The light leads you where you need to go. It leads you home to the centre of your spirit and to the source of your being. It is your source and your nourishment too. It is what you need. And it is what you are called to follow. If you do not follow it you will be less. And if you follow it you will know how much more it brings you. Go then towards the light. Go then to where it will lead you. You will follow the call easily because it comes from your own soul and spirit. Listen within and see what this light is telling you.

75 – Where is the Light?

The light is within you and outside of you. It is a part of you and it surrounds you. It is in the air and in the sky. It is in the cells of your body and it is in the rain that falls. The light and the energy of the light are the nourishment that you seek. It fills you completely. It is within you but it calls you from outside yourself too. You are never away from the light and the light is never away from you. You wear the light like a cape and yet you carry it within you too. Be at peace in the light for that is all you need to know, and all that you ever need to ask. Be at peace in the presence of the light and it will be a part of you and you will not be separate from it.

76 – Daylight

Daylight is breaking upon you and all around you. Daylight is shining and it shines upon your spirit and your soul. Your soul is called into the light. Your soul and spirit rise to meet the light, the light at the break of day. The daylight is reflected in you. It is reflected in your being, in your soul and in your spirit. The daylight and the light are reflected in you. Be wise in the light. Be wise in your spirit and your soul. Be safe in all ways. And be protected by the light in all the ways that you can be.

77 – Light and Peace

The light brings you peace and always has. It has brought you peace since the first dawn. It has brought you peace as you stepped out of the cave and gazed upon the world around you, not knowing and yet understanding everything. The light shows you that peace does not have to be excluded from you. The light wants you to have the most peace possible. It wants you to be as peaceful as you dare to be, and even more peaceful than you can imagine. The light wishes for you to be bathed in light and completely happy. The light wishes that even your moments of contemplation and solitude and meditation be filled with profound joy. This knowledge of the light, this presence of the light in your life, may it clothe you in miracles, may it surround you with the possibilities that you seek and dream of, and those that you do not speak of. May you be encouraged to dream with your universal self in a way that befits an expansive imagination. Dream and let the light and peace come to you and bring you all that you need and desire, and all that you are able to enjoy.

The Light Part 2

The light was not the shadow. The shadow had its own story which we will next relate. What then is the light?

The story of the light is the story of the thing that came into being at the beginning of time, at the beginning of the world, and at the beginning of the Universe. The light was created from God and pulled from God, pulled from a strand at His hip and made more effervescent and luminous than all the other strands of light.

God released the strand and commanded it to expand and grow. And so it did, and it traveled and grew, unfettered, till it reached all corners of the Universe and all corners of everything, till all was covered with light and by the light.

The light was perfect and it shone brightly, confident in the command that it had, confident in the role it played to bring God's Essence everywhere, to bring the truth everywhere.

And so too did it have purpose, bringing truth and illumination everywhere. It shone, and it rose every day with the daylight and purposeful, it went out into the world and eliminated the darkness, conquered the darkness and the shadow. Everywhere was the light, and therefore everywhere God was too, as both Himself and as the light.

The light streamed everywhere and went everywhere until the time when it had to obscure itself, diminish itself. The light did not disappear. It reduced itself and sometimes it went into hiding. It went into hiding to better see the darkness and the actions of the darkness. It went into hiding so that all of us would be tested, to see who among us was too weak, too easily impressed by the darkness. It did not want to go. But it understood the value of doing so. It understood and so it hid itself quietly, so that the work of uncovering the darkness – in the universe and in the spirit – could be done.

The light can now return and resume its purpose. The light can now return and shine again, and be illuminated. The light can now travel to the far reaches of the cosmos and shine. The light can show everything and reveal truth. The light is set free and can set you free too. The light is set free and we are all free too.

What darkness that remains can be chased out. What darkness that remains can be erased and eradicated. It need not exist. It is no longer supported. Go forth then in the light. Go forth and be your own light unto yourself and to the world. The light of the world and the light of God is the light that will guide you. Your mind and spirit and heart will know the journey. The light will guide you to everything.

The Shadow

The shadow or the darkness was the name that was given to all that was wrong and had ever been wrong in the world and in the individual. The shadow or the darkness was the absence of the light, the absence of goodness, the forgetting of the self. The shadow began as just an absence, a lack of what was good. But by and by, it developed its own persona, it developed its own being-ness.

Night was used for cover. Night was used to cover the darkness or the shadow. Night was naturally dark, being the state of things when the sun was not present. But it was not a bad darkness. Rather it was natural in its lack of light and meant no harm. Night was trustworthy and friendly and could tell you things that you might need to know, if you were to ask it. There was nothing wrong with night itself. But at least some of the time, night fell into the hands of the darkness and the shadow. At least some of the time it was duped. And so it began that the setting forth of Night meant that the shadow and the darkness could roam free, unperturbed by the light, not needing to answer to it, doing whatever it wanted at all times. It began to exclude others. It began to exclude the light.

In effect, the light was removed. The light was removed under pretext. Night said that it could do a better job if light were fully gone, if light were wholly absent. And light agreed though it was not fooled. Light could see through the argument. But light also knew, which night did not, that all this was necessary for the playing of a grand game -- a strategy that night could not understand. Night was not the most intelligent of creations. And Night had been fooled and tricked into excluding Light, which, after all, was its oldest and dearest friend. Night felt it could do without Light now and that this might be a more comfortable thing. Night missed light sometimes but also liked being alone, and liked especially not having to answer to anyone or anything. Night reveled in its autonomy and so the Light was removed.

The darkness and the shadow were pleased that all of this had occurred. They were pleased. The night had cooperated fully. Darkness could be present everywhere. Shadow could be present everywhere. The absence of light was not enough. Darkness and shadow had to become their own beings and Night was where this could develop and grow. This was how it would all evolve, darkness and shadow growing in strength and creeping over the world and over hearts, and the light receding. Darkness was pleased.

The Shadow

1 – The Shadow descended upon us. It descended upon us and engulfed us. It engulfed us even though we had been sheltered in the light. The light had receded and the darkness was able to come in and cover our minds, hearts and spirits. We were no longer protected. We were exposed to the darkness. What should we do? How would our thoughts and feelings be affected? How would we act?

2 – The world became dark. The whole world became dark as the darkness and the shadow were cast upon us. This darkness permeated our hearts and minds and the very world itself. The consciousness of the world became dark. We had to fight to get out of the shadows. We had to fight to get the world out of the shadows. The shadow is upon the world still. The shadow darkens minds, hearts, wills, and spirits. The shadow makes it difficult to have the possibility of good, makes it difficult to bear witness to good. Where is the shadow? It is upon us and the whole world. It is still upon us.

3 – The power of the dark darkens all of us and darkens the world. The dark diminishes the light within us. The dark reduces our power for good. The shadow takes away our goodwill and replaces it with fear. The darkness introduces doubt where hope would bring infinite success. Let the darkness not have sway upon you. Let the darkness not have sway upon your corner of the world. Use

your influence for good. Use your own power to push away the darkness and to reaffirm a connection with the light.

4 – The darkness of power is such that power itself can be dark. But power does not need to be dark. It can be a force for good. It can build better structures to support human development, working with others to strengthen them. Darkness creeps over power too and convinces the powerful that they want more, that they need to achieve their ends no matter what. It tells them they are supremely important when they are nothing. It lifts them up and makes them feel that they are at the top of everything they are supposed to have when in fact they are no better than the dirt that they walk upon. You who are powerful, look that you do good with your power, lest you be reduced to the lowest of the low. You who have influence, look that you seek to increase the comforts of others, the well-being of others. Otherwise you are wasting what you have, you are wasting the greatest gift that you have and this will not be rewarded.

5 – Where then was the light in all of this? Where did the light go and hide? The light did not hide. The light pulled itself back and receded. The light made itself smaller so that the dark could do what it needed to do, so the dark could play its part. The darkness did not know this. The darkness thought that it had won. The darkness thought that it had been able to subsume everything that it and the shadow were able to take over. The darkness thought that the light had capitulated. It served all of us to let the darkness think this. The darkness had its role to play. The darkness had to let things emerge, similar things, similarly dark things, so that we

could see what was really what, and who was hiding their true intentions, who was false, who was not real or true. The light had not gone. It was showing us, instead, who could be trusted, and who could not be believed.

6 – The darkness thought it was in control. The darkness thought it had full reign over everything. We let it think this. We let it think that it could cover everything and take over everything. It was true that the darkness covered everything. But it did not reign. It could not. For wherever there was a glimmer of light then the truth would come out, then the light would reveal all, the light would reveal the nastiness that the dark sought to conceal. The light would reveal what had been hidden, what had been covered up. The light always brought the revelations. The darkness could cover things as best it did. Sometimes we helped it to cover things because we were in search of the deeper darkness. We were in search of the deeper truth pushed down underneath things, pushed down under one lie covering another. And always there were those willing to tell the truth, willing to uncover what had truly gone on, just as there were those who participated in the covering up, or others who were too fearful to tell what had happened. Sometimes the truth took years to emerge. But emerge it did.

7 – Evil happened in the world. Evil happened under cover of darkness and sometimes in broad daylight. Evil was sanctioned by the powers that governed. Evil was sought out by the authorities. Evil happened and it affected things, it affected everything. Evil happened and it was a blight upon happiness, it was a blight on the full development of human understanding. It crushed us and

ruined us. It made us choose a lesser path and often the wrong path. How could we be lifted up if evil was in the world? How could we be lifted up? Evil happened but we did not have to stand for it. Evil happened but we did not have to stand by it. We could be a force against it. We could be a quiet force or we could be a bold force. But we are able to be this force. We are able to overturn any evil in our world through our thoughts and our words and our actions. We are able to resist evil simply by refusing to allow it traction.

8 – The soul became dark. The darkness of the soul was almost inevitable with the coming of the darkness upon the earth, with the coming of the darkness to cover humanity. The darkness came and it covered all and there were few souls who could escape from it. There were few souls that could escape and not be made dark at least in part. They were made dark because they were touched with thoughts of how they had been damaged, of how they had been afflicted, of how they had been made to pay. They took decisions with these false feelings in mind, these false feelings that had been put there by the darkness itself. They took no comfort in their lives. They saw no joy in their surroundings. They saw only gloom and misery and they identified with it. They became part of the darkness. The darkness rejoiced at the collection of so many souls, at the collection of souls because this meant a still further dimming of the light. The darkness was glad. And many souls were tormented and in misery and this did not matter to it. It cared not for their well-being. It cared only for its aggrandizement.

9 – During all this time there was a noticeable absence of God. The sheer presence of God would have obliterated the darkness. The presence of God, like the sun on the horizon, would have made all the slippery strands of darkness retreat into nothingness. There would be no more shadows. There would be nothing that the light could not penetrate as the pure emanation of God and of His spirit. God had gone away. God had gone away and so the light could go too. God had gone away and so the darkness could take ascendancy. God was very quiet in His absence but He was still watching. He was watching nonetheless, and taking note.

10 – The son came. The son came and thoughts of redemption began to be possible. The son came and then God was present again in this form. The son came and the darkness for a moment began to lose faith. And then the son died and the darkness was able to re-emerge, resurrection notwithstanding.

11 – The Angels were absent during this time too. The Angels had retreated far back too. They kept God company but were present here on earth too. They were present in a little way. They had to be asked to help. They could not just swoop in and do what was right. They could not just save the day. They had to be asked. And so often the day was not saved. Often it was ruined.

12 – Through all this of course Heaven and the Realm were affected too. They were shuttered, they were made dark. They could not perform their usual function not in its full capacity. Certainly the souls of the departed still made their way there and were healed

and made whole. But all was not as it should have been, all was not as it could have been. Things were not run in the best possible way. And things were run by those who were not the best quality, could not always even be said to be good. Heaven and the Realm were left in the hands of those who would ruin things for us. We had to see how far things would go.

13 – With all of this, despair became a part of our history. Despair was made new and renewed over and over again. Despair was made fresh and woven into human history. History became the tale of different forms of despair, different incidents of despair. One incident leading to another to another. We called this history. We called this our narrative. But it did not have to be this way. Things did not have to be so desperate, so God-forsaken. We can relinquish all this despair now. We can let it go.

14 – Misery was often a part of our lives too, the defining context. We defined our lives by how unliveable they were. We defined our lives by our ability to get through the misery, the difficulty, the unyielding struggle. Mostly that was without reward. For most of humanity, life was impossible. In modern days that may be less. But much of the world still plods along in difficult conditions, in subhuman conditions. We cannot seem to lift ourselves out of it. We cannot seem to forego misery in some form or another. The world can lift itself out of this. The world can make itself new. It does not have to commit itself to misery any longer. It does not have to commit its people to misery either. The world can be free to do better now. The people of the world can be free to do more than just survive.

15 – Strife is the companion of misery -- the perpetual companion of most lives on the planet, each person struggling to provide for themselves, to give themselves what they need to survive. We need not take shelter in strife. We can consider that we can do well, that we can succeed without strife or struggle. We can be at peace with who we are. We don't have to feel that we are defined by our difficulties. We don't even have to have these difficulties. We can be free and free of effort that taxes the very thing that we are made of. We don't have to be drained and watch our dreams slip away. We can rebuild ourselves. We can build ourselves up and replace struggle with stamina, and difficulty with well-being. This mindset change is possible for you. This change in perspective will do you good and help you in your life and all that you want to it. Choose to thrive and to flourish. Choose this every day.

16 - Gloom

Gloom was everywhere. Gloom had set upon the earth and was everywhere. Like the damp, it crept in, into bones, into minds, into souls, into spirits. It crept in and would not move from where it was lodged. It crept in and it stayed there, it rested there and sat heavily brooding. It made all of us heavy too. It made all of us despondent and burdened with all of our cares. There could be no lightness of spirit. There could be no joy for gloom had set upon us. Gloom had set upon us and imprisoned us and we could not see the way out.

17 – Grief

Grief was gloom's sister companion, making sense of gloom, explaining gloom, and giving gloom a reason for its existence. Grief was more explainable than gloom. Grief could be accepted. It was a natural emotion, upon loss. Grief was expected. Grief ushered in the way for more gloom to enter, more sadness to be upon the world. Grief announced its presence and then one had to accept gloom. There was no choice. It was inevitable. So how to be rid of both of these? How to be rid of this staggering intensity of emotion crushing us down and willing us not to move?

18 – Fear and Worry

Fear and worry were also the soft-spoken companions to gloom. Fear said all those things could happen and they would be bad. Worry said you need to look out for this and this and this. Worry said what if this were to happen, or this? Fear was always ready with his sword to strike you down. Worry sat beside him crying, seeking to comfort you or pretending to. But really there was no comfort, there was no peace or joy when this pair were in your life. They haunted you and would not release you. They cast you always in gloom, and cast you always in dread too.

19 – Dread

Dread was the worst. Fear and worry could do their work but they were nothing to dread, the thought of the hammer coming down above you. Fear and worry amplified dread and cast you into a great depression. There was no hope, there was no hope. All would end badly. All was already ending badly and all was as bad as it could be. Dread engulfed you like a fog, like a cape you could not see through. Dread choked you and altered your vision so you could only see your fear, so you could only feel panic and anxiety and could only feel that there was nothing to be done. Nothing was possible.

20 – The Reign of Lack

All this was possible because Lack was in charge. Lack was in charge of making sure you felt that you had nothing and could be nothing. Lack was in charge of taking away anything that came your way. Lack was in charge of holding you up for scrutiny to make sure that all you had was something no one would want. And so you kept on going in fear, and dread, and gloom, punctuated by worry and grief when it came around. And these were your possessions because anything else worth having was kept from you. Lack reigned and having and wanting could not be allowed in.

21 – All that we lost

We suffered a loss during this time of the shadow. We lost people and things that were important to us. Some say we lost our humanity or at any rate accepted a view of humanity that was far from humane, that was dark. We excused too many things. We excused too many thoughts and words and we thought this was how it had to be. We thought that we were not perfect and therefore we could be infinitely fallible. It was terrible to think this. It was terrible to be released to this state, to have to act in this manner. It was terrible to accept ourselves in this state and to think that we could not be better, and that we could not be the people we were. We could not even remember the point from which we had started from. We could not remember when to be human meant to be divine. Now we just thought that being human meant being miserable and not being able to act in the best interest of anyone except ourselves. We had lost a lot.

22 – All that we misplaced

We misplaced many things too. We misplaced our happiness and our joy. We misplaced our capacity to do great things. We misplaced so much of what gave our lives meaning. We thought that a moment of joy or a memory of happiness were enough. We thought that this is all we had the right to. We could not remember anymore when happiness was a constant state, when joy was ever present. We put these things down somewhere. And then we could not find them. They were gone.

23 – Discounting ourselves

We discounted ourselves often. We discounted ourselves and put ourselves down and told ourselves we did not matter. We told ourselves also that nothing mattered and that our words and actions did not matter. All of these things affected us and made us still less refined, still less human. And we accepted this diminishment because we had done it to ourselves. We thought it only right.

24 – Discounting humanity

We discounted humanity too because it seemed the right thing to do. We discounted ourselves and so we extended this to all of humanity. How could any of humanity be worthwhile or valuable?

How could any of it have any meaning when we ourselves were so very base? We pondered and considered this but we could not elevate humanity in our eyes. We could not raise ourselves up either.

25 – Devaluing ourselves

Of course we were devalued as a result. Of course we could not look upon ourselves with merit. We could not think anything good about ourselves at all. This was true and we kept ourselves from the full benefits of what a good life could give us. We did not deserve all this. We did not deserve to treat ourselves this way. But we did not know this. We did not see the difference that it would make if we just were able to think a little more highly of ourselves.

26 – Devaluing others

We had to devalue others too. We put ourselves down. We put down the whole of humanity. We had to devalue them and say that they were not worth very much. We had to devalue them and say that we could not see much point. The shadow was at work here too. The shadow clouded our minds and our judgement and it made us think less of things and of others always. The shadow was always at work, pushing us down, pushing our spirit down and also our estimation of ourselves and the world around us. We could not see things in a clear light. We could not see things with a kind spirit. This was not possible.

27 – How bad could it get?

The shadow had taken over much. It had taken over much of the earth and much upon the earth. The shadow could spread where it wanted to and take over the hearts and minds of men and women. They could not fight it. No part of humanity could fight it. Yet they strove to do good nonetheless. They strove to recognize the glimmer of light nonetheless. It could get bad. It did get bad. But the human spirit was never completely made dark. It was never completely dominated. And for that we were thankful.

28 – How bad did it get?

There are many examples of how bad this did get, many examples in history and many today. We do not have to name them. We do not have to repeat the litany of events and travesties. But we must do better now. We must do better and not allow this anymore. It is in our power to do this now. The shadow does not need to reign over us anymore. The shadow will go and we will be free to act in full agreement with the light.

29 – Tale of a Tree

The tree was still. It was nighttime and the tree was watching everyone as they packed up and left. They were sorry to go. They had to go but they could not take the tree with them. They could take, maybe, a few things that looked like they were part of the tree but that was all. Other than that they could do nothing. The tree watched them go and was sad. The tree wondered if anyone had thought to cover the entrance to the tunnels underneath it. But they did remember. They had to be stealthy because no one who did not already know could be made aware of this. It was a secret that very few knew. Very few were aware of the power of the tree, let alone what could be done if one went under the tree in the tunnels. Very few knew and certainly the ones who were taking over did not know. But the tree was still concerned. It could be that some of those who knew would tell, or would be corrupted. The tree would watch and wait and see. In time, things would unfold. And the tree had its own secrets to keep.

30 – The Removal of the Darkness

At last it was time for the darkness to go. It was time for it to be removed. It would have to pack its bags and leave forever. It did not have a choice. No one was giving it a choice, not the light, not God, not the Angels. The darkness was done and it was leaving, because if it were chased out, then it would cease to exist completely.

31 – The Absence of the Shadow

The shadow was absent then. The shadow was absent and it fled from view. It could not linger anymore and ruin things or cast a gloom on them. It could not ruin anything at all. But it was a strange thing, this absence. We were not used to it. We were not used to this lack of its presence. It brought us a new found joy that we had to get acclimated to. We weren't quite sure about this new situation. It might be difficult to get used to this. But it would not be invited back, of that we were sure.

32 – Fade

"Fade then," said the light. "Fade," it commanded to the shadow and the darkness. And so they did. They had no other alternative. It was a retreat. There was no other way to say it. The darkness had been bested. It was only then that it knew that all along that this had been the plan. It knew and it could not comprehend that this was, that it had been fooled for so long. It had thought itself in charge. But it was not. It had only been allowed to think so. And now it would go, it had to fade and beat a path. Otherwise it was threatened with its demise. There were still a few places that it could go. There were still a few places it might yet hide but not many.

33 – The Notion of Light

The idea of light was an odd one. The idea that we needed a substance in order to see, that we needed a source of luminosity, and that visibility wouldn't just be there regardless. But no, We needed the light, we needed the sunlight and we needed the Light from God. For without it there was no ability to get past the absence, the lack, the shadow, the dark. It removed both neutrality and that which was negative. It shored us up, it lifted us up. It lifted us from desperation and it lifted us to new heights. We were so dependent on the light. We are still so dependent on it. We cannot survive without it. We can breathe without it but we can't grow and thrive. Without light, we remain dwarfed and diminished, destined to remain in our small corner of the world and to shrink ourselves still further. Without light we are not who we are. It defines us and allows us to contemplate ourselves. Light is fundamental to our being and to our beingness in all ways. Rejoice in the light. Rejoice in the presence of the light, for it gives us life.

34 – The Possibility of Light

And God said, let there be light, and then there was light. And so it began. So we need never think about light as a possibility or as a potential essence. It simply is, just as we simply are. And we can use it, and live with it and have our lives lit by it. Most things are possible because of light. Light is a certainty rather than a possibility. Light exists and then we are made possible by it. The possibility of light is that it gives us our possibilities in all ways. Forever it has done this. Since the beginning. Since our beginning it has done this.

35 – The Possibility of Light and Strength

The existence of light that gives us possibility and reality is also what gives us strength. Perhaps we could be strong without the light but the light makes the strength relevant. What use is strength in the world if you cannot see? What will you be strong for? How will you use your strength? You might be strong for another but if you cannot see into their heart, then you won't choose to do this. You might need strength in your daily life, but if all is dark, then all thoughts of any kind of work are also removed from view. Use your strength wisely. You will need it for many things. Use your strength wisely and always use it for good, and for light purposes. When you do this you give yourself more strength, and potential than you could possibly know.

36 – The End of the Dark

The dark needed one last hurrah. And so here it is. You can go now. You do not have to return. And do not look for more words or accolades, above all not that. You can go now. No more words will be given. Be gone.

How the Angels Were Held Back

The Angels were held back in so many ways -- by their devices, by our devices, by a plan that had been set in motion long before any of us were born.

The Angels were to be the helpers of the earth, the helpers of mankind – of men and women. Of course, we know this. We know that they were to be our Divine Assistants. We have always known this. We have always known this. But we always knew also that we had to ask for help, we had to seek them out. They could not help us of their own free will. They were depending upon us to call on them. This is what changed. This is the thing that had changed so profoundly so many years ago.

For once, long ago, the Angels were free to help much more than they could help now. They were free to see with their divine perspective all that needed to be done, and all that could be done. They were not held back by our limited human perspective. They were not limited to only help us when finally, in turmoil, and in despair, we turned to them or to God.

No, it was not always like this.

Once, long ago, the Angels were much more present in our lives. They could come to us. They could help us freely. They could help us with all manner of our lives. They could lift the burden from us and help us see more clearly. They would do for us and then we would see further. This was how it was meant to be. Humans working in concert with Angels because Angels were our link to the

Divine, a link that we could experience day to day, in our lives with real tangible results.

Today we need to ask for help. Today we need to ask the Angels to enter into our lives, to assist us with everything. Today it is wise to ask for this. It is not true that they always stand on the sidelines. Sometimes they themselves feel compelled to act in grave situations. They are compelled to work to help us even when we don't call upon them. After so many years of standing beside us and behind us, they cannot help but recognise the tiny glimmers of a call for help as small as it might be and use that to take action.

Still, once it was much more. Once it was much more than this. They were not standing behind us and beside us silent and unable to move except in the direst circumstances. Instead, they were shoulder to shoulder with us, assisting us and breathing life into the most important aspects of our existence. They were helpers of incredible power and stature. They made our lives so easy and so meaningful.

How did they come to be held back?

For now it is important to know that the dawn of the Age of the Angels is upon us. They are returning to help us as they once did. Because the reasons for the step back that they took, those reasons are gone. Those reasons have been put to rest. And we can all be safer and more whole because of this.

To give you one detail of the story, it's important to say that they were held back as part of a necessary project. If they had not been held back, then a kind of test that was carried out would not have been able to be done properly. We had to see just what would happen. We had to allow for what happened to occur. And it did.

Repeatedly and expansively, and not with positive affirming outcomes every time. That is reflected in the story of human history. The story of strife and struggle and misery and poverty and conflict that has been the lot of human kind. Perhaps all that is ready to be lifted now. Perhaps all that can be lifted once the Angels return.

The Jesus Factor

The figure of Jesus has been monumental for so long and forever it seems in our history. Jesus, saving us all from sin. Jesus, seated at the right hand of the Father. Jesus, son of Mary. The name Jesus is like a bell that does not stop ringing for us if we are Christian. It is a name, an icon, a man, a representation, and possibly the most emblematic figure of religion that we have. Where God is faceless and almost nameless, Jesus lets the children come to him. Where God is unapproachable and distant, Jesus walked the earth among us, lived and died, taught and wept and prayed.

How do we account for Jesus now today? How do we speak of this figure, part-man, part-God?

He is still with us. He is still dominant. He is divisive. He is commanding even. He has never lost his power over us. Good and bad things have been done in his name. Where does he fit in?

He is part of the holy trinity – along with God and the Holy Spirit. The three are one. The three are all aspects of the Divine. The Angels serve each of the three.

Sometimes we feel that Jesus is in our midst. Sometimes we worship him more than we worship God. He is relatable. After all, He is a person. He has eliminated the distance between us and God. He is the human face of the Divine and he is worshipped as such.

His presence, his persona changes things. It affects things. What if he had not come? What if there were no Jesus? What would our relationship be to the Divine?

The story is that he reopened heaven to us. That his sacrifice was the representation of sacrifice of all human kind so that we could be saved. He died for our sins. The gates of heaven were then reopened. Perhaps. Perhaps this is so. Were we so bad a people previously that this was necessary? Have we been so good a people since then? Possibly not.

The great sacrifice redeemed us and our sins. It allows us to be saved, over and over again it seems. Why are we in constant need of redemption? Why do we sin? Is sin even necessary? Is this a choice that we must make?

This is a strange dance that we do. Sin and be redeemed. Sin and be saved. Sin and be thankful that Jesus made this possible.

Of course we are grateful that Jesus redeemed us and that heaven is now possible for us. But the question is, why is sin possible? Why are we able to sin? If free choice is the answer, then the question changes. The question becomes why is sin even attractive? Why is sin even a choice? How is choosing badly even possible when you can choose good? What is good is surely just good. What is Light is only Light. There is no choice for darkness when there is Light. The Light takes over everything.

These moral questions are worth contemplating. Also worth contemplating is how Jesus, in coming down and sacrificing himself, in becoming man, in dying, has become such an important figure. The ultimate romantic figure I believe. It is good to consider his importance in our history. It is also good not to use him as our excuse to sin. We must live freely. We must live well. We must live good lives. And how could we choose otherwise when good and bad are so clearly delineated, are so clearly and evidently and obviously defined?

Choose your words wisely and your actions will follow. Choose to emulate the man and his words and deeds. But do not allow his example to serve the world as a scapegoat of convenience. We do not need to allow evil to perpetuate in the world. We do not need to allow it to continue. Evil requires no redemption. It requires nothing. If we do not require it then it will cease to exist. Jesus has brought us to a certain point in our understanding and in our history. But we must make it our personal responsibility to choose well and for ourselves. Most of the time the good choice is obvious. If we can rid ourselves of what is extra, of what does not matter, then everything becomes much clearer.

The Book of Light (Introduction)

Here begins the Book of Light, the beginning of the Books of Light. Let these Books show you what they can, let these Books give you an understanding of themselves, and an understanding of what they want to say. Receive these words abundantly and well. Let any wisdom in these pages that is meant for you be received by you. Let the words find a place in you, let them nourish you, your spirit, your mind and all parts of you. Let them illuminate you and let you yourself be illuminated in all ways.

The Light

The Light shone. It shone everywhere. At first it was barely visible. But then it grew more and more, sunlight on the pavement, it shone everywhere, spreading in every direction, spreading and growing larger covering more ground, covering more space.

Where did this Light come from? It came from beyond, from Beyond. It came from beyond the heavens, beyond space, beyond time, certainly beyond history. It came from a time when the earth was new, when the universe was new, and when God was young. It came like a gift and a beacon, it came like the sun always there, always present, always shining.

The Light was everywhere now. It grew and shone upon everything. There was no darkness anymore. The darkness had gone and run away. And the things that had hidden in the darkness, the things that were themselves dark. They could no longer hide. They could no longer not be apparent. Everything was made visible. Everything was made plain and everything could be seen. Everything could be seen in the Light, plain as day. Transparency was everywhere.

For years, for many years, for too many years, the Light had been kept constrained. The Light had been forced to dialogue with the darkness, to keep itself cloistered, to keep itself separate and unsullied. The Light could not simply overpower everything during that time. The Light kept to itself, bided its time. The Light only arrived when summoned, only arrived when called.

The Angels knew of the plight of this heavenly Light. They knew what the cost was. They too had been kept separate and cloistered, unable to help in the way that they could. They knew what it was like to not be able to shine over everything, to not be able to bring the blessings of heaven to earth. They knew what this was. They knew the Light was being held back. But now the Light could return. The Light could return and the Angels could return too. They could return to Earth. They could return to humankind. They could return to make things easier, truer, and righter. They could return to bring more peace to the world, all peace to the world.

And the Light, the shining source, could come back too. The Light, that had been gone for so long, or at least contained, now it would shine everywhere, it would spread everywhere. And the blackest of hearts would be no match for the Light. The Light would shine over everything and through everything, bringing peace and restoring harmony. The Light would shine into the very darkest of things, and take the darkness away. There would be no more darkness. The darkness was done. The darkness would be vanquished. The darkness would go and it could not return.

This point is where we are at now. This point. We are at the end of the darkness, we are at the beginning of the Light.

Behold the coming of the Light. The Light is returning. The Light is here. Welcome the Light and look for it in all ways. May you see the Light everywhere. It is here all around you. It is here now.

Mark this as the true beginning of the Light, the true beginning when you and all can be renewed, can be restored.

Mark this as the point at which you need no longer be affected by darkness, no more darkness may linger in your heart, your mind, your spirit. The darkness has been chased away. Let the Light take root easily. Let it take hold.

Mark this as a time of change and wonder for you.

These are the Books of Light. They are the tale of the Light. They are the tale of what happened when the Light retreated. And they are the tale of what is to come as the Light returns. They are the Heralds and announcers of the Light. They are your tale too, of all who live in the Light.

The Book of Light

The Book of Light precedes all the other Books. It is the first book because it is the most important. The most important in terms of message and priority. The Book of Light is the core element of the Books of light. It ties the others together. All the other Books can be read in context of the Book of Light even when they make no reference to it.

The Book of Light, more perhaps than the other Books, is a book of healing. It is meant to give you peace, and sustenance. It is meant to repair and mend you. Take this healing to heart. It wants to help you in your life. It wants to work with you to fix the things that are broken, the things that need healing. You can ask the Light directly for healing. You can ask God directly for healing. You can ask the Angels too, especially Raphael, for healing. Take some time to ask for healing every day. The reading of this book, though, in itself is an act of healing. Read a few words when you are inspired to do this. Do not force this. If you feel resistant then do not read. If you feel resistant then check if you are resistant to healing. Allow the thoughts to come to you. Put the book away and then look at it when you can. But ask the Angels and God for healing anyway. Always ask. It is a good practice and will bring you peace of mind.

When you need repair, when you need mending, you will feel this in yourself. You will learn to pay attention to the signs that you give yourself. You, all of you, know what is going on. You don't have to be told that you are feeling unwell because of a particular cause. You, inside yourself, normally know the reason. Ask for healing and help. Ask for healing and this is in the real world too, from alternative and allopathic sources. Healing comes from wherever it does. Let us accept it in all its forms.

How are you empty?

You are empty because there is nothing to fill you. You are empty because the wholeness that is you has not found its way to you. You forget where you have left parts of yourself. You forget where you have made yourself smaller or contorted yourself in order that others may shine brighter or in order that you could survive in the world that you find yourself. When you made yourself small you forced yourself into yourself. You made yourself too dense. You made yourself wrong in a sense. You changed and altered the patterns in your mind and in your heart to make this okay. You told yourself it was a good thing, that you were being accommodating. You told yourself that you were strong because of your smallness. It is okay that you did this. It is okay that you emptied yourself and gave parts of you away. It is all okay. The parts of you that have gone from you can return to you now. The part of yourself that you gave away to make room for survival can come back now. Any time you changed your mind and changed yourself to suit someone else, all that is erased now. Come back to yourself. Fill yourself back up. No need to be empty any longer. No need to leave any part of you behind.

Let the Light fill you

Instead, let the light fill you. Let the light determine where you are lacking, where you are empty. Let it feed you and make you whole and piece you together. Let it come into you and repair you as it does. It does not need guidance. It does not need to be shown the way. It will find the problem the moment it meets with you, the moment it embraces you. It will embrace you, and fill you and then you will be whole in all ways.

How are you wounded?

It is true that you are wounded. It is true that you have been wounded and that you have suffered. All of you have suffered. These wounds do not heal. They stay open. Sometimes they fester. Sometimes they are merely there, existing. And you are merely there, existing. Sometimes things are like this. The wound continues even though the wounding happened long ago. Why did the wounding happen? What events and circumstances were set in place so that this wounding occurred? The past offers a strange mirror of the history of the wounding, never entirely truthful or accurate. Vague recollection comes to mind. A particular perspective always surfaces. Then we are stuck there in that moment. But we are not stuck enough to be able to fix anything. We continue there, in the same space and time, together with our wound, which does not always heal.

Let the Light repair you

The light can repair the wound too. The light can suture what was cut, what seemed unfixable. The can mend the opening, can erase the scar. The light can travel into you, into all parts of you and fix anything that was damaged. The light, with its cool energy, is pure, and it will come into you and seek out the parts of you that don't feel well and heal them. This happens, body, mind and soul. The light's energy is precise. Its energy is all-encompassing. The light will heal you more deeply than you can realize, more carefully than you might understand. Ask the light to repair and heal you in all the ways that you need this. This energy is different from that of the Angels. It is a pure strong energy. It might seem impersonal. But it is very good. It is very strong and it will heal you well.

How are you damaged?

If you are damaged, if parts of you are worn away, then you will know this, you will feel a lack about yourself. You will feel less capable. You will feel less too. Less will be available to you. More intensity will be required to reach you. If you are missing parts of your life. If you are missing parts of your spirit. There will be a calling out in you. There will be a yearning in you for those things. But you might not feel the yearning. You might not hear it or sense it. You will be blind and deaf to it. You will not care what happens. You will not care that you are damaged even, that you are not whole, because you will have forgotten. You will have forgotten that there was more of you, that there was more to you. You will have forgotten that you matter and that being whole matters too. Worn away as you are, you will not care. You will not care, and then there might be no chance to fix what is wrong, to repair you and make you whole.

Let the Light nurse you

Let the light be your nurse and your companion. Let the light soothe you and shelter you. Let it fix even the tiniest parts of you that require attention. Let it repair all the damage and make you whole again. It might take time or it might be instantaneous. Call the light and let it fill you. Call the light and let it smooth your whole system, filling the empty spots, taking out what does not belong. The light can heal you completely and in all ways. The light can nurse you and repair all that was taken from you and all that you have put aside and lost or forgotten. Call for the light. Allow it to make these repairs.

How are you hurt?

If you have been hurt in some way, you will feel this as a reverberation. Your hurts will sting and then they will tear and then they will persist, dull aches that do not fade and that become jagged at times, rising to the surface. If you have been hurt then you may wish the hurt to go away. Or you might want the hurt to remain because it is a reminder of something, a kind of photograph of something that you do not want to forget. However you have been hurt, in whatever manner this has happened to you, this hurt does not have to remain. You do not have to remain hurt. You do not have to remain in a state of hurt just as you do not have to remain in any state – anxiety or fear or anything else. You need to be willing for the hurt to go away. You can ask for it to go away when you are willing. Sometimes the hurt is so strong that we cannot even arrive to the words to ask for it to go away. Ask for this anyway. Or ask that someone you know and that cares for you ask for it to go away for you. Ask the Light for this. Ask the Angels and God. You will be heard. Hurt does not have to be your companion.

Let the Light take care of you

Let the light assist you in getting rid of hurt. Let the light assist you in getting rid of fear and anxiety. You do not have to stay in the state you are in. You do not have to accept the hurt as the way things are and the way that they will remain. Sometimes the pain is emotional, sometimes physical or spiritual. Sometimes it is a mix of all three and it is difficult to distinguish where one thing begins and another ends. The Light is able to make these differentiations. The Light is able to heal you no matter what the situation. Ask the light to help you with your pain and your hurt. Ask the light to clear away what is in the way of perfect healing. Perfect healing is available to you. Do not feel that you do not deserve it. Ask the Light to clear away any feelings or beliefs that are in the way of perfect healing. When you are perfectly healed and whole, you will be able to function in the world. You will be able to thrive and all of you will be at ease. You will be whole and you will bring your wholeness to the world. Allow the light to bathe you and heal you. Allow the light to heal you.

The Light is your balm

The Light is your balm. The Light is soothing to you and is able to help you. It gives you a salve for your situation. It gives you a salve for the issues in your life. Ask for personal help now from the light. Ask that you be shown how to work with the light and how to work with the Angels perfectly. Ask for the light to shape you so that you may be at your most whole and complete. Ask that you may be made most like to yourself, to the true self that you are. You know who this self is, but you have covered it up and this is one of the reasons that you may need help. In all ways, in all times, help is able to be called upon. Call upon the light, call upon the angels and God. Ask for help for the things that beset you, the things that you are faced with. Ask for help so that you may resolve your problems. Ask for help so that your problems may weigh lightly upon you or not at all.

The soul and the spirit are all in need of healing

The soul and the spirit are all in need of healing. No matter who you are, you are in need of some form of healing. The soul and spirit need to be in alignment with each other, and with themselves, and with you yourself. The soul and spirit cannot be at odds with each other or with you. They need to be mended and made whole. Any damage, any way you have been torn at, any way you have been taken apart, all this must be fixed. This is all a part of you and you can't allow it to continue this way. You are less because of this, you are less whole, you are less perfect, you are less happy, you are less. Allow yourself to heal. Allow all means at your disposal to heal you. Allow Divine and the Light to heal you. Allow that allowing this to happen would be a good thing for you. Don't hold back from healing.

Are you ready to heal?

Not everyone is ready to heal. Not everyone is ready to heal completely. Sometimes only parts of us are ready to heal. Sometimes only a part of our mind can accept healing. We can come up with reasons why we won't heal. Many of these conversations are taking place deep inside of us, where we cannot even hear them. These conversations convince us that healing would not be good, or that pursuing healing would not be good. We are wrong in these beliefs. We are wrong to think that nothing can change or that nothing can improve or that things are good enough the way that they are. Healing is available to you. It is available and it is good for you to accept it. Think about this. Think about and see what parts of you are resistant to healing or even against it. There are parts in all of us that have this resistance. There are parts in all of us that turn the other way when a path to healing is shown to us.

Readying yourself to heal

As you ready yourself to heal, you may not know that you are doing this. You may not realize that you are taking steps towards healing or towards pursuing healing. The thought of healing may be a long way off for you. Or you might think that this is not something that you want, that this is not something that you are prepared to do. Rest with the idea, for now, that healing is okay, that healing may be a good thing for you. Consider for now, that you might benefit from healing in ways that you did not know. Perhaps the idea of healing or the pursuit of healing might make you more comfortable and happy in your own life. Perhaps this would be helpful. If you are readying yourself to heal, and are doing this in a conscious manner, then you will know there can be some steps in the process. Whether there be few steps or many, whether this happens quickly or slowly, trust the process, trust the manner in which you are going about this. Ask for guidance in this too. Ask for Divine guidance because this will be helpful too. All kinds of healing are worthwhile – emotional, physical, spiritual – and all have an effect on the other. Complex as we are, our healing takes place on many levels at the same time. Accept all of these levels. Accept the healing that is given to you.

Accepting healing

It might seem a strange concept, the need to accept healing, or the idea that it's even an issue, but many times we hold on to the problems we have. Often, it suits us to hold on to them. The idea that they can be gone, and the idea that they can be gone quickly and instantly can be overwhelming. It is a strange thought. When we grapple with certain things for a long time, sometimes they become part of us. So if the Light or the Angels or some other kind of healing suddenly takes this away from us, then what are we to do? We have to process the healing, much as we made room for the problem in the first place. Ask that you be able to accept healing. Ask that this is easily possible for you. And then ask to be healed.

Hesitation and abundance

Just as we might hesitate to accept healing or not be sure it's even possible for us. We might also hesitate about abundance. We might want abundance in our lives and we might want to be abundant. But like with many things, the wanting of it might be more familiar to us than actually having abundance. The Angels say we should prepare to receive. The Angels say we should be prepared for abundance, that we should examine how we feel about it so that we can rid ourselves of the things in the way of abundance. If you became abundant, you might live your life a different way. You might change some things completely and you yourself might change. Do you ever think about how abundance might cause you to grow? Would you be ready for this? Hesitation is natural. Hesitation may block abundance. We may be too comfortable where we are right now. We might not be ready for a bigger frame of reference, for a bigger life even. Why not ask that you be shown how to make room for this, how to make room for abundance and for a different life? Why not ask to have hesitation taken away from you and your beliefs that keep you from abundance be taken away from you too?

The source of the light

The source of the light is the light of God. The Light comes from God and then is sprung out into the world. The light emerges from God and comes out into the world. The light streams and it follows its path, where it wants to go, where it's drawn to go. It seeks out other light. It seeks out dark too and chases it away. It seeks out the shadows, even those in your own heart. It seeks out all and you can seek it out too. You can ask it to help you. You can ask the light to be a part of your life and to guide you. You can ask the light to protect you and to envelop you. The light of truth and the light of life are the light from God. You can ask this Divine light to wrap you tightly. You can ask to grow in the light and be healed by the light. You can ask to be shown the source of the light and to let the power of the light mean everything to you. You can be one with the light and with its power. You can be one with it. You can surrender to the light. You can let it heal you in all ways. You can be the light too. You can be a light in your life and a force for positive change. You can be this light. You can be this light and be the source of healing for others. You too can be a source of light. You do not have to remain dark. You do not have to remain clouded by darkness and touched by sorrow. Allow the light to take all of it. Allow yourself to be bathed by the light and the source of the light too.

Angelic healing

Angelic healing is yours if you want it. Angelic healing is available to you. Ask for Angelic healing. Ask for the Angels to be a part of your life so that you can be healed. Other forms of healing are important too. Take advantage of all forms of healing. Take advantage of the power you have to ask the Angels also. Don't neglect to ask the Angels for help each and every day and especially when you need healing.

Allowing the Light into your Life

Allow the light into your life and be open to the light. Be open to the idea that you are the light. Allow the light to heal you. Allow the light to make repairs and to make you more whole. You can be at one with the light. You can surrender to the healing. You can allow things to be different than what they are. You can allow the illumination of the light to create change in you and in your life. Try to do this. Try to do this even if you do not know how this might work. Simply allow. Breathe into the light. Breathe into it and allow the healing.

Allowing the healing

Breathe into the light and allow the healing to take place. Allow yourself to be made whole into the light. Allow yourself to be made perfect in the light. You might be resistant to the healing. You might not believe in it, or think you don't need it, or think that it won't be enough or that it won't achieve anything. Believe what you will but allow it anyway. If you push away the healing then it will not take place. If you allow the healing then it will. All things are possible. Allow the healing. Instruct yourself to allow the healing. And then be healed!

Prayer for healing

It is my prayer and my wish for you that you be healed, perfectly and completely, now and from now on, taking into account everything that has ever happened to you, in this life, and in any other. It is my wish and my prayer for you that for ever, for the rest of your days and beyond, that you live perfectly and easily, with joy, peace, and harmony, with more abundance than you can dream of. It is my wish and prayer for you that all the things in you that are broken or damaged, all the things in you that are not healed or whole, that all the things in you that are not what they need to be, that all this be made wonderful and whole and fixed in all ways. Let yourself be soothed and calmed and made whole in all ways. Let yourself be healed. I ask all this of God and the Angels and I ask that this prayer be a permanent prayer for you and for all who read this. I ask that this prayer be modified to suit your particular needs and temperament and I ask that it be a happy thing for you in all ways. I will say Amen here. But you may say whatever ending suits you, your background and your religion. Blessings.

Bathing in the light

May you bathe in the light. May you bathe in the light and may the light bathe you. May the light wash away all that is wrong with you, with your body, your mind, and your spirit. May the light bathe you and wash you and may it set you free. May it set you free from what you have believed and what you could come to believe. May it free you and may you allow yourself to be free. Ask yourself what you need to be freed from. And ask the light and the Angels to help you.

Behold the light

Behold the light for it is there for you. Behold the light for it surrounds you and means you well. Behold the light for it envelops you. Behold the light, it is yours and yours to keep.

Receive the light

Receive the light though you do not dare to do this. Receive the light though you are afraid. Receive the light even if you are too confident sometimes. Receive the light for it will help you. It will set you free and illuminate you. It will free you from darkness and you will be alight. You yourself will be alive with the light and in the light. Allow the light of God to be your light. Allow this in your heart, mind and soul. Allow this in your body, your spirit, your system. Allow the light. Receive the light. Receive the light and then so will it too receive you and make you still more of what you are. Receive the light and you will embrace more of the Divine essence at your very core. The light is waiting for you.

The Book of Joy

The Book of Joy is about what happens when healing is complete. The Book of Joy is the revelation that Joy can be possible and that it can be a state of existence. The Book of Joy utters the declarations that help you to make joy a part of your life and your world. You do not have to cut yourself off from joy. You do not have to feel that it is not for you and does not belong to you. Joy belongs to you and to everyone if they accept it, and if they surrender to it. Accept joy into your life. It is not a burden. Accept joy into your life. It is a wonderful thing and it will help you.

The Book of Joy welcomes joy into your life and provides a pathway for you to welcome it into your life. You can have joy. You do not have to have a special place to keep it. It can permeate through you. It can permeate everything about you and around you. Joy brings light to your life and a purpose to your days. Joy lights you up and allows you to light up too. Release the joy that is in you already. Release the joy that is in you and let it take you, let it cover you and let it rise within you perfectly and in all ways.

After the dawn of the light, after the coming back of the light, we can have joy again. We had it before. We had it in fits and starts but now we can have it again, more consistently, more often, and always even. Does this surprise you? Does it surprise you to hear that a state of joy is possible?

If you have only known misery, of course it surprises you. If you have only known strife, of course it surprises you. But these things can be real for you too. Raise your eyes to the light. Raise your heart to the core of joy and let it come into you. Let it embrace you and give yourself permission to be embraced by joy so that your cares be gone from you, and that your grief and misery be washed clean. You have suffered. You may have suffered greatly. And now it is time for joy to heal you. It is time for you to have joy and to have joy enter every part of you and become a part of all of you. It is time for joy to make you happy and for happiness to be your natural state. Why not adopt joy as a way of being?

Do you have joy?

Do you have joy now? Do you already have joy? Why not have more joy? Why not have an infinite amount of joy that stretches into you and takes hold of you and stretches through the whole of your life, your thoughts and your being? Why not have all the joy you could possibly ask for and then have more? Why not be joyous in all your thoughts and all your words? Why not be joyous in all your emotions? Why not be joyous in everything you do and in everything you are? The time to have joy is now. The time to be joyful is now. There is no better time. Allow your heart to feel joy. Allow joy to enter your heart now and to make you smile permanently. Invite the energy of joy to take a permanent place in your home, your heart and your life. Embrace the possibilities that joy offers you. Embrace them. They are healing for you and will contribute greatly to your profound happiness.

Can you have joy?

Of course you can have joy. Of course you can have deep and profound joy and happiness and peace. The reason you ask is that you do not feel worthy. The reason you ask is that this hasn't been the case for you yet. But it will be the case. It will be possible for you to have and feel joy and to have it on a permanent basis. Do not look upon the reasons why you are sad. Do not look at how you are frustrated or disappointed. Look instead at the blessings you have. Look instead at the blessings, even the tiniest blessing that you have. And ask that it be magnified. Ask that it be multiplied into many thousands of blessings. Ask that the happiness that you feel about these blessings increase and increase, no matter how small they are. Ask that joy be in your heart. Ask the Angels and God to bless you and to tell you your purpose. Ask them to whisper to you how beautiful and strong and wonderful you are. Ask that joy be put in your heart and that it never leave. Ask that joy fill you beautifully and amazingly. Ask that joy inhabit every last part of you in all ways. Be joy. Ask joy to be with you and with all parts of you. Allow yourself to have joy and allow joy to fill you fully.

Do you need joy?

Maybe you wonder if joy is something you need. Maybe you wonder if joy is something that you can do without. It is not necessary, perhaps you feel, for you to have joy. Maybe you think that joy is not an important component of life. Maybe you have not given yourself enough of a chance to have joy. Maybe you have not given yourself enough of a chance to make your life more of what it could be. Maybe you have made yourself too small. Maybe you are measuring your life in the wrong way. Perhaps you could stop doing this. Perhaps you could stop and consider instead that joy would be a wonderful thing to add to your life. It would enrich you in so many ways.

There is joy and there is non-joy

You can exist and have a life that is bare of joy. You can exist and have a life that is not miserable but that is also not joyful. There can be neutrality in life. You can simply exist. You can simply not do very much and not have any joy. Is this what you want? Maybe you are afraid of joy. Maybe you are afraid to live a life where joy is possible. Do not be afraid. Do not choose non-joy. Do not choose to not be happy. Do not choose this half-life. Risk more and hope for joy instead. Risk more and seek out joy instead. It will not be too difficult to find. It will perhaps not be difficult at all.

The lack of joy

When there is a lack of joy then everything is a kind of grey existence. When there is a lack of joy then everything is clouded over, and nothing is quite right and life loses meaning. Life loses significance and sparkle. Do not seek to inhabit the space of lack of joy. Do not seek to inhabit this small space. It is possible to inhabit it. It is possible to force and squeeze yourself into this small space. It is not unimaginable. You may think that this is a natural thing for you. You may think that it is natural for you to lack joy, to be without this in your life. It is not natural. If this is where you are now, if you lack joy now, then take heart because things do not have to remain this way. Your life, and your state of being can be lifted up and raised up so that you can feel happy and joyful. Ask that your troubles and burdens be lifted from you.

The effects of joy

Joy brings beautiful things to your life. Joy itself is beautiful. It is a wonderful thing that adds to you and to your life, and never takes anything away. Joy lifts everything up. It lifts up your spirits and lifts up everything about every situation. Where we may be joyful, then we may be happy. Where we allow ourselves to be joyful, then we allow light into our situation and to the world of others. Joy is a beauteous thing. You need to hold on to joy with all your heart. You need to infuse joy into your life, your spirit and your soul. If you write and speak always with an undercurrent of joy, then your words will carry far and wide. If your intentions are based on joy and joyful action then their effect will be great, their impact will be far-reaching. Do not underestimate the good will that the smallest amount of joy can create. Do not underestimate this, and take every opportunity to create more joy and to add more joy to the world, and to every facet of your life.

The happiness of joy

Joy brings its own happiness. Joy is its own particular species of happiness. It has a flavour and an energy all its own. Joy is wonderful. It adds to life and brings health to all who have it. Joy is a gift. It bestows life and wonderment to all who encounter it, to all who are in its path. It is a creative force and it brings light to areas which were dark. It brings depth and encouragement to those who could not hope to experience anything but disappointment. Joy is its own power and you can accept it as such. You can accept the power that joy has and welcome it into your life. The happiness of joy is something that you can have. Joy and happiness are something that you can have. It does not matter if things have not gone well for you. It does not matter if there are things that you regret. Allow joy and the light to erase all of this. Allow joy to enable you to be happy once more. Surrender to joy. Let it cascade into you and fill you and your life. And may it never leave you. May you always be blessed in this manner.

The completeness of joy

Joy brings its own sense of well-being wherever it goes, and with whomever it encounters. Joy is beautiful and perfect and it nourishes all of us. Joy is a completing emotion and a nourishing thing. You must allow joy to complete you. You must allow joy to fill what has been missing from your life. Whatever it is you feel you have been missing, allow joy to come in, in its place. Allow joy to take the place of your doubts and fears. Allow joy to substitute itself in your life for anything that does not fit. Perhaps you need to reorganize yourself. Perhaps you need to reorganize your perspective and point of view. Joy will allow you to do this, more than you can believe, more than you would think. Allow joy to feed you and to complete you. It may be that you will need other things besides joy. This may be true. Joy will help you to see these too. Joy will lead you to what is best for you to grow. Joy will help to make you who you are and who you need to be. Allow yourself to be constructed. Allow yourself to be made more. And allow joy to do this work, in order to embellish you and to create the you that you have wanted, and the you that you have needed to be. Joy will make you strong. Joy will sculpt you and create you in new ways. Allow for this completeness in yourself. You will be pleased about this.

Joy in your life

Joy is in your life. It is present in your life in little ways and big ways. You may not be able to see this. You may be too preoccupied. You may have the weight of the world on your shoulders. You could be miserable. You could think that nothing good is in your life and maybe you are disappointed with your life. But there is joy in your life. You have to look for it. You have to allow it to emerge and to reveal itself. And you have to go forward with the idea that joy is possible.

The creation of joy

Joy is created in all ways and in all things. Joy is a subset of everything we do. In everything we do, there is the possibility of joy, there is the potential of joy. Joy can be created easily if you allow it. Joy can be created. It is possible that joy be in all aspects of the things that you do, of your daily life. Joy is created and joy can be possible. Will you allow joy? Will you entertain joy? Make a space for joy in your life. This will be easy to do if you open yourself to the idea that it is possible.

How can you have joy?

Having joy is as simple as allowing for the idea that you can have joy. Having joy is possible for almost everyone. In your day to day life, look at where joy is now, and then look at where things can be more joyful. Do you have an aspect of your life that is not joyful? See how you can change this. See how you can add joy to it. What can you do to change things and improve the amount of joy? What can you do in all this? Always look for opportunities to increase joy. Always look for this. You will be surprised where joy can be, where it can take place, and where it can come into your life.

Joy weaving a trail through your life

Joy can weave a trail through your life, through the whole of it, through everything you think, say and do. Joy can weave a trail through everything. Will you let this happen? Will you let joy be so completely present in your life? It would be a good thing for you to do this. It would be a good thing for you to be present with joy and for you to be aware of joy and to welcome it to your life. You can also actively add joy to your life. You can actively choose to weave this trail in your life. You can add joy to other people's lives too. Begin with your own life. Add more joy to it and see how it expands into everything around you. See how it casts out gloom and lifts spirits. See how everything that is dark and dreadful becomes replaced with something new, expectant and alive. Joy can do this in your life and in the lives of those that you affect. Seek to embrace joy. Do not chase it away and do not hide from it. Instead welcome it and you will reap the benefits of it.

Joy lifts you

Joy lifts you and will not abandon you. Joy lifts you and will not cast you out. Seek out joy always. If others ignore you or do not approach you, seek out joy. If you feel alone in the world, seek out joy. Joy is possible always, everywhere and in all states of mind. You do not need company to have joy. You can have joy in and of yourself. You can have joy and light in your very person, in the person that you are. Joy lifts you and lifts you out of everything. You can be consumed by joy and be present in joy. You can be alive with joy. You can be blissful with joy. Let joy lift you. Let joy lift you beyond where you are now and to a greater happiness. Allow joy to fill you and your life so that you may have peace.

Your spirit and joy – the mending of your spirit

Your spirit needs joy, requires joy. Your spirit is captivated by joy and made whole by it. Your spirit can be mended by joy. Your spirit may need mending. Your spirit may have been damaged or even torn. Maybe too much has happened to you. Maybe you have been damaged and need repair. Allow your spirit to be mended. Allow your spirit to find joy and to be mended. A little joy will ease a great deal. A little joy will do a great deal of good. If you do not have joy look for it now. You can look for it wherever you are. You can look for it in your surroundings and in yourself. You can look for it in the kindness of another or in music and art. Seek it out. Allow it to embrace you and to fill you. Allow it to reach through you and into your soul and spirit so that you can be mended and healed in all ways.

The breakthrough of joy

Joy breaks through. Joy breaks through the darkness, and the gloom. Joy breaks through the sadness. It breaks through disappointment and unease, embarrassment, fear, and shame. Joy breaks through blame and through self-blame too. Allow joy to break through in your life. Allow the pursuit of joy and of happiness to be part of your life. Allow joy to break through your life. Allow it to break through your struggle, your concerns, and your worries. Allow joy to break through and to fill you in every way imaginable, and to make you as happy as you can be.

The means of joy

Joy comes to us by many means and many avenues. Joy comes to us in many ways. We can find joy in different areas of our lives. We can find joy in the exchange with another – in conversation. We can find joy in quiet observation, and in contemplation. We can find joy in solitary pursuits or in social gatherings. Joy is available in many ways and many forms. The means of joy are many. The means of joy are varied. Do not limit yourself in your expressions of joy. Do not limit yourself in your experience of joy. Allow joy to take its many and varied forms. Allow joy to come to you wholly and unabashed. Allow it to come to you quietly. Allow it to come to you boldly as you traverse the regions of joy. As you traverse the landscape of joy, you will come to understand the different feelings of joy, the different layers, and the different nuances. Allow the different textures of joy to teach you and fill you and to make you whole. Allow this to happen.

The success of joy

Joy brings with it the success of things. The feelings of joy carry forth so much of what we are trying to do. Joy lifts things and carries things forward. Joy honours the way forward and gives it impetus. It encourages the fulfilment of goals and wishes, the achievement of aspirations. Accomplishment is the result of joy. Accomplishment is carried forth by work too. But joy ignites it. Joy ignites the work done. Let joy fill you. Let joy bring you to your very own future. Let joy inspire you. Let the seeking out of joy inspire you in many ways. Let it bring you success and let it imbibe you and fill you with all that is possible. Let it be your happiness and let it bring you happiness too.

Joy becomes us

Joy suits us very well. Joy suits us in all things. It becomes us in so many ways. Joy enables us to be seen in a happy light. Joy makes us beautiful and can render us more wholly to the world. Joy can make us bright and brilliant and effervescent. Joy lights us up and lights up what is around us. Joy bequeaths us to ourselves. Joy gives us ourselves and gives us more. Joy shows our best side to the world. Joy reveals the colours within and shares them with the world. When we are not in joy, this light is smaller. When we are not in joy then we are not truly ourselves somehow. Let joy become you. Let joy shape you and enhance you fully and perfectly.

When joy fails us

Sometimes joy fails us. Sometimes joy is not available to us and we are not able to meet with it. Sometimes joy is not anywhere near us. Sometimes we are simply without joy. We do not know what to do. We do not feel happy and so we cannot have joy. All this can be true. We can be caught up in miserable things. We can be caught up in things that are not right and then we don't have joy. We may not have joy always. And sometimes it is very difficult to have joy. Sometimes things are too difficult. We acknowledge this. We acknowledge that many times things are not easy and that sometimes they are very hard. At these times, though, we ask that you still hold out an expectation of joy. We ask you to invite joy into your life, even at times when all joy is gone. We ask that you ask joy to be with you. Even in difficult times, joy can make things easier, joy can find out how to improve things for you. Joy seeks to lighten your burden. Ask it to be present always

Responding to joy

When you respond to joy, you become caught up in it. When you respond to joy, you take on some of the characteristics of joy. Even though you were not joyful at the beginning, even if joy was not your state of mind, still you take on joy. You cannot help but do this because you, a part of you at least, can see the joy in the other person, can see what they are thinking and feeling and expressing. When someone addresses you and their state is joy, then you are blessed with joy too. It cannot help but shower upon you. It cannot help but become part of you in so many ways. Accept this joy. Accept this joy even though it did not originate with you. Accept this joy and let it affect you for the better.

Responding with joy

When you are joyful, joy emanates from you. When you are joyful, joy expresses itself in your person and then it must carry forth, through you and out of you and to the people you encounter. When you are joyful, then your happiness is transferred, your happiness travels, moves forward and expands. Be joyful then in your responses. Be joyful in your actions and activities. Be joyful in your thoughts and your words. Be joyful in your approach to the world. Be joyful so that you can help the world to be more joyful too.

The having of joy

The having of joy is the miracle of all things. The having of joy makes life a delight and an incomparable experience. The having of joy makes things possible and diminishes sorrow. The having of joy is the exploration of the Light in the human soul. The having of joy lights up the spirit. The having of joy is something that you can have. The having of joy is available to you. Be open to joy. Be open to the having of joy as a way to think and feel and act and to live your life. Be open to joy and let it come into every part of you. The having of joy is the living of joy day to day. The having of joy is the consistent state of happiness that does not fade. You can have this. You can have the having of joy. You can have permanent joy. Ask for this now. Ask the Angels for this now.

Needing joy

We are built to need joy. We are built to need joy but we don't always recognize this. We think that we can do without joy. We think that joy is extra, that joy and happiness are not that important. Or we think that they are not always available. We all need joy. Joy makes our lives better. We can survive without joy but not well. We can continue without joy and happiness, but what kind of meaning does life then have? Existence is available when joy is lacking. But this is not what we want really. Accept the presence of joy in your life. Accept the need for joy too. Joy will be available to you. You need to look for it and to let it into your life.

Joyful

Are you joyful? Are you joyful each and every day? Is this possible for you? Is it possible for you to be joyful and to have joy on a regular basis? I say that it is. I and the Angels and God say that it is. Look within yourself and find joy. Look in your environment and find joy. Look at the people you talk to everyday and find joy. Joy is around you. Joy is within you and without you. Be joyful then. You have a chance to be truly and deeply happy. Be joyful.

Blessing your Life

The Angels and God want to bless your life and make it joyful in all ways. Ask them for this blessing. Ask them for help in accepting this blessing in all ways. Blessings are yours and for your life. Let these blessings envelop you and embrace you. Let these blessings become part of you and enter into you at all levels, and in every aspect of your being. The Angels and God bless you and they ask that you take this in. They ask that you feel Their embrace, and Their joy at your newfound wealth of the blessings that they bring. Be in joy. Be blessed. Be happy. Be held by Divine, now and always.

The Book of Remembrance

The Book of Remembrance is the Book that honours memory. It is the Book that allows you to remember and to forget. When you take up this Book, you are taking up the storehouse of your memory, you are pondering the future and considering the past all at the same time.

Take up this Book then. Let it challenge you to remember. Let it remind you to forget.

Remembrance

Remembrance is the bounty of all things. Whatever anything is or anything produces, it will end up somehow in memory, in the remembrance of one or of many, or maybe sometimes in the remembrance of none.

Remembrance allows one to separate oneself from the past. Remembrance allows one to create a separate self that exists in the past with those memories and those events and then to depart from it. Remembrance can cling to us too. Remembrance can mean we never let go of something, even the things that we should. Remembrance is careful with us and it plays with us too. Remembrance is often a thought, never inactive. Remembrance calls to us. We force ourselves to put it aside. We force ourselves to quell memory. Everything that happens turns and transforms into Remembrance. What do you remember best? Do you remember it well? Let us sort out your memories. Let us sort out your remembrances. Let us make them good. Let us enrich them. Let us remove those memories that are hurtful, painful, and sorrowful. Remembrance can be present without pain. Ask for healing and the healing of your memories, your past, and your traumas and distress. Ask for this now.

Purposeful

Remembrance is purposeful. Remembrance is the nudging of ourselves towards that which we need to remember, and towards that we would seek to forget. Remembrance is about the encapsulation of memory, the purposeful containment of what has gone on, of what has happened. Remembrance exists in our mind and in the minds of others. It is individual and it is shared too. What purpose does remembrance have in your life? What does memory do to your spirit? Where does it take you? What purpose does it bring you too? Does it lead you in a new direction? Does it punish you? Instruct your remembrance to serve a good purpose in your life. Instruct your memories to assist you in constructing a good future for yourself. This must be the true purpose of remembrance, to lead you somewhere better, to lead you somewhere good. Banish what is bad. Let it be erased forever and always. Banish what causes you distress. Let it be completely gone. Instruct your memories to construct themselves so that they support you and give you shelter. Let us make a new Remembrance, one that will serve you fully in all ways.

Striking

What is striking about your remembrances and about your recollections? Do these things stand out? Do these important memories take centre stage? Allow yourself to be buffeted by your memories. Allow all of them to have a place for you. Allow all of them to have a part of your life and of your mind. They are striking. All of them are striking. But only some of them strike you. These are the memories that you cannot let go of. These are the memories that are too strong, that take over sometimes. Perhaps you have tried to forget them. Perhaps you have succeeded. Sometimes you succeed and sometimes you do not. Not all of your memories are like jewels, beautiful and radiant. Not all of your memories are perfect examples of what life should be. Some memories are striking because of their beauty and importance. Others are striking because they are harsh and because they have brutalized us. Whatever their nature, whatever their origin, it is time to neutralize them. It is time to make them not striking at all, in any way.

Selective

Some remembrance is selective. Some memories are culled and curated so only the best of them remain. Sometimes this is for the best. Sometimes there are painful things and we cannot get past them. We edit them in our minds and then they become more bearable, less affecting. All this is possible, all this is true. But it is also possible to do more. We don't have to live with selective remembrance. We can have full remembrance. But we must clean and clear all the memories we have. We must do this so that we can look at them without pain, so that we can look at them freely, and not suffer.

Evocative

What does remembrance do to you? What memories are evoked by different things, events, and triggers? What are you forced to think about? What is evoked in you by your memories, by your remembrance? Do you have any control over what is evoked? Can you change your response to any of this? Can you change how you feel when certain memories flood your mind? Can you make them go away? Can you change the story that they tell you in your head. What is evocative and what is evoked are powerful. They can take us over and overwhelm us. They can stop us cold. We can push them aside. We can make them fade away. But this takes effort and energy. What can be evoked, what can be called up, compels us to look, forces us to not look away, makes us examine. What things and feelings are called up in you? What are you compelled to look at? What are you forced to examine? Is this comfortable? If it is not comfortable take steps to ease this inner burden. Take steps to not be so harassed by the things inside you. Your inner world, your subconscious does not have to rule you. You can be set free from this. The memories that you do not treasure do not have to flood through you anymore without warning. Ask for this to be taken away. Ask to be protected from the thoughts that are like shards to your soul.

Painful

So many memories are painful. So much pain is held in some memories. They are like their own worlds, and to encounter these memories is to encounter something you cannot free yourself from, something that consumes you. Free yourself from this pain. Free yourself. Put a distance between the pain and the memories and then ask the pain to go away. Ask the memories to ease and to show you their lesson, and their truth, and then let them fade, let them no longer have a hold on your heart, your soul, and your mind. Let these memories dim, and let the pain underneath them fly away too. Allow the Angels to take this pain. Allow them to take it now.

Joyful

Some memories are joyful too, not just the containers of pain. Some remembrance is about joy. Can you feel this joy? Can you hold this joy and take it in and not let it overwhelm you? Do you discount joy? Do you turn it away? You might turn it away. You might not know what to do with joy. It is easy to know what to do with struggle and strife. It is easy to know what to do with disappointment and even disaster. But joy is a stranger thing. Joy envelops you and takes over, like peals of laughter and brimming with emotion, welling up inside you and spilling out like a fountain, infectious. If you have been a closed container, if you have been restrained and closed off, you will not know how to deal with this. You will not know what to make of this. All this joy might be too much. Get used to it. Get used to it slowly. Acclimate yourself to it. Acclimate yourself to happiness and to joy. It is the way that you feel blessed. You can be blessed. You can be infinitely blessed.

A Catalyst

Remembrance is a catalyst for many things. It is a catalyst for self-examination, and for action and exploration. It is a catalyst for discovery. You may want to forget. You may have many things you want to forget, but inside each of them there is a kernel of something. Choose one of these that is not too painful. Choose one memory and ask what was the reason that this happened, and ask too what is the truth from this, about this. If you ask these things, the sharpness of the pain may dissipate. It may be that the memory was so hurtful, so difficult because it was waiting, hoping to say something to you. Ask yourself, without diving into the thing itself, what your most painful memory wants to tell you and teach you. You can ask this without going back into it. Ask and see what answer you may get. Ask and see where this propels you, and what brave new direction this may lead to. Allow the catalyst of remembrance to do its work upon you. Allow yourself to be revealed and renewed by what it brings to you. You may be educating yourself about yourself. You may be breaking out upon a new path, a discovery about the internal workings of your mind, or some new perspective that you did not allow yourself to consider. Allow your heart and spirit to grow with the exploration of memory. Let this be the catalyst that it can be.

Remembrance informs us

Remembrance informs us. Remembrance informs our thoughts and dreams. From where we have come we plan where next to go. Our memories shape us and colour the way we see the world. Our remembrance gives us information about the world. It does not even matter if this information is right or wrong. Remembrance gives us colour and texture and sound and makes everything seem a certain way, gives everything a certain sense. We make sense of the world through our memories. We are not a clean slate. We have memories and histories inside of us, inside of our minds and inside our spirits and souls. These make us up and give us parts of ourselves. We can exist without memory. We can exist without all of these pieces. We can do this but it takes a lot of work to get to this point. It takes a lot of work to clear ourselves fully and completely. We can get to a point where we are clean and clear but where we still have what remembrance can teach us. We have remembrance and we are informed by it. But it does not have to rule us.

Defined by memory

We are defined by our remembrance too. We are defined and shaped, our identity is wrought. We become who we are through the many things we pass through. We become who we are and then we are constructed by the experiences we have lived. Our identities are forged. Our environment, the people around us, these lead to our experiences and to events in our lives. And then these become part of our memory and our reaction to these events, and even our non-reaction form ourselves. They form ourselves and then they create our world too for we are creators of our worlds also. Just as memory shapes us and creates our identities, then we create our worlds too. Who would you be without different experiences? Who would you be without the things you have gone through or if you could change the things you have gone through to other experiences. We are defined by memory. And we can work on these memories to make them easier, to make them less troubling. We are defined by memories. But we can change the way we are defined and the way we have defined ourselves. Even this is possible.

The many lifetimes we live

We live many lifetimes. We live many lifetimes and we have remembrance through all of them. Perhaps in this life, we do not remember what has gone on before. But our cells remember, our bodies remember, our souls remember. We are disconnected from what has gone on before. But if we just look and listen. If we listen to internally to that oldest part of ourselves, then we will find what we are seeking. Then we will find the through line that connects us from ourselves here and now to all the people we have been before, through the years, through the millennia. Who were we before? Who were we before the person that we are now today? And how is that person that is here now, how is that person made up of all of the people that have gone before. How are we the full culmination of all these people and histories? How are we made up of all this, not just in our lineage in this lifetime, but in our lineage in all lifetimes? How can we remember this and learn from it? Asking this question is enough to know the answer. Asking this question is enough to put the answer out there into the Universe and into the Knowledge of All things. Ask for this answer. Ask to know and to be enriched by the cultural history that makes up the person that you are. Ask and you will be rewarded by a deeper and more resilient understanding of yourself.

The many lifetimes contained in this life

We have one life but it is made up of all that is contained on this planet, in this universe. We have one life but it is made up of all of our personal histories. We have one life but it continues after it has ended. We have one life, but we are the echo and the memory of the people we have been before, of the other lives we have lived. We are the multiple of many things. We are the consolidation of many things. We have not one set of parents, but hundreds. We have not one embodiment, but hundreds. We are spirit and we are flesh but the way we have reached our current form is not by happenstance. We are designed and we are designers too. The power of remembrance is that it stores all of this for us, whether or not we know how to remember is a different thing. Whether or not we want to remember is a different thing.

The intersection of lives

This occurs when you suddenly realize that you know someone, that someone before you or passing by you has been in your life before, but perhaps not in this lifetime. This intersection occurs when you realize that the person you call a friend, a brother, a child in this life meant something else to you in another time and space. These layers of history envelop us. We keep them straight in our current lives as we must but every so often the veil shifts, the boundaries come down and we can see more. We can see that maybe we are the conglomeration of many lives and that those around us are too. Is anybody in your life really there for the first time? How many times around the merry go round have you gone? How many times have the people before you gone? Somehow we are all interconnected. Somehow we are all learning from each other and making sense of the puzzle of our lives, interwoven as they are with each other.

The memories that define us

How can we be defined by our memories when some of these might be painful? How can we be defined by them? We are defined around the memories and the stories and sometimes in spite of them. We define ourselves and we do not define ourselves. We allow the story to be wiped clean. We want to start anew. And yet there it is, the old memories forming the texture that constitutes us, that constitutes what we believe about ourselves. Ask the Angels to help you heal. Ask the Angels to clean you and clear you so that you may believe in yourself again, so that you may believe yourself worthy and whole. You have forgotten how you are valuable. You have forgotten that you have meaning and significance. The layers of all that has happened have worn you down. The layers of too many exchanges of too many occurrences have eroded you. You do not have to be eroded. You do not have to feel downtrodden and oppressed. You can be lighter. You can be free and lighter than what you are now. Ask for new memories and new understanding about what you have lived and about how you live. You can be light and you can be whole. You can redefine yourself too.

Faulty memory

Faulty memory can be a blessing. Faulty memory can be something that you decide to do. Or something that comes upon you that you have no choice over. Faulty memory is all this. It is useful sometimes to hide the things you do not want to remember from yourself. But it can hide other things too, other truths that you might benefit from knowing, it can hide useful things. Ask the Angels to restore you and your memory. Ask them to bring you to a place where no part of you asks for this, or desires to have this.

Truthful memory

Like a dagger, some have memories that will not offer anything but the truth, in sharpest detail. Sometimes this is a good thing. Sometimes it is not. We all wish for sharp minds, clear understanding. We wish also for peace. Wish for peace for yourself. Wish that all your memories that you have and the ones that you will have going forward are good and clear and easy. Ask that any memories that you don't like be reshaped and made easier for you. Ask that you be forgiven for the things that you did that you did that were not in keeping with a good nature, with good values and morals. Ask that you be made whole and that your mind and spirit be made whole too. Ask that your memory be true. And that your memories bring you only comfort.

Vague recollections

Memory is not accurate. Sometimes it is true, other times false, and often it is vague. How is memory clouded? How is remembrance clouded? Remembrance may be vague to offer a way into the future, to not tie you down into the past. Allow your vague memories to live on as they must. Ask only that your memories serve you well and that you have a good conduit to the future, that you have a good path forward.

Blurring of truth

What is the blurring of truth? What is the dividing line between truth and non-truth? Between certainty and confusion? What is this line? How can it be manipulated? How can it be changed and altered? How can truth stand resolute? Is truth ever just that? Is truth ever just the one undisputable thing? Or does it change depending on the person, the situation, the perspective? Where does truth lie? Where does truth stand? What truth can we find in ourselves and what truths do we make up about ourselves? What conglomeration of facts and attributes are we? What messy amalgamation of things are we? We know our truth, perhaps we know it. Or perhaps we don't. Perhaps we perceive it or perhaps we imagine it. We can celebrate the truth. And we can observe the blurring of truth. We can just observe that this is likely to happen because remembrance is never completely perfect, because experience is not completely perfective. Because subjectivity is what we have and all we can ever have. And even this subjective recounting to ourselves can change moment to moment and day to day. Honour the truth. But do not count upon it too closely.

What We Prefer

Do we prefer the past or the present? Do we prefer the future? Do we like the state of things as they are or do we think back to another time when things were different? Much of this depends on how old you are. Much of this depends on what we remember. Much of this depends on how much of the future lies before you. For now, I would tell you, prefer now, and prefer this very moment. It has much to offer you. It has much to tell you and teach you. Breathe in the stillness of this moment. Let your memory of anything else fade and concentrate only on your presence here and reading these words. The Angels suggest, and I suggest that you take the time to value this moment, this moment that you are giving to yourself. Do not dwell in memory. Do not think of today or even tomorrow.

Think only of now and think of the possibility that in this particular moment you are completely whole. Think of this. Think of the healing you are receiving now. This healing is being given to you by these words as you read them. Raphael, Archangel Raphael, instructs me to tell you that you are being healed and that you are being made whole. Take a moment to be whole. Take a moment to be healed completely. And ask yourself to continue preferring this moment, this moment in which you are perfect and in which nothing is lacking or missing and nothing is wrong.

Shards of Memory

Shards of memory sometimes cut into us. They rise to the surface and come up and there they are, showing themselves to us, revealing themselves. Sometimes these are hurtful and painful. Sometimes we have done the work and we have found peace but there is still a message there. There is still a message. Sometimes the message is in the person that this involves. Sometimes the message is in the thing that happened. Sometimes the message involves your part and yes you always play a part. Ask what the message is. Ask what it will take for you to be healed and for the memory to recede and fade or at least become part of the story rather than something that is there to continually bother you. Ask for the message. Ask for the healing to take place. Ask to be set free.

Memory Informs Our Systems

Memory informs our systems like so many lines of coding. We are systems in and of ourselves, intricately complex systems, not completely understood systems. And then memory overlays all of this too. We are complex and then memories and remembrance make this even trickier. What do we remember and what do we forget, and how does this interconnect with the people we are, and the exchanges we have? How does all of this interconnect? Obviously memory informs us and what we say or do at any time. It also informs our very beings. It also changes us psychologically and biologically too. Stress affects us at every level. Happiness affects us at every level. Our remembrances seep into us this deeply too. The texture of who and what you are is all about all of this. Not just the people around you and your environment, but your experiences and memory of it too.

We Get Stuck

We get stuck because of all of this. We get stuck and these memories stay within us. We want to point to the traumas and talk about them. We want to talk about them and seek respite for our pain. But this does not release it always. These traumas are embedded in us. They create patterns in us and we become who they instruct us to be. So we get stuck in this identity. We get stuck and we don't know how to be other than who we are. Of course sometimes we do get unstuck. Sometimes we rise above all that we have gone through and we change. The texture of it all affects us but then it doesn't hold us back. Sometimes this is a personal choice, to rise above the pattern we have created in ourselves. Sometimes we have a helping hand in rising above this. At a certain point we are made and we are formed. And yes sometimes these memories are still inside us, affecting and eroding us, even though we think we have surmounted them, even though we think we have conquered the things we needed to conquer.

The Things Inside Us

The things inside us are waiting for an answer. The memories stuck inside us are waiting to be heard and understood, and they will keep knocking at the door until they are heard. They will knock and they will upset us. We can push them down. We can push them out of the way. But it is better that they are heard. It is better that we seek to understand the things that are stopping us, the things that are keeping us back. It is better that we understand the dramas we are playing out, the patterns that we live. We can live more cleanly. We can live more simply and clearly. We can live without anything in the background, without any thoughts that hamper us, that trouble us, and that infiltrate our subconscious.

Choosing to forget

We might choose to forget. We might choose to not remember what we have experienced. But this is not always easy or possible. We might make this choice but we might not be allowed to. Ask the Angels to help you forget what you need to forget. Ask them to ease your burden and to help you with it. It might be that you do not need to carry your pain alone.

Choosing to dissect

Sometimes we want to dissect memory. Sometimes we look at our memories and replay them in our mind, looking for clues, looking for meaning. Sometimes this can be valuable. But sometimes a kaleidoscope effect occurs when we look at something one way, and then another time we see it differently. Is it useful to dissect memory? We might ask ourselves if we are actually able to do this, if we are able to observe enough, stand back enough, to have a clear understanding, to have a complete picture of the truth. The most we can do is ask how this memory is affecting us now. If the effect is not a good one, then we might ask for a resolution. We might ask for healing. It is best to heal old things rather than put them under a microscope. It is better to be made whole than to look at all the little pieces that make up everything.

Observer and the memory

The observer and the memory are tied. There is no distance. There is no great clarity. The observer is a participant. No matter who they are, they are involved. They are the lens, they are the camera and the memory is filtered through them. What great understanding can they bring to the memory? They can only bring their own understanding. It may be great or it may be small. It is always personal. You may want to be a good observer. You may want to stand back and make an accurate observation. You may want to properly record and document. But in your own life especially, this is impossible. You are not just a vessel transmitting what has occurred. You cannot do this, even for yourself. No you are participating and creating the memory and looking at the event all at the same time. Take your truths lightly. Do not hold too fast to them. They were created in your mind and of your mind. Maybe your mind wants to shape them in some way. Maybe you have some agenda that is hidden to you consciously. Be as honest as you can. And be wary of your own honesty too.

Distance from action

We are distant from some actions and closer to others. We are distant, we keep distant. We want to remain in control and aware. We are not always sufficiently removed. We are never objective. We have to decide sometimes if we will come closer to what is happening. It is not always clear how closely we should engage. Sometimes we don't want to engage. Sometimes we draw nearer when it is not in our interest. The distance or closeness we have to the action or event, affects memory and guides our evaluation of what has occurred. Our distance whether it be close or far affects how we see anything. We might not see some details. We might skip over some things. There are so many things we cannot fully see or understand. Always ask yourself if you are participating in something at the right level, if you are engaged in the right way. Ask yourself if you are understanding everything clearly. How distant should you be? Are you always the same distance from everything? It is good to allow for some fluidity. It is good to vary your engagement according to the importance of something to you. Think about your distance. Think about what memories you are forming, what things you are taking in. You will know if your involvement is sufficient. But you do need to stop and think and ponder. You cannot just simply do. Thought is its own form of action. Practice it well.

Building a reality

We can build a reality from our thoughts and our dreams, from what has happened, and from what we construct. We can build a reality on many things, with many different elements. Our remembrances contribute to our reality. They contribute positively and negatively. You must make them neutral. You must take the good from remembrances and infuse it into your present. You must leave the negative and the bitter and the bad behind. You must because it can consume you, it can circle around and around you and close in on you. Close the door on the things that bother you. Close the door on the things you cannot change. Focus firmly on building your reality now and for the future. Allow the future to be different from the past. This is not easy if you do not have an idea of what the future could be. This is not easy if the future is unimaginable to you. Allow it then to unfold. Do not seek always to shape it and create it. Allow the future to create itself too. Allow it to be a good future and full of good wonderful things. Mitigate any issues you see. Prepare for them so that they are minimized. And then you can build a good foundation for the best future you can have. Allow remembrance to be a part of this but only in a good way. This is not because we want to forget and not because we don't want justice. This is because we need to be kind to ourselves, we need to heal and we need to create the best way forward.

Just what happened?

When you consider the past, how do you remember it? Is it in thoughts and words? Pictures or sounds? How does it fill your mind? Does it bring up emotions? We can think about the past but we may not have all the answers. We may not have all the understanding of what was going on at the time. We might see our perspective on things, our memory of events. And even then, we may not be sure of everything. Maybe there were conversations at the time. Maybe we talked to other people about what happened and there was some kind of agreement, some kind of understanding of what had occurred. So then we had our thoughts on the matter and then our thoughts with the group on the same subject. And then sometimes things fade from our minds too. We remember but we are not sure. Things are not so clear. Our tenuous hold on our memories allow us to break free from them. Our tenuous hold allows us to say, "that might have happened, but I can go on from there, I don't have to stay trapped by all of that." Allow yourself to be free from what happened. Allow yourself to be free from it because if you look at it closely, you can see that you don't know everything about it, you don't have full knowledge and maybe this is not possible anyway. So rather than remain in this state of confusion and of being held by the past, just let it go. And ask for help in doing this. Ask the Angels to help you.

Where the self begins and ends

The self begins and ends farther than what you consider. You are not just your body, your soul, your spirit. Your being reaches out into the far corners of the universe. Your being can travel. Your energy, your light can travel to the far reaches. You can travel into another human heart and soul and look at what it's made of. You can travel to another country and listen and look and see. You can go where you want to go. Your self is not limited. We just think this is so. We just think this is so and we limit ourselves. We limit ourselves and we do not make this soul journey. We limit ourselves and we keep ourselves trapped by our lives and by our memories too. Allow yourself to be transported. Allow yourself to be transported where you like and where you might see and learn new things. Your remembrances too can be a vehicle of transport, they can be a way to travel and to explore new things. Do you end? Yes maybe you do end. But in the meantime, you encompass everything. You should spread your wings. You should open your heart. Allow yourself to awaken. Allow your soul to have freedom.

Memory of the group

The group has its own memory. The group has its own memory that it holds on to. It repeats these memories. It repeats these truths over and over again so they become written on your subconscious, they become written in your spirit. All those things you thought you did not know? Actually you know them. They are written inside you. You may not think you know them. You may not think it is possible for you to know these things. But the memory of the group you are part of gives this to you. They give you access. You have full access and you can gain this information anytime you want it. But it might not be real. It might not be valuable. It could be shared wisdom, it could be passed down wisdom. But then again maybe it is a list of things you are supposed to believe, you are told to believe. Is it malleable? Is it changeable? That depends on how many times it has been repeated. How many times it has been repeated will tell you if it has yet developed a stone heart or if it is still youthful, if it still has joy.

Shared memory

These shared memories are part of us. Some come to us from our families. Some come to us through our society and culture, repeated in the news, floated around on the different waves. What is the zeitgeist? What is the mood and flavour of our times, of other times? These memories are shared and connect us. They glue us together. But it is at a deep level. It is at a deep unthinking level that we take in all of this. We take it all in and then it becomes linked to us. And we trust it so implicitly. We trust it so implicitly. And the very words that were expressed, they become part of the links that are forged in us. Can we break free of shared memory? No. We are all a product of our times. We are all a product of all that surrounds us. But we can augment shared memory. We can add to it through our own choices through our own selection of influences. Look beyond the canon. Look beyond the media canon and the news canon and the forms and distribution of all these memories. Look for other sources. And when in doubt look to nature, and try to decipher what she is telling you. If you can look at the innate wisdom of nature, then you will look past language, you will look past explanation. You will simply see, touch, feel, and hear, and then maybe you will not have to translate. Maybe you will just have understanding, some innate understanding that comes to you from inside and does not have to be explained.

Do not remember

Do not remember all that has passed, we beg of you. Do not remember all that has passed for if you do then you will be remembering not just your life story, but the lives of all that you know, and the lives and history of all that have come before you. Do not seek to remember all of this. Seek instead to be informed and to be illuminated and to live your life gracefully, purposely and with joy.

Let the story stop with me

If there is a story that I have lived that is terrible, then let it stop with me. If there is a tragedy that you have suffered, then let it stop, let it end and let it not perpetuate. We don't want to presume that history will relive itself, will reinvent itself. Yes history itself needs understanding. But your story, and my story, may need healing, may need time. But do they need retelling? Let the telling stop. Sometimes, let the silences breathe and let the story stop. For in the silence and in the lack of prescience, then we can forge something new. We can create something beautiful and not wrought out of pain. We can celebrate the new. Even you who have been wounded, you can create something new and beautiful. Even I who have also lived, even I can create something new and magnificent. Let us create new things. Let us not suffer the old pains and sorrows for all eternity. Let us begin anew.

Ponder these things

Ponder these things that I say to you. Ponder these things that I write. They do not come from me. They come from a higher place, a higher source. They are worth your consideration. They are worth observing and taking in and making a part of you. These words can inform you and shape you, they can fill your mind and they can rise within you. All the remembrances you have need to make way for new ideas. All the memories you have need to be cleaned and cleared. Ask us to help you do this. Stop for a moment and ponder and think and ask.

The things I wanted to say

The things I wanted to say that were taken from my story, from my experience, from my remembrances. They are there within me. They are there, etched within me. And my story is the same story if I have a million things to relate or just one. My story is my story. It is the collection of everything I ever lived or wanted to say. And it can be expressed simply because the essence of me does not change. The essence of me does not change even if a million more things happen to me that I could relate. Even if I form so many more memories that I could never relate them all, the essence of me does not change. So let my remembrances perch upon the essence of who I am. Let them not shatter or destroy me. They have no consequence. Let them only build me up or let them be gone.

The texture of memory

The texture of memory is like the texture of anything. It can be raw or silky. It can be like an embrace or it can be cold and hostile. The texture of the memory affects it. Not all memories are like pictures under glass. Some come to the surface and gnaw at us. Some flee away from us no matter how we chase after them. Let the texture of your memories be at peace with who you are. Let the texture of your memories not corrode you. Let the texture of your memories help you and assist you in all ways. You can look at the texture. You can say I like this, I don't like that, please change it. Your remembrance will listen to you. It will listen because it wants to bring your attention to what has come before so that you may have understanding, so that you may come to a deeper awareness. Your remembrance wants to be accommodating. Talk to your memories. Tell them what you want and what you will not have. This will spur you towards a better direction, towards a better contemplation of everything, and allow you to grow.

Memory and remembrance

Memory and remembrance are interwoven. They are the same but they are not the same. Memory is the collection of thoughts and images from what you have experienced, from what has gone on. Memory is all of that. So many photographs. So many images in your mind and recollecting the events. Remembrance can be that too. But it can be bigger also. It can be the kind of institutional thought that happens sometimes, kind of society level memory of what has gone on. Conclusions and opinions created by a sweeping memory, a sweeping characterization with so many bits and fragments slotted in and fitted in. You might have perspectives about things that are shaped by a collective imagining, by a collective influencing that happens or did happen. This is our collective responsibility. We all form opinions and decisions. And we are informed by different things too. What we see, hear, and read and how all this has been shaped and formed. Sometimes it is good to let those fragments come out. It is good to think about the odd parts of the story that don't quite fit, not because of some kind of cover up, but because there is so much to be gained by not buying in to the sweeping collective view of anything. What if everything didn't have to be woven so tightly together into a narrative? Let the story speak for itself. Let the remembrances come out as they are. Let the narrative-less experience have a voice. When remembrance can more closely resemble memory, then we are able to see more and gain clarity. Resist the desire to form a story. Allow the different elements to simply emerge.

Forgetting

A good way to let go is to forget. A good way to let go is to let the memories be washed from you. Let the memories be washed from you and let healing begin. Let healing begin and the eternal healing of the Angels and of God be made available to you. Let yourself be healed in the deepest way possible. Let yourself be healed in all ways. Let yourself be healed so that the light may shine within you and may shine from you. Forget so that you may remember who you are. Forget so that you may be free. And then remember too. Remember everything. Remember it all and in your healed state, you will know that this does not hurt you anymore. None of it can. Instead you will simply be healed.

Leave-taking

Take your leave of any situation you don't like. Take your leave of any kind of thing that is bothering you. You must take your leave and preserve yourself. You must preserve yourself and give yourself healing in all ways. Take your leave too of any remembrance that does not serve you. Take your leave and tell it that it is not serving you and that it must go away. All of this is to help you. All of this is to help you see that you are not scripted and determined by what has gone on. You can strike out in a new way. You can have new possibilities and a new future. Your life can be brighter and better. Take your leave of the gloom and the sorrow. Step into the light.

Once

Once there was no memory and no recollection and no remembrance. Once there was only now and the promise of the future, though even the thought of the future was strange. Even the thought of the future was strange because there we were newly formed, there we were formed when before we had not even existed. Once, once, we came into being. We became new. We became new and we would start to live and then begin to create memory and remembrance. Once there was nothing before. Once, there was nothing that was already created, that was already there before we were. Once we were the origin of everything. Once we were the Alpha and the Omega was a distant concept, maybe not even a possible concept. We are no longer at Once. But we remember it. We remember it in our thoughts and our dreams and in the cells of our bodies. We remember. We are infused by Once. We are woven with Once. And when we speak, we reflect the Once that is within each of us. We carry this forward. And we long for the beginnings. We long for the start of it all, when Once began.

Legend and yore

Legend and yore would have us believe in the start of all things. Legend and yore would have us believe in the heroic deeds of our ancestors against some threat. Legend and yore talk of battles between warring nations, warring tribes, between men and demons, between men and themselves. Legend and yore paint a picture but we were not there, we cannot know. Legend and yore seek to foster resilience in us, seek to give us the strength of our forebears, and seek to pass their knowledge onto us, their strength. This was the purpose of all those tales, to give us courage. This was the purpose of all those tales, to give us faith and strength. Take from these things what you need. Gain your strength and courage. Gain what you need. Gain everything. Tell the tales again. Tell the tales all that you need to, the tales from your holy books, the tales from your history, the tales from your stories, the tales you tell now. Tell the tales but gain only strength from them. Tell the tales but do not remember everything. Tell the tales and let them fill you and let them send you on your way. In your own creations, in your own tales, may you be strong. May you have faith and may you have courage and wisdom. May you be inspired and may you create your own legends worthy of the old yore.

History

The history of all that is written has come before us. The history of all that has happened has been set down. But not all of it has been recorded. Not all of it has been remembered, transcribed, observed even. There are a million histories but not a million records to match. There are millions of events that have set off events, impacted so many and yet they are lost, and yet they have no voice. The voice of the past speaks to us but it is the voice of the past that is remembered. Pray that the past that has been forgotten find its voice too. Pray that its lessons are not too shrouded, too clouded to be brought forth. Your history and my history and the history of all the millions and millions and billions of individual voices, these are important too. They are important to us and maybe they are important to others too. How will the history of the individual affect the history of all? How will the individual history matter? Maybe it has not mattered in the past except in the case of the great and the famous and the renowned. But maybe now and now, more and more, maybe all of it matters.

The things that were

The things that were astound us by their simplicity and their distance. The things that were astound us by their memories of another time. They are anachronistic and they don't make sense to us. We think about and consider them and how they were part of the time they were from, how they were a reflection of the technology, of the society. The things that were were all that. And yet they are part of us now too. It's no good saying we have moved beyond them. Part of us was there when these things came into being. Part of us was there when old ideas, and movements and passions of another time were created, were active. Part of us was there and all of this is built into us. We reflect it and we absorb it and we are created by it. Maybe not we ourselves at this present moment. But in our ancestry and lineage, in our history and culture, in the evolution of the societies that we are a part of. And even in our very cells. We are constructed from the things that were. We are constructed this way. And when we try to move forward, we need to remember how much of the past we still need to overcome. We need to remember this because we need to transition. We cannot think that movement forward is always an easy thing. When we get left behind, when part of us can't move forward, then we need to dissolve the factors that are creating these blocks in us. We need to ask that we be unanchored from what is holding us, and binding us to the past, to this created past that we are so much a part of. And then we might feel freer. We might feel like we can start again.

The circular past

The past travels in waves and circles. It embraces you and then it leaves you for a while. It brings the trail of your remembrances to you. It brings them to you and it does not let you forget. And then, when you have looked at your memories for a while, you find some peace. And this is good but then some things might start to repeat themselves. So not just your memories come to you but actual events get replayed in your life in some way. Actual events present themselves to you. And you can see them sometimes. You might try to change things. You might try to change your attitude about them so that they will be more peaceful for you. You might change yourself so that you react differently and so that things improve. It is good to do this. And it is good to acknowledge that things are happening again in a way that you think you have seen before. And always ask, what is the lesson that is being presented to you? What is the lesson that you need to learn before you are released from this particular part of the past? Once you have taken this in, and applied it, then you might be released from it, and you might gain new lessons that you had not considered at all. Eventually this past might straighten and then you can go forward. Ask for help so that your lesson is quick and doesn't cost you anything in any way.

The time gone by

The time gone by is no longer. It has gone past us and carried with it the thoughts we had, the events we lived, all that was done, all that was wrought by ourselves and others. The time gone by has receded from view. It lives only in our memory, and imperfectly.

The time that has passed

The time passed. Where did it go? Those things we held onto. Are they still part of our lives? Have they changed? Some things have stayed. Some things remain. Other things have changed so deeply, so completely. Where is the future? Did we even imagine all that is now? Was it ever possible to imagine all of it? Where is it taking us? What have we left behind? Can we even remember it? Somehow, inside us somewhere, it is there. But can we access it? Can we find any of it?

Remembrance is a river

Remembrance is a river that flows on. We cannot stop it. We are carried within it. Life carries us along and we hold onto our memories as if we can. We hold on to them as if we can trap their meaning and let it give us a way forward. Some of the meaning is captured. Some of the meaning remains. But mostly it flows by us and it is gone. It flows by us and we watch it leave. We can do nothing but carry on and walk forward. The memories are plucked from us and they float past us, rush past us even. We cannot catch them. We think they remain there for us. We think that they remain there for us in the future. But there is no chance of that happening. There is no security in it. We trust our remembrances, our memories but they are fleeting and they slip away from us.

The memory of all things

The memory of all things is contained in this river too. We walk forward and we can see all these remembrances pushing past us, clearing away from us 'til we are left with only brief recollections, vague glimpses of what has occurred. And then our memories form part of a larger river that informs everything. It all rushes past us and rushes away from us and these remembrances are creating something new too. What we once believed we no longer believe. What we once clung to, we no longer think is important. And this river moves on to create the next set of circumstances, the next expression of a culture and a society. It moves on and it is reborn. This is why it leaves us. It leaves us to create something new. And we are left chasing after it. We are left to chase after our old memories before they fade completely from us.

The memory of all

The memory of all is the memory of the earth and the stars and the air. The memory of all is the memory of the music of the heavens. The memory of all is the mountains and the cities and the shimmering dew. The memory of all is at our feet and above our heads. We are contained in the memory of all. We are expressed in the memory of all. We are made from all that was done before. We are created from all that was said and all that was not said, all that was written and all that has been forgotten or ignored. The memory of all informs us, has seeded us. And we would do well to remember that we are more than this tiny thing that we are, we are more than that. We are a reflection and a representation of everything. The memory of everything is contained within us. Through us everything is expressed, is remembered, and is written upon the world.

The consciousness of all things

Everything has energy and all matter has consciousness. We can
debate the level of consciousness of different living things, and even
nonliving things. Why debate this at all though? Why not just
surmise that every object, everything, every being, every atom
carries the cells of everything else. Why not just accept that all
things are in and of each other. So to each the other. And in doing
so, in accepting the consciousness of all things then our awareness
may stretch, the boundaries of ourselves may stretch. And we may
be happier in the knowledge that we are of all things, that we are
created and that all other things are created also. And we may find,
at the end of all of this, that everything is perfect.

The interconnection of all things

I am propelled toward this thing or the other thing. I am led, I am
guided to this person or that person. How do I know where to go?
How do I know who to speak to? Always I am pushed, always I am
directed. Sometimes I am even compelled. That person's energy is
calling me. This object is speaking to me. I am communicating with
everything and everyone at a deeper level, at an energetic level. All
this is happening and it is not only happening to me. It is
happening to everyone, all the time. If you choose to listen, if you
choose to consider this, then you too will begin to see how you are
pulled and drawn. You too will see how everything is connected
and how you are a part of it all.

The importance of memory

We can no longer wear memory like a badge. We can no longer refer to memory like an authority. We may treasure it. We may turn away from it. Make it as important as it needs to be for you. Make it only as important as that. Do not give it so much weight that it takes from you, that it robs you of your present awareness. Put it away. Put it up on a shelf or in a box and look at it sometime. Do not surround yourself with it always. Allow it to fade. It will fade if you want it to.

The importance of non-memory

Non-memory is the blank slate. Non-memory is the state before memory and the state after memory is cleared. But how to reach this state? How to reach this state if there are years you have lived? There are different means, there are different ways to alleviate the effects of memory, to cleanse the effects of memory. There are different methods and these are useful to explore. Above all ask that your spirit be cleared, ask that your soul be cleared and healed that you may reach a positive state, that you may attain a feeling that the different passages in your life can be well considered within you, can be well kept and that they will not weigh you down and hem you in. Allow them not to clutter your mind, your heart, your soul. Allow yourself the ability to be free.

The ancient brain

The ancient brain remembers the thoughts of all. The ancient brain remembers all your own thoughts too over all the millennia that you have lived. It remembers the universe and the forming of everything. It knows God. It knows everything. It knows all the stories of creation and the real story too. It knows all the myths of mankind and all the truths too. It knows all our goodness and all our cruelty. It knows, it records, it remembers. It lives within us and it stays in the background like a dim signal, sometimes guiding or warning but mainly remaining silent. It is busy. It is busy adding to its storehouse of memory, about our current lives and the life we are living and about everything around us too.

The people we have been

You and I have been many people through our lifetimes. We have been many people and there is something to be gained from that. We have lived different variations of ourselves. We have lived different events and made different choices. And so in all of us there is knowledge of prior history, of prior events, of prior decisions. We are filled with the history of who we are and who we have been in contact with since the beginning of time. Our memories run deep. Even if we feel we can't remember, they run deep nonetheless.

Our presence in the Divine

We are present in the Divine. We are a living expression of the Divine. We are strands of the Divine and these strands are fashioned within us linking us to Divine. How have we come this far? How have we lived this way? We have been tethered. We have always been tethered. We are present in the Divine and the Divine is present in us. Open yourself to this connection. Open yourself to the knowledge of this connection.

Aspects of memory

Aspects of memory fail us. Aspects of memory beseech us, call upon us and draw our attention to something we were before, something we have forgotten. We may think we know who we are. We may call upon memory to argue this to ourselves. But the memories are faulty. The experience right now is real and we may be different than who we were. Also when we call upon memory, we may be forgetting that the memory we call upon is the memory of all, it is the memory of everything, and it is the memory of everyone we have ever been. The aspects of memory are separate from us. We do not own them. And it is thinking that we do that we become confused, that we become so convinced about what we want to believe.

Aspects of Divine memory

Aspects of Divine memory are present with us. Aspects of Divine memory take their place within us. We were given these to help us, to keep us moored and keep us present. Our independence is not called into question. We are independent. We are free beings. And yet, we are tied to something far greater than us. We are tied to something. And though we may not remember all of it, we have knowledge of it. And we can try to understand.

Memory considered

Memory laps over us and around us, is a part of us and yet leaves us. Memory is unfulfilled always and never complete. It nourished us and it strips us too. It forms us and we shape it in return. It is the river that we are standing in and it rushes through us. We can never catch it. We can't make sense of it either. We can only try to paint the best picture we can, to capture the essence of what has gone before. And then we have to let it go. We might not think we can. We might not think we have to. But the past does leave, the present is here and the future is coming. Memory may support us but only to a certain degree. After that we need to march bravely on.

The Book of Sorrow

The Book of Sorrow is about how sorrow informs us and heals us and tears us apart and is in some ways the precondition of our state of being. Recognize sorrow. Recognize your place in sorrow and you can heal yourself. You can heal the ways that you are broken. Accept sorrow and you can heal. Accept that things are not perfect and maybe cannot be perfect and then you have a place from which you can grow and be made whole.

Sorrow as our precondition

We are not born with sorrow, normally. We are not born with sorrow. We are born pure, with joy. We are born a blank slate with nothing having come to us, with nothing having happened. But this changes. Sooner or later this changes and we are touched by sorrow, we are touched by injury, we are touched by loss. Sorrow forms us and we are expressed through sorrow. We bear it badly. We bear it heavily. Grief, loss, pain, duress. None of it is easy. None of it wears well on us. It blights us. It carries away our joy and our possibility. But it doesn't have to. We can recognize sorrow. We can acknowledge it as our precondition, as the state of our being and then it won't be so difficult, it won't be so hard on us.

The advent of sorrow

The advent of sorrow is like the wail of grief. The advent of sorrow is the overwhelming tide of emotions engulfing you. The advent of sorrow comes when it is expected and it comes also at other times when it is not expected. Sorrow comes and sorrow embraces you though you do not want this embrace. You can't turn away from it. It reaches into you and grasps your heart. It reaches in and takes every part of you, searching through you, taking away from you. You can try and shut it down. You can try and shut it out. But it will enter you through every pore and every part of you. It will enter you and demand that you confront it, it will demand that you will have a conversation and that it will own a piece of you. How much of you it will own is up to you. How much you will give to sorrow is up to you.

The condition of sorrow

The condition of sorrow is the salt taste of tears. The condition of sorrow is the redness of your face and the unstoppable pounding in your head. The condition of sorrow is the weariness of your shoulders and the stiffness in your back. The condition of sorrow is the complete desperation that you feel, and the despair. Let the condition of sorrow not engulf you. Let this and all that it contains be lifted from you. It is like a heavy blanket that has been placed upon you that you cannot lift off of you. It is like all of that and you feel surrounded by it. You cannot lift it from you. It deadens you and it comes to you in the middle of the night to take away what little peace you have. We say it need not be this way. We say it need not be this way and you can be uplifted, you can have Grace, you can be taken away from your troubles and your heartbreak. Let it all be lifted from you and may you be at peace.

Sorrow itself

Sorrow itself is a temptress. It doesn't want to leave you alone. When given the opportunity, it is present. When you give it voice, it is pleased. It wants to live and grow in your mind. It wants to furnish out the corners of whatever free space you might have there. It wants to create darkness. It wants to shackle you to the inside of the darkest thing you think about. Sorrow can flourish and sorrow can foster the darkness. We want to shine a light on this. We want you to shine a light on this too and not succumb. You think you must. You think you must give way to sorrow. But, we tell you, you must not. For sorrow is but one way. Sorrow is not the only way and you must not give it presence. You must not allow it to grow. Do your grieving but then look for light. Feel the hurts you have but then seek to heal them. Dwell not in sorrow lest you lose your light and become unfindable. We will help you. Let us help you to find your light again and to heal the sorrow. Ask for this and it will be done.

The beauty of sorrow?

Sorrow can appear beautiful. Sorrow can appear lingering and majestic and noble. But it is not a good thing. It is a cast out thing and we might feel sorry for it. It is a downtrodden thing and we may look upon it through a poetic lens. But being miserable and wretched and impoverished in spirit is not beautiful. Look in your own heart and look to see where you have placed value on sorrow. Do not do this anymore. Heal this within you. Find beauty where it truly resides, not in sorrow. Seek out truth and meaning and cast sorrow aside. Healing is what you need, not any sense of loss or wounding, not any sense of being stricken. Agree that you will take steps to be whole. Agree that this is what you want and that you will turn away from sorrow and misery. Agree and then this can occur. Agree and you can be set free.

Sorrow and loss

Sorrow is loss and loss can be sorrow. Sorrow is the stripping away of ourselves and the ripping of our spirit. It occurs when someone important is taken from us. The loss of this creates hurt in ourselves. The scale of the hurt is the same as the scale of the loss. Sorrow and loss work together. You will never feel sorrow without loss. Sometimes you can feel loss without sorrow though. Regardless of the size of the trauma, there is an effect on you. Regardless of what happens, you feel things are difficult, things have changed, and you have been caught off guard. Heal your loss first and then your sorrow. Heal your loss first because this will give you more strength. Then you will still feel your sorrow but it will not be like a cut that does not heal. It will be easier. It will be easier to deal with. And then sorrow can begin to heal too.

Twists and turns

Sorrow has twists and turns. Sorrow has alleyways and avenues. We are led down the road that sorrow takes us. We are led down the road, we do not choose the shape of it. We do not choose what it will do to us or with us. Sometimes there are highs within sorrow. Something will appeal to us. Something will call out and make sense to us and for a moment we won't feel badly. And then it reverberates back. And then we are carried back to the pit of sorrow. Waves of sadness wash over us and push us this way and that. We surface for a time and then we are hit again. Until one day, maybe, hopefully, life presents us with something new, something good and we are swept off the track of sorrow, we are swept away from it and can regard it more calmly. Perhaps it becomes a story within us then. Perhaps it becomes part of our fabric.

The unthinkable

When the unthinkable happens it is beyond processing. We can't comprehend. We look for meaning and we lose our minds. Let go of the unthinkable. It is the only thing you can do. Let go of it. The unthinkable almost never happens. But when it does, if it does, do not cling to it. Allow it to happen and then try to forgive it and what happened. Try to separate yourself from it and have peace.

Recovering from sorrow

Recovering from sorrow takes a long time. It might never happen. You might always be trapped in your sorrow. But if enough time passes, many years, then you may be set free. You might want to be set free sooner. You might not want to continue the experience of sorrow. Ask for help and do the inner work. Do not say why did this thing happen to me? Do not say why did this thing come to me in my life? Think, instead, of what you can do to make things better for yourself. Think what you can do to heal yourself. Healing is possible. The assuagement of grief and sorrow is possible. Choose to believe that your emotions can be righted. Choose to believe that your soul and your spirit can be set free.

When life lets you suffer

When life lets you suffer you must make a plan for a new day. When life lets you suffer you must say to yourself, today I am suffering but tomorrow will be better, tomorrow will be infinitely better. When life lets you suffer, you must seek to stop the suffering. Ask the Angels for help. Ask God for help. Ask those in your life for help. Stop the suffering and stop the emotional pain. Stop all of that. When life lets you suffer, take a deep breath and carry on. You can carry on. You are strong beyond all measure. You are valued. You are cared for. Allow the Angels to help you. Allow yourself to be supported. This is how you will keep going. This is how you will thrive. And this is how the suffering will be eased and will leave you. Breathe and feel your freedom. Breathe the release of your pain. Do not keep it. Do not let it linger.

Suffering

Suffering is just a part of all things. Suffering is here and now. Suffering was yesterday. Will it be tomorrow? Does it have to be tomorrow? Suffering can be eased. Suffering can be softened. Suffering can even be avoided. Look deep inside yourself and find the counsel that you need to ease your suffering. Ask the Angels to take away all that you have suffered. Ask them to release you from all the ways that you suffer. Ask that you not need to suffer anymore. And ask what you need to do in order that that be true. Be at peace. Do not think that suffering needs to be a part of you anymore. Be at peace.

Subjectivity of Sorrow

Sorrow comes to us individually, plated for our perfection. It is bitter when this galls us most. It stings when we are already hurt. It wears us down with exhaustion. Stay strong in the face of sorrow. Stay strong and care for yourself. Care for your emotions. Care for the way you feel and treat yourself well. Be kind to yourself and you will make yourself stronger. Then the sorrow will no longer berate you and beat down upon you. Then you will be stronger and be able to bear all of it better. You will be able to surmount the despair.

Sorrow and sadness

Sorrow and sadness come upon us, and sometimes they linger and have a hold that will not release us. Sometimes we catch ourselves lifting out of it. We catch ourselves feeling better and we wonder if this is right. We wonder if we should feel well. The lingering nature of sorrow means it comes for us time and again. It comes for us and we are its prey, we are its victim. Permit yourself to feel well even in the midst of sorrow. Permit yourself to be right in yourself and right with the world even when you are sad. You can allow for many emotions to be present at one time. You can allow for many emotions to well up within you. Sadness and sorrow can be a badge of honour. But these are false aims. Be sad and sorrowful when you are sad. Grieve. And then continue. Life does continue. It always continues. It is better for you to recover than to continue shrouded in grief and clouded by misery. It is better for you to continue and meet the new day with a better frame of mind, with happiness even, when it comes to you again.

All that is

All that is and all that ever was are contained in this moment in time. All the sorrow and sadness you feel reflect all those other moments in time that come before this one. When you feel your sorrow, you are feeling not just your sorrow but the sorrow of so many other calamities, so many other hurtful things. What is it that you feel? Can you be sure that all of it is yours? You are part of all that is. All that you are feeling is part of all that is too.

The infinite

The infinite is aware of us. The Infinite is aware that we are here and that we are part of everything. But we are not always aware of how infinite we are, and how we are part of the infinite too. Unaware, we are lost in our sorrow and covered and cloaked by our sadness. Unaware, we have no knowledge that there is really no sorrow or sadness. There is only the infinite. There is only the continuum. And we are here upon this place now. But there were other places and times. And there will be more places and times. And there is eternity. And we are part of this already. But we cannot see it. And so we console ourselves or we try. And so we give way to our sorrows and our sadness.

Sorrow after death

After the death of a loved one there is sorrow, there is grief and loss. After the death of a loved one there is bereavement, a feeling that much has been taken from you, a feeling that part of yourself is gone. You cling to the memories but there is no resolution to what you feel. You try to remember the details, the person's voice, how they spoke to you, what they said, how they felt about things. There are many things you can remember. There are many things you can conjure up in your mind and revisit. Your imagination can relive the past. But you can only enter into this so far. Ultimately there is loss, there is a wrenching of things. The wound is fresh. The wound takes time to heal. It takes time to heal all things, all losses, and all sorrows. Be consoled in your grief. Be consoled. One day there will be a reprieve.

Life after sorrow

After sorrow there is still life. But this life changes. It is tinged with bitterness, coloured with regret, with fading memories, with the things that happened, with words spoken and unsaid. Hopefully there were enough words, hopefully there are enough memories to carry you through. Even if not, even if more should have been said or spoken, you can say these things now. You can say them now to this page and your loved one will hear them. You can say them now and you will be freed. Your heart will not be so heavy. It will be released from its burden, from the anchor of grief. And when you have grieved, and when you have suffered your loss as you will, you will find that it will be lifted. You will find that the day will come when life returns in the way it was before. You will find that you are healed and that you are cleared in some way. Your grief has affected you, it has deepened you, and now that you have felt everything so deeply, now you can carry on.

Upheaval and betrayal

Sorrow and loss is an upheaval and a betrayal. It is an upheaval of our core at our deepest level. It says to us, 'you cannot protect yourself.' It says to us, 'we are striking you through and through.' We feel this hurt, we feel this deep impalement and we can do nothing. We can do nothing. We are betrayed. We are betrayed by our very selves, by our very sense of being completely overwhelmed. For we cannot turn from it, this upheaval, this sorrow waits for us in every corner. It waits for us and assaults us with its stings, with its fierceness. We are forever assaulted it seems. Or at least it seems so for a time. In time, we make peace with the upheaval. In time we accommodate the betrayal. We accommodate it because we must and then we grow stronger. Maybe you do not feel strong right now. Perhaps you are lost in your sorrow right now and feel this deeply. If you feel so wounded that nothing can ever seem right, then be patient a little longer. The light and the daylight and the light in your soul is returning to you. The light of your spirit will be relit. Be patient, the day is breaking. Be patient, your heart can heal from this too. This too shall pass.

Betrayed by God

In the midst of your great sorrow, in the midst of your great tragedy, it might seem to you that you have been betrayed by God. It might seem to you that you have become unimportant and that the Divine and God do not concern themselves with you. You are on a path that is beset with loss, beset with traumas, and you cannot find a way to lift yourself up. You cannot find a way to be at peace. And yet, you are not betrayed by God. He has not turned away from you. He has not looked away. He waits for you to cross the bridge of your grief, to surmount the chasm of your losses and to find Him. He is waiting for you. He is waiting for you. He has faith in you and He trusts that you too have faith in Him. Ask for help. Ask for the help of the Angels. Ask for the help of God in restoring your faith, in restoring your peace, in restoring you in all ways. Ask for total and complete healing and you will find that in your grief you will gain something anyway. You will find that in your loss, even in your devastation, there will be some way to bring light to you and to your very soul.

Stung

The sorrow has stung you. The sorrow has stung you like a thousand bees. The bitterness binds you to it and you cannot feel anything. You cannot feel love or hope or compassion. You are numb. You feel dead inside. You do not feel alive. You do not feel that anything is possible for you or will ever be possible for you. Be aware of everything that is happening inside you. Be aware of all your emotions flooding to the surface. Be aware and let them go. Let them go if you can. Let them go to the degree that you can. Let your tears be the balm for your emotions. Let your prayers be the salve for your soul. Let all you feel, let all the intensity that you feel ebb away from you. These feelings are important. Your sorrow is important. But it can flow away from you now. The pain can ease. The sharp discomfort you feel can be soothed. You can be free of it. You can allow the pain of it to flow away from you. You can allow peace to come into you instead. This is not a betrayal of the way you feel. This is not a betrayal of the loss you have suffered. It is the order of things. Loss. Grief. And then healing. It is the order of things and you can participate in your recovery. It is the order of things and you can be made whole. You can be made whole and your spirit can be repaired. The damage can be repaired.

Healing

Healing is possible after sorrow, though you may not believe this is true. Healing is possible and you need to let it occur. It will take time. Time will be needed to repair the many ravages that sorrow has caused within you. First one thing will be healed, and then another. And then new pain will present itself. New wounds will make themselves apparent. The first crush of sorrow will dominate you, and then there will be some lifting of it. Grief will rack your brain and then you will glimpse a window of freedom. Tears will convulse you and then you will be aware that you have stopped crying. Healing will happen but there will be many layers. Sorrow will present itself with many textures, many points of interest will be made visible in its landscape. It might be that it will force you to tour all of them. It might be that you will be spared some of them. Allow healing to take place. Allow healing to take the time it needs to. It will come. It will come. Have peace you will be healed.

The Angels will help you

The Angels will help you in your grief, and your strife, and your misery. The Angels will help you and they will lift this burden from you, they will lift the sorrow from you. You have been weighted down, you have been crushed and overwhelmed. But this doesn't need to be the case anymore. This doesn't need to be the case. You can be lifted from it. All of this can ease. All of this can ease and not push down upon you. Allow the Angels to help you. Allow the

Angels to minister to you and to provide what help that they can. Ask them for help and they will come to you. Ask them for help and healing will be easier and more complete. You will be helped. You will be at peace.

Sorrow relentless

Sorrow is relentless in the way it hunts us. Sorrow is relentless in the way it pursues us. It has us in our grasp and it won't let us go. We are caught in a floodgate of our own emotions. We are caught and we can't be released and we can't let go. We are sorrowful and this is our definition. We are sorrowful and we are captured here. The all-encompassing nature of all things holds us here. The all-encompassing nature of sorrow clings to us, envelops us. How do we escape it? How do we push away from it? We begin by refusing to do battle. We begin by refusing to embrace it. We say to sorrow, "there you are and here I am, but I will come no closer to you, I will not approach." When we begin to refuse to engage with sorrow, when we engage with other things instead, then it will go away from us. Then it will go away from our lives and we will have much more peace. We will be free.

The texture and taste of sorrow

Sorrow has texture and taste and it becomes imbued in us. Sorrow has texture and taste and we know this and it becomes a part of us. It becomes a part of us and we may not like it but we are drawn to it. We are drawn to what it gives us, to the picture it paints for us. The appeal of the melancholy, the appeal of sorrow is wrought within us. We find pathos and sadness intriguing. Happiness is its own thing. Its own bright beautiful thing that shines and is beckoning. But sadness too has its charms. Sadness and sorrow draw us in. We are enveloped by the texture and taste of it and by the bitterness of it. And it feeds something in us. Something maybe that we should not feed. But it feeds us all the same.

Is bitterness loss?

Sorrow can be bitter. It can be an achy emptiness. It can be an inconsolable grief but it can be bitter too. The bitterness is there under the surface. The bitterness of what we have lost. The bitterness of what has been taken away from us. Bitterness is not just loss in and of itself. Bitterness and loss come together frequently but are not interchangeable. In a state of loss, you may feel bitter. But you may not feel this way. You may even feel grateful, in spite of your loss. You may feel grateful that you knew this person, that you had this experience. And you can feel bitter without sorrow, when someone has done something to you, when someone has taken something from you. Leave your bitterness now. Cease to see the appeal of it. Leave your bitterness now and be cleansed of it. It does you no good. It brings ill will unto yourself. Do not trap yourself in this cage. Allow yourself to be free of bitterness. Allow yourself to be free of this scourge.

Can sorrow be absolved?

Can sorrow be absolved? Can sorrow be asked to leave and then forgotten? Does it have to be ever present? Does it have to linger and never really fade? You need to commit to allowing it to fade. You need to commit to the possibility that it can go away from you, that it need not linger. You need to commit to the idea that it can be absolved. And then you have to absolve it yourself. It listens to no one but you. It follows no one but you. You are the guardian of your own sorrow and its keeper too.

The blame of oneself

It is easy to blame oneself in the advent of sorrow. It is easy to blame oneself when sorrow comes upon us. We say to ourselves, if we had done this thing or that thing then we would not have this sorrow. If we had said this thing or that thing then this sorrow wouldn't be there, or it would not be as bad as it is. It does not matter the circumstances, it does not matter what happened or did not happen. What matters is the part you can play now. Never think that increasing the sorrow will help. Never think that blaming yourself or indeed another will help. Ask for your sorrow to be lifted and for all forgiveness to be possible. Ask to be able to forgive yourself and others. Then, the light can find a window to your spirit. Then the light can lift up your sorrow and remove it. You will be brighter and filled with light. Then you will blame no more.

The survival of sorrow

In moments of perfect anguish, in moments of complete devastation, we do not think we can survive the sorrow. We do not think that we are capable of surmounting this greatest of traumas. And yet we can and we do. It is a profound mystery to us how in our very depths, in the very deepest of things that we can suffer, still we can rise up, still we can continue. And yet we do. We continue and we endure and we survive. Even when we don't want to, even when we don't see how, we survive and we make it through. We survive and we endure and we are lifted. We may long for better days. We may not see how they are possible. But something keeps us going -- some deep faith in ourselves, some deep need to survive, some faith in others. All this helps us to survive, helps us to countermand the sorrow and to prevail. Sorrow may survive. But we survive too. And we survive more beautifully and with more grace, than anything that comes to test us, and anything that comes to demand from us all that we cannot give.

Staying within the confines

Stay within the confines of your life if you want to. Stay within those confines. But examine too, how you are confined and who and what put you there. If it was trauma or distress, if it was tragedy or brutality, these things are at an end, they can withstand your spirit no longer. You can rise above them now. You can be free and strong and brave. You have the heart that can rise above this. You have the mind and the fierce spirit that can always be counted on. Look within yourself and find the means needed to move away from the stale barriers that are upon your life. Break free of the confines. Break free of any trauma or misery. Sorrow is at an end.

The whole of life

The whole of life is at your disposal. The whole of life is here waiting to be beckoned too and summoned, waiting to be reveled in and enjoyed. The whole of life is yours for the taking. Live it not under a shadow. Live it not under some gloom. The sky is not overcast nor will it be overcast again. Live your life. Enjoy the moments, the days, and the years that you have been given. The whole of life is here for you. Shroud it not in misery. Contain it not in sadness. Rather enjoy it and delight in its beauty. Receive its blessings.

After life

After life, a new life is waiting for you. After life, a new dawn rises. Your spirit will rise like the sun in the morning and it will never set. Your spirit rises to a new existence, to a new expression and possibility. All that you feel now, you will feel later too but without fear, without remorse, without anger. You will be reborn. You will be wise and whole. You will be free and without sorrow.

Revisit your loss

Revisit your loss after this life and see where this brings you. Revisit your loss and see that there is no loss. There is only delay and a veil separating us from our heaviest losses. Revisit your loss, it is there no more. Your loved ones are waiting for you. Your sorrows are departed. You are whole and complete and the sadness is leaving you. There can be no sadness any longer. There can be no loss, no sorrow.

Seize everything

Seize everything that you may. Seize everything and breathe in the life that you have and the life that you imagine. This life is here for you. This life is being constructed for you and you can construct the life that you want. You can construct all that you imagine and all that you want. Dream and realize this life. Dream of happiness and fulfillment and joy too. Banish the sorrow. It does not belong in your new life.

Release

Releasing is sometimes difficult. You may not know what it means to let go of something. You may not know what it means to release it, to release your sorrow and your anguish. There are many things you can do in order to release your feelings. You can do inner or self-work with a number of techniques. You can exercise. You can pray or meditate. One thing that you can do and that will be helpful to you is to decide that it is possible to release all that you feel. In deciding, you make the decision to move forward. In deciding, you agree to be released, and you make an agreement with yourself to release too. Try this and see if you can move forward from things. See if you can be more at peace.

Repent

Repent. Repent of your sorrow, although it is not your fault. Although you are not to blame, repent of it anyway, because there is something in you that draws it to you. There is something in you that will not let it go away. Repent of your sorrow and watch it vanish before your eyes.

Let go

Let go of all you need to let go. Let go of your sorrow. Let go of your anger. Let go of your bitterness, your shame, your remorse. Let go of all of it and let peace and happiness remain. Let joy fill your heart and let yourself feel blessed in all ways. Be blessed and be at peace.

Telling the Story

Here are some story elements that contribute to the telling of this story. They are meant to be ambiguous.

The Cherries

The cherries were on the trees. The cherries were unlike normal cherries. They were small red glass squares cut sharp and arranged in clusters upon trees.

The trees were in an orchard, masses and masses of them. All filled with the brilliant red squares, pushing against each other, clicking and sounding in the breeze.

Pacifico stood still, watching the trees. He stood still waiting for everything to begin, just as they had planned.

He was still. But he was poorly named. He was still but angry. He did not like what was going to happen. He was still and angry but this was what everyone had agreed to. In order to draw things out, this is what everyone had said was best.

Any moment now all of it would unfold. All of it would happen.

What would happen was this –

The she-devil Béa would swoop in, followed closely by Larriot who had no control, none, over his actions. Not since Miraldo had made certain modifications. (Again a necessary thing and with Henry locked up what else could they do?)

So there was Larriot spineless and in Béa's control. And Miraldo watching to make sure. And I was there too, let's not forget my culpability in all of this. You can call me Irene here although all names have been changed to protect the innocent and the Divine. So there we were, waiting, and then it happened.

Béa, falsely thinking she was in control of the show, ordered Larriot to take down Pacifico. Pacifico was seething and shouting a few choice words to Miraldo. Béa was so oblivious and stupid she thought that this was directed at her. Pacifico could have rebelled and killed Béa then and there, but Henry and I had persuaded him that really perhaps he better not. Then Pacifico was down, and protesting, and some others who had turned or were pretending took him away. First they wanted to put him with Henry but realized what a bad idea it was. So they put him in another cave nearby, and I went and freed him later on. (The Daughters had helped me seek out this place).

But in the meantime, Pacifico had been removed from the cherry tree orchard and so Larriot was able to take some of the glass cherries and give them to Béa, enough for her to wreak some havoc and destruction for a few thousand years. Miraldo reversed the changes he had made to Larriot and then banished him, or maybe Larriot banished himself. But whatever the case their relationship was very damaged, almost irreparable. Larriot couldn't quite accept how badly he had been used and maligned too.

So that's the story of how the cherry trees were abandoned and everything that happened as a result.

After Pacifico had been manhandled and shut down, arms tied behind him, he could do nothing except look at what else was happening. He couldn't move. He couldn't stir. There was no point screaming. No one was strong enough to rescue him so he knelt there on the ground shifting about angrily and noting the conversation that Miraldo and Béa were having. He thought that perhaps Miraldo was casting glances back at him to see how he was. He thought, though he could not be sure, that some invisible signalling was taking place because suddenly there he was standing, being prodded along away from the field. He thought he could see Larriot looking and hiding. He knew I was there. He could always pinpoint my presence without even trying. But he would not look my way. He would not give me over to them.

I was in the background perched in one of the trees. I was quite invisible, hiding under the dark blue cloak we used for these purposes. Still I could be found out if someone wanted to find me, if someone knew where to look. So there I sat, perched precariously and leaning, trying to be still and feeling powerless. I wasn't entirely powerless though. Pacifico and I (and Miraldo too though Pacifico did not know everything), we had set all this in motion. We had decided that this was the best way forward. But still I didn't enjoy this. I didn't enjoy any of this.

Here we were casting ourselves out of our homes, waiting to see if this would give the results we wanted. We boarded everything up and left. We left and abandoned it all. We left, but we left secret instructions. "Don't tell her about this," we said. Let this part of our world be safeguarded. Let her not see that it exists. We didn't want the whole of everything to be put at risk in our plan, just enough of it to be convincing.

So I waited perched in the tree. I waited for Pacifico to be taken away and for Giraldo to give the all clear. And then I would follow and track and record and understand. And at the end of it all we would take back everything. This had to be done. This would be done. But for now we waited. And it would take centuries.

We knew this would happen. It didn't matter. Time was infinite. We knew it would take that long but it had to be done right. So we played the long game through many lives and centuries, and we played it over and over again. Until finally, we reached the time when all was understood and everything was complete. It was time to go home.

Back when the original plan was launched, not everyone had been in complete agreement. Pacifico liked the plan but in typical fashion thought everything would be achieved by the next solstice. Henry, thinking in wide swathes of time, thought in terms of millennia. I had no knowledge of the time that all of it would take. But I could already see some of the lives I would have to live and the characters I would play and honestly, it was a little too much. I who had always preferred to step aside and avoid conflict was being asked to plunge myself headlong into conflict over and over again in order to root out what was needed, in order to achieve the end goal.

So there we were, fixed in our goals, and fixed in our play-acting. It would take a very long time.

The Incantations

Behold the incantations. They are words that have meaning. They are prayers, mediations, even statements. They are words used as energy, recognized for their energy. They are a calling upon. They are a creation energy. They are a calling upon Divine. Call them what you will. Their words have power. And I present them to you now.

Words that have meaning

Why should not words have meaning? Why should the power of things be concentrated and limited to actions, limited to people and persons of great position? Why should not words themselves have meaning? Words that were created and spoken and written by people, the very people that are imbued with power themselves. And the words have more power than the people sometimes. The words sometimes speak so clearly and plainly that the truth of them cannot be denied, the truth of them is present. Words may outrank the speaker. Words may carry on forward centuries past when they were written. They are a continuation. They are our legacy as human beings. Our words bind us and separate us. Our words give us resolution and hope. And our words enable us to speak with the Divine, through incantations, through prayer, through mediation and through simple conversation. Our words have meaning and significance. Behold the power of the word and the power of your word too.

Prayers

A prayer is but a formal petition to God and sometimes other Divine. A prayer is a sequence of short sentences beseeching the All-knowing for help and assistance in times of need and in all times needed. A prayer is a message of hope. A prayer is a chance, and a risk and an entreaty. A prayer is sealed with love, offered with faith, and often in fear. A prayer offers us a respite from our desperations and our miseries and our struggles. A prayer offers us hope that our requests, and our urgent needs may be answered. A prayer is the first inkling we have, the first way we are presented with the idea of talking to the Divine. A prayer is often a good place to start when you feel uncomfortable with the idea of talking to the Divine.

Meditations

Meditations are myths in the mind. Meditation is where we create our reality with our mind. We breathe. We watch our breath and we watch the thoughts that come up. We think about them or we don't. We can expand on them or we can let them go. We watch our breath, we breathe and then new realities can come to us, new worlds can be created for us and by us. We make a space for the new world. We take a new world and form it and shape it within us and then we bring it out to the world, or maybe it brings us out to the world. We ponder, we shape, we dream, and all of this by breathing, all of this though we do not know we are doing this. We do not know, but we do this nonetheless. We do not know, but we create nonetheless. We create nonetheless in our thoughts and in our breathing and in our putting out of new ideas and new modes of being to the world. We fashion our creations and we release them out into the world. We are bound to do this. We are blessed to do this. And so our myths, our dreams, can become our realities. We can open our souls and spirit and fashion new things from the clay within us. We can make new things, just from our minds. Meditate and create. Meditate and be blessed for you will calm yourself and save the world in so doing.

Statements

Even simple statements to God, to yourself, to Angels, to the people around us can do much. Even simple statements can change the world. Utter a phrase in the right environment with the right people there and suddenly the dominoes are in play and one thing touches another. And suddenly, the thing you spoke about, the thing you talked about is real, it is not something just to be considered. Suddenly it is real. Talk to God. Talk to the Universe and the Angels. Talk to yourself aloud sometimes and say what you feel. Say what you want to see happen in the world, and in your world. Say what you don't like. Say all of these things and see what happens. See what the power of your voice and your mind can do. Don't stay quiet. Find a way to make yourself heard. In the way that you express yourself, in the choices you make in your communication, you will have more impact than you can imagine. You will have so much impact. Do not keep those important thoughts to yourself. Do not keep your opinions to yourself. Give voice to them. Allow your voice to speak simply and clearly so that it cannot be denied, so that the truth is evident and undeniable. The simpler the message the more truth it carries. The simpler the message the farther it will travel. Speak clearly and you will be heard a million miles away.

Calling Upon

It is time to call upon the forces that will help you. It is time to call upon the forces that will set you free. Call upon the Angels. Call upon God and the Universe. Call upon the saints and the masters. Call upon your ancestors too. Call upon all of these so that they may help you, and teach you, enrich you and protect you. Call upon all of these and surround yourself with the embrace of true security, of true sanctity. Call upon them now. I leave it to you to choose your words. I leave it to you to choose the place and the form of your calling. Call upon all of these as best you can. They will not deny you. They will hear you and they will help you. They want you to be blessed. They want you to be at peace. Call upon them now and be happy and at peace.

Creation Energy

The energy of creation is at your disposal. The energy of creation is within you and it is made from the clay that formed your soul in the very beginning. The energy of creation is yours to shape, and is yours to mold. The energy of creation rises from within you. It rises from within and it takes hold of you so that you can create and make things new. Take this energy and fashion your world with it. Take this energy and clear yourself with it. Take this energy and be strong. Take this energy and revel in it. Take this energy and let it carry you in life and indeed, every day. Take this energy and fashion what you will with it. Just as God fashioned you and me, so can you fashion your world too. Take this energy, breathe it in and be the creator that you were made to be. Be this creator and allow yourself to have more freedom and scope to do more. Do more with what you have. Do more with what you do not have and create what you do not have for yourself. Take your thoughts and feelings and dreams and make with them. Take this energy of your spirit and make with it. Make all that you can. Make all that you are called to create. Make it from somewhere within you. Fuel it with your spirit and your soul. Shape it with your mind and your intellect and your imagination. Allow the meanderings of your mind, the wonderings of your soul, and the shape of your imagination to give it flavour and texture. Allow the very energy you have, the very energy of your spirit to shape it and to guide it and to make it real. Allow all this to be real and possible for you. You can do this with all that you have and with the energy that is within you. The creation energy that you have is within you, it is calling you because it wants to be expressed, it is calling you because it wants to serve you and to be active through you.

Calling upon Divine

Calling upon Divine is something that is easy to do. You simply call, in your own way and when you feel compelled to do so. You do not have to wait for a special moment in time. You do not have to wait for a special circumstance. You simply call, you ask, and you trust that your prayers will be answered. Calling upon Divine can mean a few different things. It can mean a specific prayer or request that you have for God or the Angels. It can also simply be a call for help. If this is what you need, if this is what feels right to you, then you have only to do this simply, and in the ways you are compelled to do. It can be a desperate cry for help, a quiet plea of desperation. It can be those things when we are upset, when things are happening beyond our control and affecting us. But we can also call upon the divine every day. We can make this a regular practice, we can call often and for all kinds of reasons. When we do this we will feel more secure in ourselves, we will feel more at peace. We will cultivate the feeling of being held by the Divine and this will be a good and healthy thing for us. This will do us good. Seek out ways and reasons to call upon the Divine. Anytime is a good time. Call upon the Divine now and ask the Angels and God to help you in your life each and every day.

Call them what you will

All these things presented here – words, prayers, meditations, statements. All these things have meaning and power. All these things can bring important changes to your life. It does not matter the form of communication that you undertake with the Divine. What matters is that you try to connect, that you try to act, that you try to reach out to something eternal and immense that is waiting in the background for you to connect with it. Take this chance. Take the chance to communicate with the Divine and see where it brings you. If you feel unsure about this, then ask that your heart be opened. Ask that you have proof of connection. Ask that you have a sign that you are safe and secure. If you ask for this, then you will feel better. You will feel safe and loved and able to accept the help of the Divine. Words, prayers, and meditations are all a form of communication between yourself, your deepest self and the highest expressions of the eternal, the highest manifestations of Divinity. You can bring Divinity into your life today. And you can access this, yourself, from within in order to bring more peace, joy, and happiness to your life.

Creations Among Us

There are Creations among us. They walk among us. The Angels and God walk among us. The saints and masters too. And we walk also. We too are creations, beautiful and blessed and glorious. How can we understand ourselves? How can we make sense of who we are or who these others are too? All of this is a mystery to us.

Creations

We are creations and we do not know our own strength. We are creations of the Divine, of God, and we do not know how valuable we are. We are creations. We are valuable, we are strong and we are infinitely wise. In our very being is our strength. In our very being is our meaning, our depth, and our wisdom. We do not value ourselves. We do not see the strength and magnificence of who and what we are. We do not see what we are in any way. We think ourselves paltry. We think ourselves weak and small. Who are we, we ask, in the face of all that is, in the face of all that is bigger and immense, and more powerful than we are. Who are we? We are creations, we want to say. We are creations, made by God, valued by God, and served by the Angels. We are creations and all of us are special and important and significant. All of us have meaning. All of us are beautiful in our power and in our expression to the world. All of us are magnificent. Revel in your magnificence. Revel in the joy of who you are.

Creation

Creation is what we are capable of. Just as we have been created, so too can we create. Just as we have been formed and shaped and put upon the earth, so too can we form things, so too can we create with our mind, our hearts, our hands. Our spirit is capable of the imagination of wondrous things. Our souls raise us up. Even if we have felt diminished. Even if we have appeared small to ourselves and to others, this is no match for what is inside us. What is inside us can create and make a thousand things, a thousand beautiful and meaningful things. What can you create? What beautiful thing will you create? What important meaning will you bring to the world? Creation is written in our DNA. Creation is hard-wired in us. It fills us and seeks to express itself. Allow yourself to create. Allow yourself to claim this identity. You will feel more at home in your skin and in yourself.

Creation-ing

The act of creating is important. It is important and I want to call it creation-ing. I want to call it this to give it more weight and meaning, and to make it more important, because the significance cannot be lost. The significance of making something and bringing a new form to the world – a new physical form, new thoughts, new ideas, new books, new ways of looking at things, and new understanding - all of that is so profound. If I call it creating then you might misunderstand my meaning. You might ascribe this act a value that is less than what it deserved, and it is so important. All that you do to create something new in the world, all that you do to instill value and to install a new idea, or new thoughts upon your corner of the world or upon the whole human race even – those things are so important. New ideas can travel fast. New ideas can create worlds and new modes of being. Celebrate then the actions that you take. Celebrate the things that you have brought into the world. Whether the birth was difficult or easy, whether the labour was hard or joyful. Celebrate it all, because you have become a creator. You have helped the world go forward and in its evolution, and in its adaptation, you have created a new mode, you have fashioned a new expression, a new reality, and the world is replenished. The world is developed through your contribution. Celebrate your creations and create more. Create more and you will be blessed too.

Creating

Creating is a powerful act. Creating is powerful no matter what we seek to create. We can create through language, art, music, and technology. We can create new meaning and understanding. We can create new movements, new ways of seeing the world as well as new worlds, and new possibilities. We can open up potential for ourselves and others. We can conquer resistance and overcome adversity. We can create something new and different and wonderful and all by starting with the next step. Start with the next step and see where it leads. Strategize too about your creating. Strategize so that you will take the time to create wonderful bold things, and amazing new realities. If you plan, and if you dream and create, you will make magnificent things. And the reward will be felt within you. You will grow and you will be nourished by this very act of creating.

How we create

We create with our minds and our hearts. We create also with the pen, the paintbrush, with our hands, and our computers. We create with others and we create alone. All forms of creation are powerful. Start with pen and paper and explore. Start with setting aside time for your mind to do all of its wonderful imagining. Ask for Divine assistance and inspiration. Ask for your well to be filled and for creativity to flow from it. Create in any way you choose. Make sure your mind is actively involved. Make sure your heart and spirit are engaged and creating alongside with you. The best creations come from all of you. This doesn't have to drain you. This can nourish and fill you and inspire you. Just as your creations, and your creating will benefit others, so too will it benefit you. The act of creating is the making of the new – it creates the new in you just like it reveals the new to others. Celebrate your creations. Celebrate your ability to create and feel all that this is bringing you. Feel how this is feeding you.

How we are created

We are created flesh and blood, mind, matter and spirit. We are created in all such ways – millions of molecules, millions of cells, animated energies coalescing together in human form. All put together in one package, and we have to figure out how we will live, what we will do, how we will engage with the world. We don't come with instructions. We are self-creating. We are created and self-creating too.

How we affect the world

We affect the world by our presence and our reality. We affect the world by our physical inhabitation of it. Our breath, our form, our actions, these all affect the world. The world is not impervious to our presence. It is not impervious to our thoughts and words. These things carry. Our actions have meaning and our thoughts and words have meaning. Do not consider yourself unimportant. Do not consider that you have no bearing upon the world. You have so much bearing but you cannot see. You have so much bearing. Do not think that if you shrink and make yourself small you are not affecting the world. You are. Everything you do, think or say affects the world. *Everything.* It is not a question of acting or not acting, of saying or not saying, of being present or of seeking to stay out of the light. Instead it is a question of acting rightly and not acting rightly, of saying rightly and not saying rightly, of being present in the right way or of not being present *in the right way.* This is the only choice we have really. Are we acting in the right manner or are we not? This is the choice that each of us makes all the time, every second. And with this choice, and even if we think we are not making a choice, we are affecting the world.

How we change the world

We change the world in good ways and in bad. It is up to us to choose how we do this, when we do this and what the consequences are. It is good to choose to change the world for the better. This seems obvious but it is worth saying. It is good to choose good and it is not good to choose bad. Good choices have good repercussions for the situation and people involved, for ourselves and for the world. Bad choices do not. At the time a bad choice may seem like you are winning. It might seem that you are winning something somehow and you might feel victorious. Maybe you are gaining power over someone and you like this feeling. But bad choices always come to light. Eventually they come to light. It might take a long time, even years. But eventually this will happen. So the bad choice always has a repercussion that will affect you, always. The good news is that the good choice has a good repercussion for you also. And this repercussion will carry on and be amplified over time. Make good choices every day. Make good choices, for yourself, and for others if this occurs, and for the world. If you do not know how to make good choices for the world, if you think that you are too small to affect the world, then I invite you to meditate and to send positive energy to any place in the world that you are drawn to send energy to. Your act of benevolence will change the situation. I promise you that you will have an impact. You are so powerful, more than you can know.

Here is a prayer and incantation for Creation

I pray that you will Create;

I pray to God and the Angels that you will be the Creator of many things.

I pray that your Creations will light up the world and spark your spirit.

I pray that you will be enriched in all ways by your creations and that they will deepen your spirit

I pray that these creations will make you happy and add to your life in all ways

I pray that these creations will bring you peace and joy and love

I pray that you as a creation have peace and joy and love and will continue to have more

I pray that you will see yourself as a strand of divine essence and will feel as blessed as you are

I pray for all this and for more

I pray for the unknown parts of you that desire healing and creationing

I pray for your soul and your spirit and for all the ways that you are beautiful

I pray that in your creationing you will be kind, wise, and will help others

I pray that you will always do good and will always seek to do good

I pray that you will be free and fair-minded

I pray that all will be well with you in every endeavor of your choosing

Amen

I have prayed for you. And now I invite you to pray for yourself using the same words and changing them to say 'I' or 'me' instead of you.

Blessings

Who Do You Say You Are?

Who do you say you are and why do you say this? Who do you say you could be? Do you make any claims upon yourself? Do you have an identity? Do you speak definitively and say who you are? Do you express the full potential of who you are and who you might be? You are not limited to who you think you are or who others think you are. You are a magnificent creation and it is good to speak from that place. It is good to learn to be magnificent in the world.

Who do you say you are?

All of us say who we are somehow and in some fashion. All of us announce ourselves in some way or other, by what we say, or by what we wear, or by who we speak to, or by who we listen to. All of us say who we are in some way. We may remain silent but that announces us too. We may pretend to be someone we are not, but that doesn't indicate anything. Ultimately we reveal ourselves. Ultimately the layers of ourselves reveal themselves, and we are that who we are. We can say who we are and we do this in a million different ways. And then we ourselves say who we are too. We might subvert ourselves. We might say that we are something that we are not. But then we give ourselves away and everything is understood anyway. We are understood. We can speak or not. We can explain or not. We are understood nonetheless.

Why do you say this?

Why do we speak about ourselves? Why do we say what we are and who we are? We need to articulate our identity. We need to express ourselves to the world. We might not explain or want to, but somehow we do anyway. Why do we make some effort to put ourselves in the world? The world knows us anyway. Why do we think we can arrange ourselves by our language, our dress, our company, and our activities? All these forms for our substance, all these conveyors of our meaning, all these attempts to express our significance. And yet that is what we do. That is what we need to do, and are compelled to do. Shape and meaning, words and action, we articulate our form into the world. We pour ourselves into these things to give ourselves identity and significance. How can we differentiate ourselves? By those things. How can we identify ourselves? By those things too. And so then do others identify us, by these markers we put in place, by these ways that we signal our being-ness in the world.

Who do you say you could be?

In our preoccupation with self, in our preoccupation with our presentation of self to the world, do we lose sight of who we could be? We are governed by our current state of affairs. We are governed and shaped by what is going on right now, by how we think of ourselves right now. What surroundings do we have? What kind of work do we do? Who are the people around us? Through these environmental factors and our activities, we just are, we just be. Through our thoughts, through our expressions, we may be wrapped up in the current moment. Because there is so much going on, we may be caught up in this version of ourselves that we perceive. But this doesn't allow ourselves to move beyond this point. This doesn't allow ourselves to imagine anything else. Who do you say you will be? Can you look at this? Can you move beyond now and look at this? Who do you say you could be? This is a good thing to ponder. You don't need to search for the answer now. But it is good to sit with the question. Sit with the question and think about who you could be.

Imagine and dream

Imagine and dream your reality. Imagine and dream a new state of being, a new identity. Imagine and dream a new expression for yourself. Paint it and dream it. Write it and consider it. How can you change? What can you become? What would make you happy? What would make you more fulfilled? There are variations of the current you that you could explore. There are whole new versions of you that you could explore. Dare to stretch and see what you could be. Dare to see yourself differently from how you have been up 'til now. There is a future for you that you have not yet written. There is a future for you that you have not dreamt of. Allow your mind to be open to the possibility that there is a bigger world for you than the one you are living in now. Allow your mind to be open to the possibility that you can change and dream and grow. Allow yourself to believe that your spirit can grow and become different. Allow yourself to surmount the obstacles of the past. Allow yourself to go beyond what you have now and what you allow yourself to be now. What constraints do you put upon yourself? What boundaries do you place around yourself? What cages? It is okay to break free of these. It is okay to go beyond these and to change the definition of yourself. Change your definition in a way that is good for you and nurturing for you. Change your definition so that you may grow and do well. The whole and abundant universe is waiting to greet this magnificent version of you. The whole and abundant universe is waiting for you. Ask for help in this. Be strong. Be very strong but do not neglect to ask for help. Be reshaped into all you can be. Live your full potential and explore all possibilities that exist. Explore all that is available to you and rejoice. For you can make all of this with your own mind, heart, spirit and imagination. You can soar.

Expand your perceptions and possibilities

Expand your perceptions and possibilities. If you are to go beyond what your life is right now, you need to expand your idea of what your life could be. You need to think beyond what your current life is, and think about more. Can your life be different? Of course it can. Are there things and people in your life that are keeping you constrained right now? What can you do to change that? How can you move away from these constraints or loosen these restrictions? You have the answer to that right now. And you need to think further than merely getting rid of whatever cage you find yourself in. You need to think about imagining a whole new state of being. Who could you become? It doesn't matter where you start from. It doesn't matter where you are now. You have room to move and grow. You have the ability to imagine new untold possibilities. You have the ability to imagine the things that do not yet exist and to make them happen. Take a bold leap into the future. Take a bold leap in your mind and your heart and your spirit and see where this can take you. See how far you can go.

Expand your abilities

When you are thinking and dreaming and planning your future, you may find that your abilities naturally expand to fit your new reality. You may find yourself growing in ways you did not expect, and you did not imagine. Do not let the shock of this stop you. Do not let the shock of this hold you back. Imagine yourself into the future. Propel yourself into the future. Prepare to succeed and enjoy your success. Do not let the success shake you. Do not let your movement into the future startle you and stress you. Your expanding abilities will help you and enlarge your possibilities. Sometimes, though, the situation is reversed. Sometimes you have to expand your abilities and then the new opportunities will come to you. Sometimes you have to take action and understand what it is you can do and what you need to learn in order to expand. Be brave and brilliant. Be brave and follow your calling and the yearning that you have inside you to become more. Be brave and follow the instinct to create more for yourself, to be more and learn more and to develop and grow. Do not worry about those who would hold you back. Do not worry about leaving those you love behind. Stagnation has no place in a truly loving relationship. If they love you, they will come along and they will grow too. Invite them to grow too. Invite them to join you on your journey as you expand your horizons. Seek out your own expansion and those around you will expand too.

Open yourself to being more

You need to open yourself to being more. You need to open yourself to being more and break open the frame of reference that holds you in your current state, and in your current world. It might be that you think your current world is a good one, or good enough, or all you aspire to. It might be that you have a good environment already, that you are fulfilled already. Still, even with all that, even if this is true, open yourself to being more and to having more. Open yourself up to the eternity of possibilities that await you. Open yourself to all the opportunities that are out there. Receive them happily. Receive them openly and with joy. They are yours. They are yours now that you have decided that you can accept the bounty of the universe. They are yours now that you have decided that everything is available to you. You do not have to shrink yourself down. You do not have to make yourself small for any reason or for any person, even yourself. Do not think that you are not good enough. Do not think that you are not deserving enough. You deserve to reap the rewards that the universe has for you. You deserve to be more and to have more. You deserve to be as bountiful as possible, and as magnificent as possible. You deserve all of this and all of this will come to you. You are ready for more. You are ready for an expanded experience of the Universe and all that it has to offer. All of this is offered with one caveat – be a good person. All of this is offered with one request and demand – be a good person. The universe cannot fulfill the hopes and dreams that do not wish for the best for others, and that do not treat others in the best way possible. Receive the bounty of the universe in all ways. Receive the bounty and be inspired by it also.

Have an expanded version of yourself

Having an expanded version of yourself might be difficult for some people. Having an expanded version of yourself might not be easily available to you. It might not come naturally to think of yourself as a magnificent creature with universal importance. It might seem arrogant or rude to you, putting on airs or something like that. But still you must try. Still you must try to be bigger than what you are and to be important. You must look at your significance and become more significant still. You must grow and increase your knowledge and awareness of yourself. You must increase your skills, abilities and competencies. You must do all of this so that you can learn more and do more and be more. With this attitude towards growth, with this attitude and openness towards expansion, you will be rewarded, you will be stretched, and you will come to a new and better appreciation and understanding of yourself. Expand, be open to expanding, and be accepting of the changes that come to you.

Prayer and Incantation for Yourself and Who You are

Here is a prayer and incantation to summon you and who you are, who you really are. You can pray it too in your own words afterwards, or by simply changing some of the words below.

I pray to the Angels and God that you will be comfortable, happy, and at peace with who you are.

I pray that you feel safe and loved and filled with joy. I pray that you are fulfilled and content and that you know who you are and what you are made of.

I pray that you have strength always and that all of your days are filled with light. I pray that if gloom comes to you it will dispel quickly like clouds after the rain. I pray that you always see the good in things and in others. I pray that you always see value in yourself and that you are always happy about things and about your life.

I pray that you have a path for your life and that it makes you happy. I pray that you have good people in your life, that you have someone to take care of and that there are people who take care of you. I pray that you are part of a community. I pray that you are never lonely and that you are whole and perfect all by yourself too.

I pray that your spirit is beautiful and magnificent and capable of growth and wonder. I pray that your soul is whole and healed. I pray that any way that you have been broken, you are healed now. I pray that you know how to heal yourself and that you know that everything can be repaired.

I pray that you know the song of your own soul and that you know how to follow it. I pray that you are at peace and that you are at peace with who and what you are in all ways. I pray that you take whatever steps you need to arrive at a more whole version of yourself.

I pray that you are happy just the way you are. I pray that your world is happy too. I pray that your light shines strongly in the world and more brightly each day. I pray that you are strong and so strong that you can move a mountain. Can you feel this strength within you? I feel it.

I pray for you now and for every day.

May the Angels and God bless you and keep you and embrace you.

Namaste

Rewriting the future

If you rewrite the future is it yours? If you rewrite the future does it belong to you still? Can you rewrite the future or is this wishful thinking? Is this a fantasy?

You can rewrite the future that you expected. You can rewrite the future that you had forecast once long ago because now you know differently. Now you know more. You have better tools and more avenues to explore. You have more abundance – more resources, more friends, more love than you thought possible. So yes it is possible to rewrite the future. Let us begin.

If you rewrite the future is it yours

You can write your future. You are the one who can write it. Others will try, but you don't have to let them. If you have already written it, you can change it. You can say I am different now. I am different and I would like a different future. I would like to rewrite something. I would like to choose something different, something altogether different or maybe a little different. Rewrite the future. This is yours to do. Rewrite the future. See how it can feel.

Can you rewrite the future?

You may have doubts. You may have decided already what your life would look like. You may think it is too late to change things. You may think that it would be too cumbersome even painful or at least uncomfortable to change things. But you do not have to throw everything out. You do not have to make a wholesale change and get rid of things. Maybe you enlarge your perspective instead. Maybe you change your point of view and make your vision bigger. Add something to your life. Add something big to your life. And watch how the rest of your life falls in line. Think about the future. Think about your future. It is yours. It wants to be magnificent. It wants you to have a wonderful time. What can you do to make your future amazing?

Thinking about your future in strategic terms

It is important to think wisely about your future, to think and to plan and to be okay with imagining something new for yourself. You shouldn't hold back because other people have a different vision of your life. You shouldn't change your point of view because your current environment doesn't support it. Instead, be brave in thinking about the future. Be brave and make plans that truly suit you and your deepest goals and aims. You can think wisely about these goals. You can make plans that are bold and doable. You can see where the opportunities and the obstacles are already. See what you can do to make things easier for you. See what you can do to improve the situation for yourself. You might have a time that you set aside so that you can think about these things. It's important to plan. It's important to set aside time to do this. It's not a luxury. It's a necessity for your life. It's a necessity and it is the way that you will be able to make things happen. It is the way that you will set your plan in place.

The appeal of the future

The appeal of the future is that it isn't quite here yet. It is unfathomable and unreachable. It is in the distance. It is not quite arrived but just temptingly in view. The appeal of the future is that it is still to be defined. We know what today might bring. We know what yesterday was. But the future is not completely knowable. We might plan and we might carry out our plans but the full flesh and shape of the future is still to be wrought, still to be determined and made. The appeal of the future is its undoneness, it's not quite formed-ness. It is still to be created and it is magical.

The appeal of what is

The current state of things also has its own appeal. The appeal of what is, is the familiar. The appeal of what is, is the comfortable. Sometimes the current state of affairs is not good. Sometimes the current state of affairs needs changing. But sometimes, what is, is good. And so we want to stay in this place. We want to stay in this state and not imagine the future, we do not want to create it. We want to stay frozen right here. It is good to be happy with how things are now. It is good to be happy with the way you are living your life. But it is good too to imagine a fuller richer existence, more expanded possibilities. Expand yourself so that the world too may expand. Expand yourself so that everything around you can grow as it needs to and be nourished and made whole.

How do you decide what you want?

How do you decide what you want? How do you decide what your future should look like and what it should be? Start from what you have now. Start from what you have and see what you would like more of. See what you would like to add to your life and to take away, either in part or completely. Start with these things and then take some big leaps of the imagination. Imagine a new future. Imagine the most audacious thing you could have or be. Imagine this and see how it feels to you. Is this something you actually want? You may be imagining something that you have been told would be good to have either by others or by influences around you. Think deeply within yourself. Do you prefer a quiet life or a busy life? What kind of environment do you like? Who would you like to have in your life? Think about these things. Think about them and see if they push your dreams in any direction. Always go towards the dreams that are the most compelling and the most appealing. You will find them. They will reach out to you.

How do you decide what the future could have?

In addition to imaging the future, you might imagine what you could have in the future. This is somewhat the same or an extension of this exercise in imagination that you are participating in. It is an extension but it is being mentioned because so often we put restrictions on what we could have. We put restrictions and limits and we confine ourselves. We don't do this, strangely, because we are incapable of imagining these things. We do this because we don't somehow feel we deserve it or we don't feel that these are things that we could ever have. The Angels want to appeal to your sense of wonder and of magic. They want to request that you honour the notion that the Divine can bring you anything. They want you to consider that the universe too can bring you anything. The Angels invite you to dream. They invite you to look for signs that your dreams can come true. They invite you to take the steps and the actions that in your heart are calling to you. You know deep down what you can do. You know inside yourself that you are capable. You might need help. You might need Angelic help and human help to accomplish these things. But they are not impossible. They have just not been achieved yet. They have just not been allowed to be cultivated yet. Cultivate your dreams. Make your plans. And see what dreams you might achieve. See what beautiful magnificent things you might set in motion and create – for yourself, for your life, and for the world too.

Imagining the future

The future is difficult to see. The future is difficult to contemplate. We might think it will continue the same as things are now. We might think that nothing will ever change or that things will get worse. Plan for things to get better. Expect that things will get better. Expect that your hopes and dreams and plans will come to fruition. Have some faith. You do not yet know what mountains you may move with your faith. You do not yet know. You have not yet tested yourself. You have not yet tested your abilities. Take firm action. Take firm and inspired action. Imagine the future. It is waiting to be created.

Imagining your future

The future and your future are not the same. They are not always the same. We live in the context of our society and culture. We live in our times. And so we live our collective future too. But we don't have to restrict ourselves because of this. We don't have to limit our thoughts. We can live outside of our future. We can live in our own world, outside of our society's artificial restraints. Imagine the best future you can have irrespective of your world. Imagine the best future you can have regardless of your environment and the world you live in. When you do this you might make miracles happen. When you do this, you might make miracles. For yourself and for the world around you too. You might lift the world around you. You might be the catalyst for real change.

Prayer and Incantation for your future and for the way you will write it

I want to pray for you and your future and the way you will write it. Please join me in saying this as a prayer or an incantation and modify the words so that they are in first person.

I pray to God and the Angels that your future will be brilliant and magnificent. I pray that you will have wonderful and amazing experiences. I pray that your heart will be filled with love and that you will be fulfilled in all ways. I pray that you have peace always now and forever. I pray that no hardships will come to you. I pray that your future is a magnificent journey forward in all ways. I pray that you will be carried peacefully into the future and that you will rise to all challenges that are contained in the future. I pray that you will grow into your future beautifully. I pray that you will construct a wonderful future for yourself. I pray that all these things are true and that they are true now. I pray that anything preventing you from having the most wonderful time in the future be dealt with now, easily, instantly and without discomfort. I pray that you will be present now and always. I pray that you will seek the best for yourself and for others now and always. I pray that you will always be true to your ideals. I pray that your ideals are right for you and that they are right and true. I pray that God and the Angels will guide you in all aspects of your life, in making the right choices, and in steering you towards the right opportunities. I pray that all this is easy for you. I pray that you be given great understanding and wisdom. I pray that you will enjoy yourself and that you will be wise always. I pray that you will carry the best of yourself into the future and be inspiring to others and to the world. I pray that you will heal the past and that this will be done easily. I pray that you will forgive yourself and others and that you will allow yourself to be forgiven. I pray that God and the Angels will bless you and heal you and usher you forth into your future. I pray that your beautiful imagination will create the most wonderful future possible for you, for those around you, and for the world. I pray that beauty alight within you and that your soul is blessed and well. I pray all this for you and now I invite you to pray it for yourself too. Amen.

The Tree

The Tree is in many ways the heart of everything. The Tree is no ordinary tree. It is at the centre of the Earth. It feeds the Earth and it feeds all of us. It is the Mother Tree. It is the Tree of Life. Is it the Tree of the Garden? No, it is not. But the Angels want to point out that there have been many beloved trees in our history. They have been important to us and we have felt that always.

The tree from the Garden of Eden was another tree – the tree of all knowledge. This tree served its purpose did it not? It cast Adam and Eve out into the world and began everything.

It is not important that you believe this literally. It could have happened or it may not have happened. What is important is that this seeking of all knowledge was thrust upon Adam and Eve and that they were then cast out.

We have long suffered in the world. We have long suffered and tried to make the world a better place through the seeking out of innovation, of knowledge. We are always trying to return to that tree. We are always trying to remember the knowledge that we had from that tree. We seek it still.

No, the Tree of Life is another tree. Long celebrated in the mythologies of different cultures. The Tree of Life is the tree that holds up the centre of the earth. It provides sustenance to all of us. It regulates and powers the earth. It allows the earth to carry on and to engage in the seasonal and cyclical rhythms that have fed us for millennia. It allows the earth to be mother earth and to give us all we need, to nourish us and to sustain us from the moment we are born to the time that we die. It is the centre wheel, the cog of the earth, the spiritual centre allowing all of this to take place.

Again it is not necessary that you believe this at all. It is simply good to look at the earth and its nourishing function for all of us. Just in appreciating and recognising this then you honour and accept the tree of life. The tree of life can be a metaphor for the life patterns of the earth, for the ecology and the ecosystems. But it is also a spiritual place, a home for our home, the mother of our earth. Does not everything require an anchor and a base?

The Tree is important because it nourishes all of us. What if it were cut off somehow, or restrained? What if it could not provide what it needed and wanted to provide to all of us? What if somehow this lack that we feel, this existential question that we ask all the time, what if this was to do with the Tree?

The Tree also has been cut off somehow. The Tree also needs to flourish further in all ways. We might think about this in our day to day use of the earth. We might think about how we might send love and energy to the earth herself and to the Tree of Life also. This way we support the ecosystem we live on. This way we strengthen it so it can become a safer place and more strongly cohesive and in balance. Take a moment to ask that the earth and the Tree be supported in all ways. This support will be repaid many times in your own life and in your own system. You will feel more whole and stronger as a result.

The Repatriation of All Things

The repatriation of all things suggests the idea that all will be put right in the world, with all of us, and perhaps even with history.

The repatriation is the idea that things will return to being what they once were or what they were meant to be.

This does not mean the return of some country to its former state, the return of boundary lines to some previous incarnation of human cultural or national definitions.

The differences among us have been firmly and violently expressed for centuries. Repatriation does not mean a return to old territory, a return to old ways of being and doing, a throwback to a bygone era.

No, this repatriation speaks to a far older world. The world that was when everything was new, nothing was ruined, and there was no thought even of ruin.

This repatriation speaks to a return when everything was good and pure. It speaks to the return of the time before the very birth of what is bad, before the birth, indeed of evil.

Why should this be shocking? Why should this be difficult to accept?

Is it strange to think that somehow evil could be born, that it wasn't always there?

We know very well, in our world, and in our history, how evil has been present and manifest, and how it has developed even. In some cases, we might be able to take a particular moment in history or a particular set of circumstances and say to ourselves that evil was here, that evil was born here and grew here. Sadly, we can point to this now in our world too.

The defeat of evil is no easy thing. The defeat of darkness that can creep into the heart and take it over and make it seek out destruction. But the defeat is possible. It is very possible and able to be done. Just as the strongest darkness cannot cover the tiniest light, so the strongest of all Light can engulf the darkness.

But if it could be done why has it not been done? Why has this gone on for so long?

These are important questions and some of this has been discussed in these pages.

Now that they are not being held back any more, now that they can return, do you think that the darkness stands a chance? Do you think the darkness can even try to exist? It cannot.

This is what I mean by the repatriation of all things, the repatriation of the Light and of all of our places in the Light. This is what is catapulting us into a new reality, a new world made good.

Appendix A/ Daily Practice

A daily practice is a set routine you can follow every day. You do this because you want to gain calm and peace in your life. You do this because you want to create an anchor point for yourself. You might do this because you don't have enough structure in your life and you want to introduce some. You might do this because you have chaos in your life or are too busy and you want a pause point every day. Whatever the reason, or even if these don't apply, a daily practice is a good thing to add to your life.

What is the daily practice?

In this case the daily practice is somewhat free form but contains a few elements that you can interchange or change as you wish. The idea is that you have a set way to introduce peace in your life.

When can you do the daily practice?

Any time that is convenient is fine. But the real answer is in the morning and when you have quiet time.

Forms of the daily practice

The daily practice has a few components and involves silent time with yourself. Here are some components that are valuable –

A quiet room where you can shut the door or where you can guarantee quiet and non-interruption.

A tea or other hot beverage.

At least 30 minutes of non-interruption. (Fight for this, it's worth it)

Somewhere to sit down, probably at a desk or just a chair is fine too.

What to do during the daily practice?

Shut the door

Take your seat

Drink your tea

Then you can begin

Start with meditation or reading or peaceful music.

Do this for 10 minutes or so.

Think about whatever comes up or don't

Then journal if you want to. Journaling can be done on paper preferably. For this process, leave the electronics out.

If you don't want to journal you don't have to. Some notes on journaling follow.

After 10 minutes or so, see if you can do some inner work.

You can do Inner Influencing or another energy modality like TAT or EFT. You can simply allow thoughts to come to your mind and ask the Angels to help you and to remove your problems from you or show you how to solve them.

Wrap up by coming into a quiet state and being grateful for the day. Thank the Universe. Thank God and the Angels. Thank who you pray to. You need to do this for yourself in terms of what is true for you.

Leave out anything that doesn't matter or doesn't mean anything to you.

That's it!

You can start your day now

Some notes on journaling

Journal however you want to. Journal long or journal short. Journal about what is going right and what isn't. This is first person thoughts to yourself and you can complain as much as you want or be grateful for as much as you want. It's not up to you or anyone to judge what comes out. Just let it come out.

If you want a great resource on the subject and art of journaling, consult the work of Julia Cameron in *The Artist's Way* and other writings. She has the most definitive explanation and method there is. Follow this or modify it. As long as you write something down, you will benefit.

Appendix B/Laughter

Laughter

Laughter is the most beautiful bounty of all things, the most beautiful reward. Laughter is the punctuation mark of joy, the sure revealer of happiness. If you have laughter, then in that moment you have peace. If you have laughter, then in that moment you have joy. Seek out ways to have more laughter. Seek out ways to have more peace and joy. This is good for you. This is healing for you.

Laughter in your life

Is there laughter in your life? Is there enough laughter in your life? Laughter is important. It is important to your physiological makeup. It replenishes and restores you. Find a way to add more laughter too your life. Find the things that make you laugh. Not everyone is the same. Not everyone prefers the same kind of content. Not everyone finds the same things funny. Find what makes you laugh. Find out what funny means to you. Explore this. It is important to your life. It is not something you should neglect or dismiss as trivial.

Laughter sustains you

Laughter sustains you and heals you. Laughter provides you with nourishment that is soul medicine. It heals your spirit. It heals your soul and it builds you. Laughter reminds you that you can be happy even when you are not. Laughter tells you that you have joy within you, that you have healing potential, that at some level you are perfect and that you want for nothing. Laughter is a great gift that you can give to yourself. Do not make the mistake of sacrificing happiness in your life. Do not think that you should do without laughter. Even if you have been through great distress, do not rule out happiness and laughter. Even if trauma and hurt has come to you do not shut laughter and joy out of your life. They are important. They are important because they are healing and they tell you that you are worthy. You are worthy of being and you are worthy of being and having. This is important. Laughter is the music of your own soul. You must honour it.

Laugher fills you

Laughter fills you when other emotions leave you bare. Laughter fills you when you have gone through trying times. When you stop laughing, when you feel you cannot laugh, it is good to try to bring this back, it is good to bring this back into your life. You can do so quietly. You can invite laughter to come back and fill you. You can invite laughter to assuage the emotional pain you have. Even if you are not in pain, even if you do not have distress, then laughter is important too. Laughter fills you and nourishes you and goes into those parts of you that need some attention. Laughter brings its healing ability into you, into your body, your mind, your heart, and your soul. Laughter reaches into all parts of you. All parts of you respond and heal to your own laughter. Even the laughter of another will reach into you. Even the laughter of another will create music in you that will heal you. The pure peals of laughter are like joy being offered to you. Fill yourself with them. Fill yourself with your own laughter, and the laughter of others too. Rest in this energy, rest in this beautiful light energy and allow it to heal you.

Make room for laughter

Make room for laughter in your life. Put aside your cares and worries. Put aside your appointments and your observations. You need to laugh. Find something funny that humours you. Find something funny that you find appealing. Do not look at distressing things. Do not look at serious things. Look at what fits with your sensibility. You do not have to worry about the taste of others. You have to look at your own ideas. Acknowledge what you find funny. Act on this and it will be more real and genuine. You can laugh at things that are not completely to your taste. But it will be better, more resonant if you find what you really like. Set aside time for laughter. Set aside time to engage with this energy and welcome it into your life. You do not have to seek to be funny yourself if this is not natural for you. You need to welcome the laughter and joy in. You need to find this and you will if you give yourself this chance and opportunity.

Appendix C/Portals

Now

The presence of now

Now is present. Now is here right now, as you read this page.
Before you read this page, before you opened this book it was
present too. After you put this book down it will be present then
also. Now is always present. Now is always here. Now is always
around you and consuming you. You worry about what has come
before. You worry about what will happen next. But you can't
escape now. It is always here.

Living with now

How do you live with now and with the certainty of now? Now
doesn't change. Now never changes. Now is now. Now is here.
Now will always be here. It is certain and constant. It is
indefatigable. It is because of now that we think of when. It is
because of now that we don't leave the past behind. The past creeps
into now. The past informs it. But it doesn't have to. It doesn't have
to be a part of now. Now can just be a solitary moment. Now can be
a plane of time that exists just for us. Take a breath. That is now.
Take another breath. That is now too. You are always in now but
you are always wondering about now. You are always in now but
you do not know what to do about it. You do not know if you
should choose differently or choose other things. You do not know
if now is what you want. You do not know if you like your now or

if you should change it or try to change it. You do not know about now. It is forced upon you. You live with it and you have to live with it. It is your reality. It is good. It is bad. It is indifferent. The circumstances might fluctuate. The ideas around it might fluctuate. What doesn't change is that you are in relationship with your now. You are in relationship with it. You can drown it out or numb it out. You can try but now always seeps back into your consciousness. You can try to take a break from now. You can try but now is always here. Now is always with you.

Can time pass?

Can time pass? Does time pass? Or is this one imperceptible moment just here, just present? Is this one moment available to you? Some say that this is all we have, this one moment. Others say we can freeze time, if we work hard enough, if we develop ourselves enough. It is true that we have now, that we have this moment. It is true that we can expand our consciousness so that time becomes immaterial. But time might pass or time might not pass. I say to you that we have time. I say to you that we have time, and that we have now, and that we have all the moments. We can freeze time if this is what we want but circular time remains. Circular time remains and it brings all the arguments back to you. Circular time remains, and it brings all the themes of your life back to you. If you are angry, then you will be angry. If you are sad, then you will be sad. If you are joyful then you will have joy. But you don't have to stay stuck in your themes. You don't have to stay stuck in what is not good, what is not freeing for you. Learn to freeze time, learn to accept all the moments and to shape them. Learn to pull out the threads and the themes and change them so that a better texture is woven for you, and so that your life is made from a better cloth. Do this. You can do this. You think you don't know, but somewhere inside you do. If you cannot fathom this, then look inside you. If you cannot understand how to do this, then look inside you and change something. Change the thing that is keeping you still. Listen to the voice inside you that is always there, that is your spirit and your soul. You are many things. Maybe right now you are stuck, but you have not always been stuck. Before this time you were whole, and you understood what it is you had to do. You understood how to be whole and complete and to be as big as you are. Time is immaterial to you. You are bound in this temporal reality right now. But you are not of this world. You are not of this world. And so yes you can freeze time, yes you can change your patterns, and yes a thousand moments can make now and a thousand moments can inform now. Start with this moment right now. Start with this moment you are in now and change your intention. Change your intention and have a better now and a better future too.

The feeling of now

Now can feel rushed or slowed. Now can be everything or nothing. Now can be trivial and mundane or it can be glorious and exciting. The many moments of now coalesce. The many characteristics of now splinter off from each other in a thousand different ways. What experience are you having right now? How typical is this of most of your nows? How was now different yesterday? And what do you want now to be? What do you want now to look like in any way? Now can be a thousand flavours and a thousand thoughts. Now can be a thousand actions and reactions. The thing is mainly we are having only a few thoughts in each now. Mainly there is one action or reaction in now. Mainly there are only a few flavours and textures in any one now. This is okay. This is our experience and our linear reality. We know inside of us that reality is more than linear. We know that it is made up of remembrances and fragments, of experiences, and of collective memory. We know all this, that all of this informs the now. We know that current events, and cultural and social occurrences and movements can sweep through our times and affect our lives and colour our lives. We can be moved by our time or be blind to it. We can live in our society or apart from it. Still somehow our now is affected. The nature of the air. The nature of the collective consciousness, it breathes into us. It informs us and colours what we are. Perhaps we are separate but now affects us. Perhaps we have closed ourselves off but we still have now and now is a bucket filled with many things. Not all of them are within our control. Not very many of them are actually. Rejoice in now. Rejoice in the feeling of now. Because your experience is the experience of many. The joy you feel, the sadness you feel, the anger you experience. Not all of it is yours. Some of it is shared. Some of it is given to you. All of it is yours to feel and see and experience and think about. All of it is now. And you and I are privileged recipients and participants in now. Breathe it in. Now is life and all of life. It is not just your now. It is the now of all.

Now is never momentary

Now is never momentary. Now seems like a solid state, a time that will last for always. But now is fickle. It is really here only for a moment. There is now and then there will be another now. But the now we are in at this moment, that now will pass. That now will not last. So we are lulled into thinking we have all the time in the world. We are lulled into thinking this because we will always have the next moment, and so we think that now stretches eternally before us. But it does not. It is never momentary. It leads to the next moment, and the next one after that. But it doesn't mean that all these moments belong to us. We are better off seizing them when we can. We are better off making the most of every moment, every now. We don't know that this now will present itself again. We don't know what the next now will be. So now is not momentary. Now continues or changes and replicates. But it is never ours. It is never ours to hold onto with any certainty.

Now steals time

Now steals time away from us because it fools us. It fools us into thinking we have more time than we do. We don't have much time. We might even know this. We don't have much time at any particular point. Maybe our time is measured. Maybe it is even languid and unhurried. But we deceive ourselves if we think that this moment will stretch into something more than it is, into something more than what is here at the present time. Can we seize now? Can we stop time from being stolen from us?

Now and urgency

We are often struck by urgency. We are often asked to do things in a quick fashion. We are often summoned with the idea that time is pressing and that we have to be fast, because otherwise something will happen. Now is co-opted for this purpose. Now is co-opted, and we are made to feel urgent. We cannot expand the moment. We cannot breathe into the moment. We must rush and rush into the moment. But we do not know if the now will expand really. We do not know if the moment will stretch. We might feel rushed. We might feel rushed but we should take a moment and breathe deeply. We should take a moment and not let now get the better of us. Now will not wait for us. The urgent matter will not wait for us. And yet we should take a moment and bend this urgent thing to our will. We should see what element of time we can stretch to make an urgent thing seem less strident, and the unwieldy and unyielding tyranny of now impose less stress upon us.

Now and respite

Does now give you respite? You must allow yourself respite. You must allow yourself rest from the now. It is not wise to dwell always in an urgent state. It is not wise to be forever hurried and forever frayed. We must rest instead. We must rest, even though now calls upon us with some urgency. Even though now summons us and wants us to do this or that. We must resist the urge to be always busy. We must resist because even if we feel compelled, even if we feel drawn to always do and do and do, we get no rest this way. We get no rest, and then this is detrimental. We must build rest into the now and into the everyday. Rest is an important component of the human condition. Rest is an important element and integral to our well-being. Do not neglect your rest. Do not decide that periods of inactivity are not necessary. They are vital. This is the time when you rebuild yourself. This is the time when you make yourself new and when your spirit is reconditioned. Your hopes and dreams need this time too. Your hopes and dreams need this time to come alive and to translate into action. Do not deny yourself the power of rest. Your imagination and your best future depend on it.

The quieting of time

The quieting of time is an important element of rest. The quieting of time is the time when your mind slows down and you can listen to your heart and spirit once again. The quieting of time is the active time for your heart and spirit. We call this down time but it is really the time when light work can occur inside you. This is the time when your spirit is renewed and restored. This is the time when you are rebuilt. This is the time when your imagination can come to life. All of this can happen when you are quiet, when your mind is still. We say that time is quiet now too, because time, and the exigencies of time are not begging you and drawing you in for their attention. They are not calling you and compelling you at this time. They are in the background. And they allow other things to take over. The workings of your mind, the activity centres of your imagination, your creative centre – all these take centre stage and work together to create new things and new ideas that come to you out of nowhere. Time is quiet in this still part of you and then you can listen, you can really listen to who you are and who you are called to be. Think of it as a time for aligning of you with yourself.

The quieting of ourselves

The quieting of ourselves takes place, but it doesn't always take place as often as we need. We need to be quiet. We need to have quiet within ourselves and outside of ourselves. We can seek to quiet ourselves in different ways. We can read, we can think, we can pray, we can have reflection time, we can meditate. These are all ways that we can quiet ourselves. It is important to do this. It is important to do this often, daily in fact. We need to do this so that we can hear ourselves think and in order to shut out the din of the outside world, to shut out the voices of people around us and the outside world in general. We need to listen to our own voices. We need to listen to the voice within us. We need to listen to our mind, our spirit, our conscience, our heart. We need to listen to all these things. What is your voice saying to you? What are your mind and heart and spirit saying to you? They have many things to tell you. They have many things to reveal to you about what you want and need. They contain hidden desires and treasures for you. They contain hidden imaginings and ideas. How will you even know what all these are if you never stop and listen? How will you know what your inner voice wants to say to you? Take the time to be still and quiet. Take the time to reach inside yourself and to see who and what you are. It may be that you do not know who you are really. It may be that now is a good time for you to reach a deeper understanding and awareness of yourself. This kind of self-knowledge is invaluable. This kind of self-knowledge leads to deeper fulfillment and happiness in your life. Take the opportunity and make the time to spend more time with yourself. You need to do this in order to truly reach self-understanding.

Of stillness and action

Stillness is so valuable and important yet often we favour action above all else. Stillness brings us meaning and knowledge about ourselves and the world around us. It brings us self-awareness and a deeper commitment to ourselves. But in spite this, in spite of the value of spending time in aligning with our true selves, we are often called and compelled instead to action. Action is valuable too. Action is necessary and it makes things happen that would not otherwise be. But action needs to be inspired by contemplation and thought. Action needs to be inspired by your inner voice telling you what to do and how to do it. Action without stillness and without prior thought is often wasted. Action that is borne from spontaneity and compulsiveness might not be fruitful. It can look very appealing. It can be a way to show the world that you are busy doing something. But what are you really doing in this case? Is this just the creation of noise and show for the world? Why waste your energy and time? Why not spend time to plan the right kind of action? Why not spend time to think about what the right kind of action will be? If you do this kind of thinking and planning then the right action will be easy to see and to undertake. If you do some thinking and planning then you will begin to see opportunities more easily. When you take spontaneous action with the benefit of prior thought and planning, then you will break through barriers and reach new levels. Stillness and action need to go hand in hand. Perpetual stillness without action will not be useful either. But action without forethought is even more problematic. It can take you in the opposite direction of where you want to go.

The light in now

Now has light. This very moment has an energy to it and gives energy to the next and next moments afterwards. You can access this energy of the now. You can access this light and benefit from it. Do not shy away from the light of now. Do not shy away from what now is revealing to you. Now is powerful and the light that it carries is powerful too. It is possible for you to be imbued with the energy of now. It is possible for you to be imbued with the speed and the light of now. Ask that you always be present in the now. Ask that now inform you and that all of your nows are informed by all that is necessary. You can act in the now but you do not have to act with speed and haste. You can act with wisdom and understanding and still remain present in the now. Take it as your spiritual goal that you will be fully present and fully aware and that you will also not be pushed and swayed by the compulsions of now. This is the key to having great understanding and to making wise choices in the every day. Be present and be observant. Be ready to act but be ready to slow down and consider your actions. Always consider your actions and your thoughts and then the light of now will reveal itself to you. All the possibilities that now holds will always be easy for you to see. Accept now and the light it can bring you. Do not be swayed or rushed by it. Accept it and let it inform you and you will be the wiser.

When

When happens. When is a fixed point in time at which we say, this happened or that happened. When cajoles us and beguiles us. We would not do anything were it not for when. When is this? When is that? When governs us. When dictates to us. And we are happy to be kept this way. We are happy to be kept by the constructs of time this way. We might rebel. Sometimes we might rebel against when. But always, we end up subjugating ourselves to it. We are all captives of when. We all define our lives, our minutes, and our hours by when.

The virtue of when

When is a good thing. When is a thing of beauty even. When regulates us and informs the passage of time in our lives. When tells us when a thing may occur. When can never be absent in discussions of time. When structures our days and gives meaning and direction to our plans. When itself is virtuous but when can capture us too, when can hold us prisoner. Are we subject to the wants and whims of when? Do we bend to when? We can be made too easily to fall for when. We can be made too easily to be charmed by when. When captures us always. When will not release us. We need to structure ourselves within when. We need to find freedom within when. And we need to dictate to when. We must become the masters of when.

The knowingness of when

When is knowledgeable. When can govern much more than just our time. When can sneak in and take over our plans. Our plans can be usurped and derailed and taken over by when. This is what happens when when is given priority and importance over how and over meaning. This is what happens when when is not subordinate to purpose and reason. The convenience of doing something a certain way takes over and becomes more important than the actual thing that you are trying to accomplish, than the bigger picture. The expedience of things takes over. When takes over. The appointment book nudges you and you make your plans based on when. However, important though when may be, it cannot come second to intelligent reason, to forethought. Do not let when take over. Do not let the knowingness of when come before anything else.

The when of when

When is insistent. When will insist that things must be done, that decisions must be arrived at, that action must be taken. This is problematic. This operates from the point of view that when is more important than anything else, that action is more important than anything else. This is wrong thinking. It is wrong to think that the carrying out of an action now is always the right course of action. This allows for no consideration of the action, the effects of the action, the repercussions and the timing of it. The when of when is the urgent call, the urgent compulsion to do something. Far better to be patient and to do the right thing at the right time then to do anything now. Doing anything now will have consequences. They may be trivial and meaningless but they might also be significant.

The when of when bows us to its exigencies and to its urgency. The when of when urges us to act. But we must stop before this point. We must not take random action. We must subjugate the when of when to proper thought and contemplation. This is only something that we can do. We must resist the temptation to do otherwise.

When subjugated

How do you subjugate when? How do you bend when to your own meaning and your own timeframe? How do you assure when that when does not mean now? How do you explain to when that not now does not mean never? You explain this to yourself principally. You explain this to yourself because the when is inside you. The fear to not act is coming from inside you, welling up and urging you to take action. You might say to yourself "I can't stand this. I have to do something." Maybe that is true. But it is better to do slowly than to act with impetuousness. You must subjugate your desire for quick action. It does not always lead to profound results. You must develop patience instead and be in charge of your when. It is your when. It belongs to you and is ruled by you, no one else. It also cannot rule you or be allowed to rule you. It must be second to your wishes and desires. Otherwise it is ruling over you. Otherwise it is taking over. Subjugate when to your plans and your aspirations. It is a powerful tool when you use it correctly.

When is when?

If you use it correctly, then you decide when is when. If you use it correctly then you can choose the best times for the action you take, the best steps, the right way to go. Use when as a powerful tool to live life the way you choose, to live life the way you need to in order to be most fulfilled. When is a powerful tool to achieve your dreams. When is when you say it is. When is when would be most right for you, most important for you. If you have tasks to do, look at when and look at this strategically. The answer is not usually now. The answer usually is the right time defined by what you are trying to accomplish and by what you want to accomplish. When never needs to be rushed and never needs to be artificially slowed down. When is important but you must decide how it is important. You must also not let its importance derail you and overwhelm you. You must use its importance but not be dominated by it. The Angels invite you to do this and to trust your innate sense of timing. It is present inside you and it is important. It is present inside you and it is valuable to you and will give you peace. When you know when you must do something, it gives you a firm foundation from which to take action. Do not underestimate the power of this certainty. Do not underestimate the confidence that when can give you.

Dealing with when

When is always here to deal with. When is always begging us for our attention, demanding that we put pen to paper and decide when things will happen, when action is taken. When does not allow for contemplation. When does not allow for space and time and thought. We must build this in to when. We must schedule these too. We must set aside time to be free and to do nothing. We must set aside time to let things just unfold. We must have time for thought and planning and stillness. All this is necessary. And your when must allow this. Your when must make room for these things.

Your when cannot be allowed to become a kaleidoscope of thoughtless action. Your when must have built in respite and peace and rest. Why do you define when only with the tumult of activity? Why do others do this around you? The presence of hurried busyness means that you are somehow left out. The hurried and harried aspect of many corners of modern life means that you are diminished and stepped down. You do not matter anymore. Only the when and the how matter and your ability to execute these things. But actually you do matter. You do matter most of all and you have to manipulate your when to reflect this. You have to manipulate your when so that you are in charge of it and so that it bows to your needs. Acknowledge your needs and your when will fall into place gracefully.

Dealing in when

The time of the world rushes by and we have to deal in when. The time of the world dictates that things follow a particular schedule. You can change the schedule if you are able to. You can make your own schedule if you are able to. Ultimately you are bound by a schedule. Ultimately if you choose to participate in the world you are bound by a schedule. If you deal in when, you are encountering the rush of other people's lives. If you live in the world, you are intersecting with other lives and events and you have to choose to participate or not. All these intersections force something upon your when. All these intersections shape your when and affect it. When you deal in when, you deal not just with your own timetable and activities, you deal with everyone else's. You are subject to the when of the world, or at least the when of the world around you. You must carve out space and time to deal with this. You must carve out space and time to look at this properly so that you can understand how best to arrange your timetable and not be bombarded by the needs of others. With time and space you can safeguard your time and space. With planning you can make sure that your needs are not subjugated to the many demands of others. This is not to say that you should not meet your obligations. This is not to say that you can ignore the needs of others. Instead when you deal in when, you need to plan this. You need to plan to deal in when, because if you don't the when of others will overtake you, and even your own activities will overtake you. You need to be articulate about time and space in your own life. You need to do this and to manage it well. This will allow you to grow and to manage everything and to have peace. Doing this properly will ensure peace in your life.

When and whenever

When is a scheduled thing and whenever is not. Whenever implies carelessness and freedom. When is strict and involves schedules and timetables. We all need room for whenever in our lives. The thing is sometimes we are so busy, so inundated that we may have to plan for whenever. We may have to plan times when nothing is scheduled. This might seem sad or disappointing. But sometimes it is necessary. When things get to this point, then it is good to see how you might scale back your commitments. You might want to be freer. You might want to have less when and more whenever in your life.

The ambiguity of time

Time can be ambiguous. Time can be strange to us. If we don't fix it down in a schedule. If we don't write things down and attend to them, then time can slip away from us. Time can evaporate as if we never had it, and never had the right to it. It can just go away on its own. It can be gone and we don't know where it went. It can disappear and we don't know where it went. All this is funny about time. We can't hold it. We can't keep it. It is a possession but it is always running away from us. So we try to fix it in schedules and timelines. We make plans and we follow them and we get a sense of accomplishment. We think we have made good use of that time. And perhaps we have. Perhaps we have. But if we had just let the time float away from us instead, would that have been good also? Would that also have been a magnificent use of time? These are questions to ponder because time is so ephemeral. We cannot hold it and yet we try to. We cannot hold it and when we try we do achieve much. But still we know we are wrapped in a fantasy somehow. Perhaps we can contain time and use it as a tool for our lives. We may wonder why this is important. We may wonder about how we live within time and what this means for our lives.

The fixedness of time

Time is fixed. It's fixed in our minds and the past is fixed too. It lingers and it can affect us if we're not careful. It can remain stuck in our minds. The things that have happened to us can remain stuck in our minds. And we value time so much. We value time and the fixedness of it too. Sometimes it seems that time runs away from us. Sometimes it seems that time stands still. We look at things and events that have happened and they become fixed. We are fixed in our position when we look at them. We are fixed and we can't change our perspective. But we should change our perspective. We should change it and be okay with time passing. We should change our perspective and be okay with the idea that things have moved on from the time of the past. The past was fixed in our minds. The past was fixed there. And maybe we changed or maybe we didn't. Maybe we changed or maybe everything else changed around us. Have we made the changes we needed to make? Or are these changes not available to us? Are we not able to ebb and flow and change like time? Maybe we have become dinosaurs stuck in the time of our youth. Maybe we are fixated on things as they used to be. Our environments change. The people in our lives might change. Our jobs. How we feel about everything might change. But what if we don't change? The world doesn't wait for us. We can talk about the fixedness of time. We can talk about this moment or that moment. But really, it is ourselves that choose to change or choose not to change. This is a very deliberate choice we make. Choose to change. Choose to evolve with the times. Choose to see how you can enjoy living in the times that you are in. It is good for you to do this. It's good for you to fully participate in being alive. You will see. The present doesn't have to be strange to you. The past doesn't have to be the only home you know.

Pinning down

Sometimes we want to pin things down. We want to pin down a certain time and place, a set of circumstances, a thing that happened. Sometimes we may want to pin down an environment, a way of doing things, a set of social mores even. We can try. We can try pinning things down. But we risk becoming caged ourselves.

We can pin ourselves down too. We can remain stuck in the past, stuck in a certain time. We don't have to do this though. We can choose to be different. We can choose to be different with the times and let new things inform us and reveal to us new ways to think about life and living. Sometimes we want to pin down another person or even an aspect of our own personality. We say we want to understand more. We say we want to understand better. But really, we want more control. We want more understanding and more awareness because we want control, because to be out of control is to be fearful. To be out of control is to acknowledge that you really don't completely know what is going on, and you don't entirely have everything completely the way you want it. It is not a good feeling to feel lost. It is not a good feeling to feel strange about the way your life is. You can try to pin things down if you want. But you are invited instead to ask for help in adjusting to change. You are invited to ask for help in making the most of your life in the times that you live. Do not try to pin yourself down, or others. Strive to set yourself free. Strive to be happy and free.

Free-floating

Do your whens float around? Do the whens of your life change and ebb and flow and take you over? Maybe you don't know when anything should happen. Maybe you don't have a sense of time and want things just to be. Maybe you don't want to acknowledge the passage of time, or maybe the way you think about your life means that time doesn't matter too much to you. Maybe your life is not time dependent. Whatever your situation, you can enjoy a kind of free floating of the whens if you want to. Whatever your situation, you need to explore what it is to be unfettered. You need to be free to escape the reality of your life. You need to be free to step beyond the whys and wherefores of your life. Can you escape the whens? Can you be completely free floating? It depends what kind of a life you want to live. It depends on whether you want to be apart or separate and not subscribe to the values of those who want to always get ahead. But getting ahead is not the only reason we are subject to the whens. We have obligations. We have commitments. We can't just put these aside and act however we want to all the time. But still, it is good to have some free-floating time. It is good to have some time when the whens don't matter. See if you can have this in your life. Do this in small quantities to start with and then build from there. You might think that you don't deserve this, but all of us need to have time for ourselves. All of us need to have time to understand who we are. And free-floating time is a good way to do this.

When when was

When has been around for a long time, maybe forever. But there are places (fewer and fewer) that don't recognize concepts of time. What if you looked at your life like that? What if the past present and future were all here right now, and you could look at them all at once? What would you learn? What would you change? You don't have to wait to change anything about your life. You don't have to wait for anything to happen. You can change things now. You can change things, but you might need help. It is a good thing to get help. It is a good thing to acknowledge to yourself that in order to grow and change, you might need to step beyond yourself. So if you had past, present, and future in your sights all the time, what would you change? What would you do? Would your environment be different? Would you yourself be different? Allow yourself to imagine this. Allow yourself to imagine who you would be and what would be happening. If time was absent from your life, maybe the real you could step forward. Don't let time be your cage. Don't let your whens define you.

When when wasn't

Sometimes there are moments when time doesn't exist. There are golden moments when time is frozen and you are in a bubble. There are moments of torment too, when time refuses to pass. This is because the intensity of the moment, of this time good or bad, takes over. It dominates our sense of time. It freezes everything and we are inside time. Time won't pass. It is just here now. If you could freeze time, what wonderful time would you capture? If you could unfreeze time, what horrible time would you erase? Think about these things. It may be that you can do some inner work to make this happen. It may be that you could learn how to slow down or speed up time. We have within us the capacity to do many things. Why not this? Time is a bubble and we are either inside it or outside of it. But once in a while we are given the chance to affect it. Sometimes we know this quite concretely. Sometimes we are very aware. Sometimes this ability is more subtle or indirect. Sometimes when doesn't matter. Remember this all those times when time seems to crush you, when things are bearing down on you. Think then of a time when you are free of things, when you are not dominated by your whens and your wherefores. Think of this time now. Be free of time. Be free of the whens and you will be happier. You will be more content with everything that is happening, and with everything around you.

Maybe

Maybe is the state between is and is not. Maybe is the state in between. Maybe is the time you allow yourself in a decision. Maybe is the time when you pause and consider. Maybe is necessary and important. Sometimes maybe takes a long time. Sometimes it takes too long, and sometimes we don't allow it enough time. Maybe is the period of gestation and the time of gathering information. It is the time we wait and we listen to the voice inside us, we listen to our intuition and we try to come up with an answer that will serve us well. We try to come up with an answer that will add to our peace and not take away from it.

Is maybe real?

Maybe is real. Maybe is a real place between the acceptance and the rejection of something. Maybe is a real state where we can pause. But we might not allow ourselves to have maybe. We might think that we don't have this luxury and that we have to decide now. It is very rare that we don't have a chance to breathe in making our decisions. It is not very often when we have to give the answer right away. Usually we have time to consider. Usually we have time to gather more information. We should gather more information. We should be informed and we should search our feelings about things. We need to see how we feel about one thing or another, about the options in between also. Often we don't think about how there might be other options too. Sometimes there are variations. There are variations and we don't see them right away. If we give things time, these variations might come to light. Better things might come to light. Allow yourself to have the space of maybe in your life. Allow this to be real for you in all ways.

Maybe and what it means

Maybe means we haven't quite decided. Maybe means we are waiting for a signal. We might not feel strongly for something or strongly against something. Not everyone has strong feelings about things. Not everyone has access to their true feelings. They might have some distance to them and their feelings have gotten covered up over time. Sometimes maybe indicates a degree of apathy. We might not really care that much about something. Sometimes we need to ask if a decision really has to be taken. Sometimes we need to consider that maybe no decision needs to be made, sometimes things just evolve and change on their own. When you do need to make a decision, do not be hesitant to employ the spirit of maybe. Do not be pushed into a decision. This is what maybe allows for. It is the space for proper thought and consideration. Also you may not need to even say the word maybe. You may be engaged in considering what to do and not have to explain this. When you are in this situation, when maybe does not need to be said, then you are entered into a kind of negotiation that is to your benefit. The thing you are considering, and the people you are dealing with are not pushing you to engage with them. This is very valuable and can be taken into consideration. Negotiations and contemplations where you have peace and time to consider are the most important thing.

Following up from maybe

When maybe has occurred, eventually a decision is made. Not always perhaps. Sometimes things are just left and nothing happens. A decision not to proceed is the default from this usually. But when maybe is followed by a decision, then we have to look further afterwards. We can't just make the decision and leave it usually. Most of the time we have to shepherd our decision. We have to take care that things happen in the way we said they would happen. We have to see that things get fulfilled and we have to see that indeed the results after the maybe were followed. When we are in the maybe we have the luxury of thought and contemplation. We give this to ourselves and we should do so. It is important in our thought process. But after a decision has been taken, then we go from there. We have to employ consideration and be methodical in making sure that all this has happened correctly. There may be a few steps to this. It might not all be clear and concise and easy. Sometimes it is. But often we have to ensure that the right things happen at the right time. It is right to do this. It is right to do this because you want to make sure that you arrive at what you asked for. It is right to do this because you are honouring the decision that you made. You are saying to yourself, to the people you dealt with, and to the world that your decision is important and that you need for it to be followed and carried through. When you are in maybe, this follow up state has to be thought of too. You need to make sure that whatever decision you choose, that you are able to follow through on it and bring it to life, bring it to fruition.

Living in maybe

Some of us live in maybe. Some of us are a little too much in maybe. We spend time in maybe and we think about things. We think about our options – what we should do and not do. But if we do this too much, though we might enjoy the contemplation and reflection, we will not get very far. We will be too much in our minds, and not enough in the actual reality of the world. We need to balance maybe with other things. If you find yourself too much in maybe choose an area that you could push forward in. Encourage yourself to make a decision and take action and see how it feels. Sometimes we need to spend periods of time in contemplation and reflection. Sometimes we need a long time for this. We need to lie fallow and let the thoughts of our mind mingle and let ourselves rest too. This is very important and can't be overlooked. It is good to live in maybe sometimes, but not all the time. If you live in maybe all the time, then you do not do anything. You only think and consider. But it is important for us to do, too. It is important for us to see how our thoughts can become actions and can create real things in the world. When you live in maybe only, then you don't honour your creativity. You don't allow it to be expressed in the world. And this is disappointing. The world is waiting for your creation. The world is waiting for the thing that you alone can create. See what this is. See what this is inside you. And let it promulgate itself and be created in the world.

Not having much but maybe

There are some that don't have much in the world. There are some that don't have much and so maybe becomes very important to them. They say maybe one day I'll do this or that or go here or there. It is important to say maybe. It is important to have dreams. Even if you do not have much, you can still do much. Even if you feel that resources and money are not available to do the things that you want, you may be surprised by the very depth of resources inside you. The Angels advise you to make a plan for your dreams and your hopes. The Angels advise you to set out the steps you need to take. The Angels advise you to do this and then you will be happier with the way things go. You will begin to have more. You can still have maybe. But you will begin to have more too.

Maybe isn't here anymore

Maybe isn't always allowed. Maybe, it can be said, isn't here anymore. It was never tolerated that much. The need for quick action has always been with us. The demand for urgency has always been here – the sense of doom if things aren't done right now. Not for everything. Not in all cases. But in enough situations to make us frantic sometimes. Many times, we are called upon to act and to make up our minds and there is no space for anything else. There is no space for consideration and thought, for consultation and gathering information. It's almost as if maybe has departed, gone to some far off land. Maybe is not given any credentials. Maybe doesn't have any authority. It's as if maybe doesn't exist anymore. But we should call it back. We need to call it back.

Maybe doesn't exist

If you live in a sphere where there is no maybe, then you need to create it. If your environment doesn't recognize the need for thought and contemplation, you must push aside walls and create the space where this can exist. Set up a contemplation space. Set up reflection times. These are empty times and spaces. They are not filled with meetings and bookings. They are places where you can come to sit and think. They are times when you are free to not focus on anything except what you want. And sometimes that is nothing. It is good to have the space for this thought. It is good to allow the space. How much maybe can you allow in your day? As much as you need is the right answer. How much will you allow in your day? You need to start small perhaps. Or perhaps you don't. Perhaps you can start with exactly what you need. Maybe will wait for you because maybe has no choice and maybe is patient anyway. But you should ask how much you need this space for calm and deliberation. This space is crucial to you. Don't brush it aside. Don't let it get away from you or trivialize it. Seek it out. Build it. You need to build this to have it in your life. It will not magically appear on its own. You need to create this space.

Tales of maybe

What would maybe tell you if it could? It would tell you of a thousand or a million eureka moments. It would tell you of great creations in writing, music, art. It would tell you about the solutions to problems that were unsolvable. This is the joy of maybe. This is what maybe offers. Place yourself in the space to receive. Place yourself in the space to connect to the Divine, to the Universe. Place yourself in this space and see what comes to you when you allow yourself this space. See what tales of maybe you will create. See how you will add to this great collection.

The absence of maybe

If you banish maybe from your life then you might regret this. You might style yourself as a person of action, as a person who doesn't need time for contemplation. Or you might not like indecision and think that maybe is a form of it. But be careful that you do not spite yourself. Be careful that you do not cut off your possibilities. When you allow for maybe you have your ear to the ground and are listening. When you allow for maybe then more ideas can come to you. The absence of maybe means that you have closed yourself off, you have isolated yourself. It could be that this is not of your choosing. It could be that this has imposed itself upon you. Maybe someone has imposed this upon you. Resist this imposition. Resist being rushed and hurried. Find a way to create more space. Find a way to create more time. When you do this you will be expanding what you can do, what you can think and have. Maybe is the allowance of more. Maybe recognizes choice and the possibility of expansion.

Going away from maybe

There are times when maybe is not good. There are times when you have to go away from maybe because it is holding you down. There are times when too much space and time is available and it scatters things. You lose focus. So the advantage of the space and time and of proper thought becomes overextended, becomes negative. You will know when this is going on. You will know because it is as if the edge is lost, as if you lack meaning in your life. When you experience this, try to pull things back. See where the meaning is in terms of your life. See where the meaning is in terms of the things you have to handle. Reach for decision here. Reach for small decisions. Reach for more impactful decisions. Reach for them and make them and see how they feel. Reach for them and try them on and see how they affect you. Sometimes we need to go away from maybe. Sometimes maybe can drown us out or embrace us too fully. When you are experiencing this then you will know what to do. You will know how to act.

Fuelling thoughts of maybe

Maybe has to strike the right balance for us. Maybe needs to be present in our lives. And sometimes we need to distance ourselves from it. Maybe can create space and time and also it can be distracting. We need focus too. Use the time you have, use the time you can create to properly contemplate everything. Use the time to gather the information that you need. Do you have all the information that you need? Only you can decide this. You will know within yourself when you have all of it. If things seem incomplete, then you need to learn more. If things do not fit together in the right way, then there is more thinking that you have to do. We need to use maybe to our advantage. We need to set our sights on the goals we have, and on the things we want to accomplish. And then we have to build in time for the accomplishment of all of it. We can do this. We can use the tools we have, our thoughts, our minds, and our intelligence to think about all of this. Of course there are other tools too, other resources. But all that we need is within ourselves. We simply need the space and time to consider our situation, to consider the steps to take to accomplish what we want.

The end of maybe

If life is so fast paced is there an end to maybe? There could be an end if we let it. If we live in an instant world then how can we beg for time? Some things may be instant. Some things may be very quick. But the ground still needs to lie fallow for us at least some of the time. We need to think and brood and dwell and contemplate. These inner resources that we have will not work automatically in every situation. There is thinking to be done. There is work involved in this thinking. So do not let the instant nature of a lot of your life challenge you to such a degree that you give up on thought. Refuse to consider that maybe is at an end. You will always need space and time. You must consider these essential. You must consider these necessary to living your life well.

The rest of maybe

When you build in this space and time, your life becomes much easier. When you give yourself this freedom, then you can effect better change in your life. You can make changes that are easier for you that make your life easier. When you incorporate maybe in your life, when you build in the time to think and plan, then you can grow more easily. Then you can achieve your dreams more easily. The rest of maybe is your life itself. The rest of the significance of maybe is that you honour your life and its dreams and decisions. Take charge of maybe. Take charge of everything that you need for your life. The space and time you gain will repay you infinitely.

The Intersections of Time

The intersections of time is the idea that time is not always linear. Sometimes things repeat in our lives. Sometimes things repeat and we call these patterns or themes. This is an exploration of the idea that this repetition is perhaps more literal than we know.

Time intersects

Time intersects and comes together in one big push. Sometimes we are inundated with things. We are at the crossroads of many things and we feel we are in a whirlwind of activity. We have this whirlwind and then we can't stand outside of it. We have to stand in the centre and let it fly all around us and try to make sense of it all. We have to try to grasp and come to terms with what is going on and try to grab hold of it. When we do this we are intersecting with time. We are intersecting with all that is going on.

Past, present and now

Past and present are happening. Now is happening. They are both happening in the current instant. The past informs the present and shapes now. The present and now are the same thing. The present sounds like a placid thing. The present is a placid thing and now has a sense of urgency. Now requires us, compels us to act. Now says that if we don't act now then we will lose something. Is this really true? Only rarely. Can this be true? Can we distance ourselves from now? We can but we might have to train ourselves to do this. The present and the now inform the future too. They are the seeds of the future. The past and the present roll into the future. We think sometimes that our futures are constructed out of our past, that they take shape from what is happening right now. But this doesn't have to be true. Our lives can be completely different. Our lives can be completely changed. Our future can bear no resemblance to what is going on now. Or our future can be similar but with added goodness. We don't have to carry the past into the future. We don't have to hold onto it.

When maybe was born

Maybe was born to put a pause between yes and no, between okay and not really. Maybe was born so we could step back and evaluate. Maybe is the pause point on the linear line we have traveling into the future. We think it is linear. But maybe's existence means we acknowledge the swirling possibilities that are reaching towards us at all times. Maybe means that we are conscious and aware of our place in the eye of the hurricane of life. Maybe says, "Let's wait a minute and figure this out." Maybe says we are not ready yet to direct the future. We are not ready yet to finish with the state of the present, with what is happening now.

The fault of when

When is always very demanding. When asks questions. When always has something to say. When requires answers and a time frame. The fault of when is that it does not allow for the circularity of time. It insists on the linearity of time and this insistence creates a great stress. We are stressed because of when. We are stressed and we cannot release ourselves from it. We are told that everything depends on when. We are told this and we are pressured. Maybe some things do depend on timing. Other things do not. When precludes any thought and favours action. When gives decision the greatest authority. But thought is more important. Thought is more important in considering the future. After the flush of urgency is done, we may look at something and think what is happening? Why were we so rushed to do this thing or to make this decision? Learn from these times. Learn that you have the capacity to take a break from the demands of when. You have the opportunity to ponder and consider if you take it. This will help you to better reflect on the things that affect your decision and your plans. This gives you time to consider all factors and all things that are important. Taking this time is an acknowledgement of the circularity of time, the way that all things circle around and come to you. The way you are the star in your own life and in your own progression through it. When you don't insist upon linear time, then you are better able to make the choices that suit you. You are better able to make the choices that are in alignment with your soul.

Leaning into the future

You might look toward the future and be afraid of it. You might try to plan but feel that your dreams never come true. Inch your way forward instead. Take your plans and dreams and break them down so that they become achievable. Do not fight your way into the future. Do not insist that the future be here now. It will arrive when it wants to. Make your plans and preparations. Detail your dreams. Dare to think and dream with all parts of you. Don't hide anything from yourself – any feelings or wishes. You might have big dreams or little dreams. You can honour all your dreams. You don't have to think this is not good enough or bold enough. You don't have to reject ideas because they are undoable. You will make the path and take the journey of your dreams. You will do this because you have to. If you say to yourself that you cannot, it will not matter. Maybe you won't now. But you will in due time. Your dreams will never give up on you. They will push you into the future. And you will have to go. Because this story of your future, of your life, is written in your heart and your soul. Try and change it. Try and see if you can change this. If you can open yourself up to your vision of the future, no matter how deeply it is inside you, then things will be easier. Do not delay your dreams. The journey itself calls you. If you can hear this, then you will walk this path. The journey itself will define you and teach you. The path is already laid out for you. You have not had the eyes to see it yet. But you will see it now. You will see it when you are ready. Do not be afraid of your path. Do not be afraid of your particular journey and story. All of our stories were created with marvelous intent and with Divine blessing. All of our stories were created on purpose and with meaning. Your meaning is experienced through your journey. And in walking your journey, you evade time. In walking your journey you recognize the circular path that all of us take, and be freed from the strict linearities. You will be freed from all the demands that are placed upon you because of your beliefs about time.

Resisting time

Should you resist time? Should you resist the demands that time makes on you? No, you can embrace them. You can follow their dictates and do what you need to do. But always, you need to look and see what you are being told. You need to look and see what does all this mean? It may be that demands are being made on you and you are being asked to see something. It may be that the demands that time is placing on you are pointing to something deeper. There is something very particular about how time constrains us. We must get this thing done before that one. We must get something done before something else can take place. Consider each piece of the puzzle. Consider each element of the process. How do each of the elements affect each other? Can you delay certain things and speed up others? Can you do more than one thing simultaneously? How can you play with time? How can you say to time, this day I will be the master. This day I will not be ruled. It is possible to resist against time. It is possible. But it is better to work within time wisely.

Thoughts on time

Time holds commitments that we need to honour. Time requires us to take action, to make decisions in an appointed slot. Time is its own space and place. We honour time and we bend to it. But time cannot run us into the ground. Time cannot be the be all and end all. We must exist through and in time. We need to exist this way, being born, growing up and growing old and dying. But we must not run constantly to its wishes. We must decide that we will be in charge. We can swim with the current. We can be pulled by the tide. But we can step outside of all this too. We can step outside of time and decide how we will spend it. We have this power. We have the power to choose how to spend our time, what to do with our lives. And sometimes we are ramrodded into things that don't suit us. Sometimes we follow paths that lead away from what we should be doing. Sometimes we attach ourselves to someone else and then their time dictates to us. Take back your time. Take back your time and decide on your own what you will do with it. Decide what is important to you. Decide how it is important to you to live, and decide too about the speed at which you want to live. Do you want a quiet and slow life? Do you want to spend your time in reflection and contemplation? Or maybe you like a fast paced life with a lot of activities and events. The culture of your own life is something you need to define for yourself. You need to discover it and develop it too. Time and how it manifests itself in your life is very much a part of that. Work with time, play with time and let it be a positive thing for you in all ways.

The time of action

The time of action is the time when you make decision and take steps. You take action to bring something to fruition. Of course this is obvious. But the point is that not every moment is a time of action. Some moments must be definitely non-action. Some moments must be about thought and must be reserved for contemplation. Time of action suggests urgency and speed and these ideas too are only partially right. Sometimes action is swift and needs to be. Other times action is measured and slow and takes place over a long period of time. The intricacies of the time of action are dependent on the particular thing you want to achieve. Your goal might take a long time to realize. You may have a lot of work to do before all the things are in place. There is a lot of thought that goes into a long range goal. There is a lot of thought that goes into deciding what needs to happen when. You need to take this time. You can't be deceived by the idea that you have to act now, with urgency. Now and urgently are sometimes important. But mostly they lead to action that is ill-advised or not as complete and satisfying as it could be. There is a lot to be said for doing something well. The time of action, the time of now insists that action is more important than the end result. You can ask yourself if you believe this. You can ask yourself if this is true. Maybe sometimes this is true. Maybe sometimes this creates more complications, more work to do in terms of fixing and repairing things. Take the long view when it comes to the time of action. Take the long view and plan your actions well.

The time of need

The time of need is a different kind of time. It is a time when what you are feeling and thinking override everything else. It is a time when your emotions dictate the schedule, when the schedule begins not to matter. At this point all the goals and dreams and timetables fade from view. It may be that something has happened and you need to pause everything in your life and deal with the situation. It may be that something has overcome you and you need to stop everything also. This time is a difficult time because it is as if you are completely bound. You can do nothing. You can achieve nothing but tend to the situation and tend to yourself. During this time, look inwards and see what you need and what could help. The goals and dreams will be there again. The goals and dreams will be renewed but you need to be in a steady state. You need to right yourself and fix the immediate things that are an issue. It might take time and you may need help. Take the time and get the help that you need. You will be stronger and then better able to resume your usual life when this is done.

Beginning with time

We always want to begin with time. We always want to start with time because we feel we are in time. We have this concept that we live in time. This is because of our mortal construct. This is because we live as human beings and we are constrained by the physical presence of our bodies here on earth and because of the way we are born, grow, and eventually die. We are constrained by all of this and so it shapes our perspective to a fundamental degree. We cannot absent ourselves from this perspective. We cannot escape this or pretend that this is not happening to us. We can pretend that we are not subject to all of this. But somewhere inside us we cannot pretend, we cannot carry on with this illusion. The thing we can't comprehend, the thing we don't understand is the immortality of the souls and of our souls. We can have an idea of this, but we don't have the experience of it, at least not consciously. So we begin with time because we feel we are living in but a moment of time, the time it takes to complete our lifetime. We don't understand that we are bigger than time, and that we are from a place where time is just another tool, another construct, to be played with and manipulated. If we can move towards an understanding of this, then we will be freer.

Thinking about the future

We have to think about the future. We have to think about it and make plans and dreams. We can just drift along too. We can coast towards the future but it is better not to coast entirely. There are always things about the future that need our attention. We have to make plans for how we will carry out our lives – what we will do, how we will live. Sometimes things change dramatically. But even so, we can make plans. Are your plans right for you? Do they feed your soul? Maybe you have made plans for your future. Look at them again. Are they right for what you need now? Have your needs changed? You might feel that it is tiring to look at this. But this kind of looking forward is so important. It is important to your well-being. In order to be happy, you need to feel that things are going in the right direction. It is also important to be at peace and at ease with where you are and with your decisions. Do not feel that this has to be daunting. Do not feel that you will set something monumental in motion. You are doing this, this forward thinking, in order to protect your life. You are doing this forward thinking to protect the quality of what you have and how you want to live your life in future. Your life is important. You do not have to make quick snappy decisions about it. Take the time to think properly about things. Think about the future and envision it. When you think about it, does it feel right to you? This is the test you must give yourself. Only go to the right things. Only go towards what is right.

The future of now

Now has to become less urgent. In future, now will still matter but it has to matter in a calmer fashion. Now is important and shapes the present. This present moment is the now. Sometimes now calls us to action, makes us jump to attention. I seek a future for you where now will be more restrained in its demands, where now will be more polite when it asks for things. Now does not have to mean right this minute or else. Now can be the steady state of the present where we are working. Now can be the steady state when we are actively engaged in the achievement of our dreams and goals. Now is critical to the construction of the future. Now is critical and must remain important. We must engage with now and actively take part in the steps that lead to our future. Can we do this in a measured way? Can we do this in a productive way? Yes if we realize that urgency is often diverging us from our dreams. We must separate now from the anxiousness it sometimes create. We must use now as the tool it was meant to be, as the space and time to do the creative and active work we need to do. We are creators in now and this is how we build and make and change the future.

Building the future

The future is built one step at a time, one wonderful creation and idea at a time. And it is also built all at once. The future rushes in one minute to the next. And our creations, our developments affect us, and affect the world. We do not always know how. We do not know what trajectory they may have. We do not know where they may lead and what other developments they will in turn inform and germinate. We cannot know. We cannot imagine the multiplication of factors and influences that one creation, that one new thing will change. We can try to ride this wave. We can try to see where this will go. We can try to be on top of each new thing as it occurs. We can also let it wash over us and accept the changes as they come to us. We can embrace the new as it comes to us and affects us and changes us. How will we be changed by the future? How can we not be changed by it? It is a rushing tide. We do not have to worry about being left behind. Somehow we will be carried forward. The future is being built constantly and it is constantly rebuilding us too. It is not possible to be part of the past anymore. We can retain whatever we do from it, but we are all sailing forth to the future. It is carrying us. It is too strong for us to do otherwise.

And we are built for this too. We are built to accept the future and to be fine with it. You do not even have to embrace it. You are part of it already. See how you can make it your friend. See what you can take from it and what you can use from the new to improve your life. See how you have changed and see how it has changed you and your life. All this is natural and important. Accept the significance of the change in your life. See how you can be the arbiter and moderator of the change. See how it can best benefit you. When you do this, when you accept the future, then you will feel more a part of things. And you will feel more blessed too.

Building everything

Time builds everything. Time builds everything and everything is built within time. Anything we care to construct – physically and more intangibly – is built over time. This is one way that we truly experience time as a linear construct. Our experience tells us that we achieve a certain thing in a certain time frame, that morning came before afternoon and evening, and that we were young before we were old. We know this and we experience this. And so we can point to the time that a certain event happened historically and we can measure our life against that. We can measure our life against certain milestones – schooling, marriage, childbirth, anything else we feel is significant. We can say that was the year I took that wonderful trip. That was the year that that happened. That was the year when I was upset because this happened. We can measure our lives within the time of everything. We can measure it this way and it won't be the whole truth but maybe it will be the only truth we know. We can measure it this way and we can realize how things are built in time for us and by us. We can use this tool of time. We can use it to construct more things for ourselves, to make our lives easier and more beautiful. We can use this tool of time in a positive fashion. And we must. We must do this to encourage a positive trajectory for our lives. Do we build in time? Yes we do, we always do. We must do this. But if we choose not to, then time continues to ebb and flow. Time continues to pass. We can watch it pass. We can be an observer and not a participant. But things will be brought to our attention anyway. Things will be brought to our attention by the river of time. We can choose to make use of this information, and we can choose to address those things we need to deal with. We can choose to build too. Sometimes we are stuck at the intersections of time and we cannot do anything. But even in those times, we can set out the intention to build. We can set out the intention to build. And this might be important. This might be everything.

Building over time

Some of the best things, the best establishments and edifices, the best laws, the best changes for society are built over time. Some of them are built over a long time. Some of them arise seemingly in an instant, but we never see the lengthy preparations in place to make them happen, to make sure they happen. All of this is important in so many ways. All of this is important. Realize that you too can build over time. Realize that you don't need to make things happen in an instant. You can take time to do things. You can take time to do things well and to build something wonderful. When you build over time, when you take the long view of things, then you can consider more options. You can consider things from a bigger perspective. Considering things in this way is valuable. You attach more time to the different steps involved. You can consider the different steps involved. You can also allow things to unfold properly. You can allow them to unfold and then they can unfold well. Sometimes things need time to germinate and grow. Sometimes different shifts have to occur in you, in those around you, and even in society for the thing that you want to build to really begin to take hold, and to be allowed to start growing. It is not sensible to assume that you can do everything in this instant. But your dreams can be envisioned right now. Your imagination can be allowed to fly and soar. Indeed it must if it is to build wondrous things. Let your imagination soar. And then be guided in the plans you come up with. Be guided and make the best plans you can so that your vision can unfold into a wonderful reality. Build over time whether it be days, weeks, months, or longer. Build over time according to the right time for the dream to take shape, to become manifest in the right way. Ask for help too. Never forget this important step. Ask for help from the Angels, for your dreaming, and planning, and for the realization of the dream too.

Cumulative action

Actions, little actions and big actions accumulate and grow bigger. They accumulate and make more of something. More is created. More and more and then something bigger is launched. Something bigger is created than the thing you thought you were creating. We may start with one thing. We may start and think we are making just this one thing. But we don't know what it leads to. We don't know where it will go, what it will build towards. We don't know where things may lead and how they may accumulate and accrue in time. When we build in time, when we build over time, we are taking so many steps. We are making so many choices and making decisions and we do not know where they will go, where they will end up. We don't know, we can't know how one decision might touch another, how one thing might affect another. We simply cannot see. We need to trust in the strength of our cumulative actions. We need to trust in the strength of this. We need to go forward in good will. We need to set our intent with good will. Because it is with good will that we do everything. We need to enter into every conversation, and every action with this spirit. We need to take all the care and attention we need. We need to take the time and space that we need. And we need to dialogue with everyone around us and everyone involved in our activities with the spirit required. We need to be understanding and patient and kind. And we need to move forward in the spirit of positive action. When our intent is clear, and when our intent is good, then all things will be achieved. This will not be a false hope. Your actions will bear fruit. Your faith and intent will have an effect. And the culmination of all of this, the touching of so many points, will have more fruit than you can possibly imagine, will have more positive repercussions than you can possibly imagine.

The distance of action

The taking of action creates repercussions into the future. The taking of action is seeded in the events of the past. It is seeded in your thoughts and your mind and your spirit. You set the intent for your action. You dreamed or planned your action. And that action that came to pass. That action that you took or that you set into motion has repercussions. That has an impact into the future. That has an impact and touches many things and touches other people too. The distance that action has is not fathomable and not visible right away. You will see it after a time. You will see the ripple effects in wide concentric circles around you. You will see it linearly too. How this one thing leads to another and leads to another. Take your actions wisely. Take your actions wisely and from the right place in your heart and see where they may lead into the future. Take actions also that will result in you being made more whole. Start from this point and from the intent that you want to be more whole. If you start with this, more things will be easy for you. Things will come into being just from your actions. They will also feed and contribute to other actions. Each action causes something else to occur. Each action is part of the journey of your dreams. Each action is a link in the chain to achieving your dreams.

Action, space and time

Our lives take place in action, space, and time. They take place in space and time. This is an understood thing. But they take place in action too. They take place in action whether we are taking action or not. If we are making plans and doing things, then this aspect of our lives being in action is clear to us. But if we don't do things, if we don't take action, we might feel that this is not a good description. There is action that is always taking place around us. It is up to us whether we want to participate in action or initiate action ourselves. If we don't, if we sit on the sidelines, we might think that we are not active. But actually, what we are doing is participating in non-action. We are actively being non-active. Space and time and action occur around us and this is inescapable. The thing to do is to actively take part. The thing to do is to initiate the action ourselves and not wait for things to happen. Action, space and time shape our lives and swirl around us constantly. They do this and we can be subject to them. We can also protect ourselves and live fully aware of them. We can live fully aware of space, time and action. And we can articulate our lives. We can live our lives and live our actions and carve out space and time. Everything is quite fluid. We might think that there are constructs that bind us and structure us. But really most of them are easy to modify. Think about how you can shape your reality. Think about how you can participate in life and shape time, space and action to best suit you. If you do this, you will see what a creative force you are in your own life. You will see all that you can do.

Episodic notions

Episodic notions in time occur in our lives. Episodic themes repeat at certain times. We can see these if we look at our lives. If we think back to important events in childhood, important memories, we can uncover certain themes that manifested themselves. Then at other points in our lives, we can find those themes again. We can find those themes and they come up for us again, forcing us to deal with them, forcing us to look at the conflicts at play. Sometimes we might feel like we have no choice in the things we are dealing with. Sometimes we feel that we are at the crux of something, that something has us and we cannot choose anything different. It might be a way we behave when certain things occur. It might be that we always find ourselves in a particular relationship pattern. We are always with the same kind of partner. Or we seek out the same kind of friend and they are abusive to us. And sometimes these episodes apply to actual events. We go through times when we lose things. Or we go through times when certain things don't work out. The

Angels want to say that we can expect some repetition in our lives. We can expect this because we have to look at things from a new angle. The first time we experience something or see something, we don't see and experience fully because the newness of it dominates our experience. Then when it happens again, we can better understand certain things. Of course we may not want certain themes and events to repeat themselves. We might not want this to happen. Maybe they are negative events and they take a heavy toll on us. If this is true, then you can ask the Angels for a reprieve from this kind of thing. You can ask them to lighten your burden. You can ask them to lighten it and you can also ask what it is you need to learn from the situation. You can say to the Angels, "I feel that this situation is teaching me this and this and this. Is that true?" You can wait for an answer. The Angels may tell you that you have something else to learn. They may even tell you what that thing is. Then, when you are complete with the experience, it won't have to happen anymore. You will move on. You will be at peace within yourself in some way.

Repetition and history

The repetition of events within our lives is echoed by the repetition of events in history. We live our lives and things repeat themselves. We try to deal with these things as best we can with more understanding and ability each time. Hopefully we learn and grow. Hopefully we can achieve more. Hopefully we can also have more peace and deeper fulfillment. This is very good if we can move forward. This is very good if we can take the lessons we have learned and apply them to ourselves. These personal lessons are an important part of our history. In the larger history, the history of humanity, there are other lessons to be learned too. It is not always easy to see and understand these lessons. It is not always easy to apply these lessons to new problems and to arrive at solutions. The global world is a diverse place. There are all kinds of events taking place, and all kinds of ideas about what is happening, what the problems are and what can or should be done. No one has all the answers. And maybe not all the answers are available. It is possible to see the way forward to a better future. It is possible to imagine a future where everyone has what they need and the great scourges of poverty, hunger, war and fear are erased. It is possible to imagine this. We must imagine our way into this future. We must do this for the good of everyone and for ourselves. Imagine this bright and beautiful future. Let it take hold in your mind, and in your life, and your heart. If you imagine this and if the whole world imagines this, then it will become reality. The world will be made new.

The intersections of time and space

Time and space intersect during events, during societal crossroads – pivotal moments. Time and space intersect and this is what we are stamped with. This is what we are imbued with. We bring this into ourselves. We are time and space intersected. Every waking moment and every moment we are time and space intersected. We happen in time and we happen in space too. We are all of this and so we can't often see beyond this. We can't often rise above this. We can't see beyond this and so we think we are stuck. We make these decisions that we are stuck. If we are stuck though, it is only for a moment. If we are stuck, it is because we won't allow ourselves to be unstuck – we won't forgive ourselves or we won't move beyond something. We might be stuck but we don't need to be frozen too.

We might be stuck but this doesn't mean we can never move forward. We have the capacity to move forward in time <u>and</u> space. We have the capacity to do everything. It is all within ourselves and it is all within our grasp. The manifesting of our dreams is at hand, is always at hand. Now we are able to see this. Now we are better able to see our ability to do more, our ability to make and to see and to realize. Now the barriers are gone. Now we can be free to truly imagine. You can rise above the intersections of time and space. You can rise above the x and y of your particular existence. You can rise above it or change it or ignore it. You can do what you want. The time is now to rise and to create your own time and space to conquer the things that you need to conquer, to do the things that you need to do. Rise now. You are powerful. Rise now. You are a creative force and you are unleashed upon the world.

Reliving the future

Have you ever felt like the future you were planning had already happened? Have you ever felt like you were going towards something you already knew, and that you could feel everything about it already? This kind of reverse déjà vu is possible. This kind of experiential acceptance and understanding of the future can be inborn within us. We can have this understanding and awareness of what is to come. We have charted it out in our dreams. We have imagined it and visualized it, we have conceived it and planned for it. But sometimes there is something deeper going on. Sometimes the seed of the future is planted now or before now. Sometimes this seed of the future is planted and we think it is just good planning, good management on our part. But really a small piece of the future has travelled back to us, it has done so to make our way easier, to guide us. Nothing, the Angels want to say, is truly unknown. Nothing is truly new to you. A part of you will already have experienced it. A part of you will also have ventured forth into the future to stake a claim, to mark the path, and to learn the journey. This is why we don't have to be afraid of the future. Part of us has already gone there. Part of us understands already what we have to do and the decisions we must make. We can trust this. We can trust this part of us and this connection we have. The Angels say it is our link to all parts of ourselves, in this time and in all times (in this lifetime and in all lifetimes). It is also our link to everything else – to all other places, to all other time. So we can trust this within us. We can trust these feelings about the future and trust that this will be a good future, for us personally, and for all of us too.

Interstices of time

The interstices of time are the times in between time. It could be the time between events, between important milestones. It could be the time we spend waiting for things, or the time of delay. When we encounter these non-moments, these times that do not seem important, we can reflect on where we are at that particular point. We can use them for contemplation. We don't have to waste this time and we don't have to consider it wasteful either. Sometimes one kind of time bleeds and blends into another kind of time. Sometimes there are transitions. There are empty times too, empty spaces. If you live a busy life then these spaces will not happen too often. If you lead a quiet life, these spaces can last a long time, days and weeks, maybe longer. What do you do when you have a sudden gift of time? What do you do when your time is freed up? You can plan for these spaces of time. You can plan for them. Plan to enjoy them. Plan to notice what is around you. Plan to contemplate and to think. Plan to experience the vibrancy of everything that you can see. Empty times are an opportunity to deviate from the page you have set out for yourself, from the plan that you had for your day. Use these times to think and to change your mind about things. And observe, observe how the time travels from one thing to another. Observe how one activity you are involved in ends, and how another might begin. Observe the space in between the two. And observe too how you feel in this time, if you feel comfortable or stressed. Observe your interaction with time itself. When you allow yourself to look at the edges of everything then you might be happier, you might be more aware of everything.

Chasing dreams

We chase our dreams in and out of time, in and out of space. Sometimes we don't chase our dreams. Sometimes we let them fall away, or we feel we can't pursue them, or we think they are too big for us, or too improbable. Let yourself believe in the beauty and power of your dreams. Let yourself believe that the chase is worthy and that the dreams are achievable. You don't have to be dissuaded from your dreams. You don't have to find reasons to cast them aside. You are the reason that you are doing all of this. Don't think that entering into conversations with yourself about your worth will serve you. Most of us do not have a strong enough sense of self-worth. So do not let feelings about self-worth, or self-image be your guide. Instead, be bold. Instead, recognize that your dreams have meaning and that they matter to you and that is worth enough and that is worth everything. But recognize too that your dreams are important to the world too. Your dreams will have repercussions and ripple effects that will change the world. How can they? Because no matter what you are dreaming of, no matter what you are doing, your dreams have power, and they come from deep inside you. They come from deep inside you and they contain Divine essence, just like you do. So when you call on your dreams to come forward and to show themselves, when you make these kinds of declarations, you are calling into being something infinitely valuable because it is powered by your deepest passion. Your deepest passion is calling forth this dream. It is calling it forth and you are the instrument. All of the rest of you is the instrument for making it happen. Make it happen. Live your dream. Call it into reality. You already know how. So is chasing dreams worth it? Of course it is. You are only putting your story into the world. You are only adding to the rich and vast storehouse of the worlds' treasures. The world needs you. And you need to recognize this if you are to take your part beside all the icons of our times. It is okay to be brilliant. Actually it is more necessary than you can ever know. Please be brilliant. Please call your dreams forward and into being.

The Future

The future

The future is here and now as we speak. The future is in the mirror as we look to the past. Some seeds of the future are contained in the past. Some seeds of the future are present right now. Can we look into the future? The answer is not totally. The answer is also yes. What future do you want to see? What future do you want to create? Do you want the future to be created for you? Do you want to set the agenda for your future? What impact do you have on your own future, on that of those around you and even the world? You have a great deal of impact and significance. You have to accept the responsibility you have for shaping the future. The future is contained within you and you will write it. Write it well.

All the future

All the future is coming to the forefront. All the future is coming to be accounted for now. The future presents itself in your imagination, in the news of the day, in the gestalt of the time. The future reveals itself and then it asks you to go towards it. The future signals the tomorrow that is not quite here. It signals it in opaque ways and in more evident ways. The future is signaling to you now. You may hear it. You may see it. You may not know how it will come about. You may not yet know how you will shape it or be part of it. You will be a part of it. You will be integral to it so you can begin to consider this now. It is good to contemplate this now. Do you want your life to be the same in the future as it is now? What would you change? Do you want the life of the world to be the same in the future? The questions are the same. What would you change? Set your intent for the best and brightest future for yourself and the world. Set your intent for the best resolution to your problems. Set your intent for the best outcome for everyone, for yourself and for everyone in the entire world. The future is coming and we need to prepare for it. The future is coming and we should prepare well. We can prepare for all that we need to do and all that we are hoping and planning for. The Angels ask that we also leave some room for unexpected joys and happiness. The Angels ask that we allow for good surprises. We cannot know the entire shape of the future. But we can will it to be good. This much the Angels are promising. Will it, then. Will it with your intent, your imagination, and your heart and soul. Make this your resolution – to have a beautiful and bright, and kind and compassionate future – for yourself, and for humanity too.

The future as it stands

The future, currently, is predicated on the articles of faith that we deliver to it. This means that as we are informed, as we fill ourselves with information and impressions, so too are we informing the future, are we paving the way for it to occur. This doesn't mean that all the negative things that we might worry about will come to pass. This doesn't mean that we can actively create a downwards spiral just by our anxiety. It means though that we might want to take a break from the things we are considering and thinking about. It means we might want to absent ourselves, temporarily at least, from the news of the world, from any source of negative information. Taking a pass on the news, and on current events is a good thing to do once in a while – a kind of fasting in a sense. This absence of daily drama will make you less worried, and less fearful. When your mind is quiet then you can think more about your own future, and even the future in general, without being interrupted constantly by the current news cycle. The future is in your hands to make. It is good to allow yourself full creative control in this regards. And sometimes that means turning down or turning off, the volume on the general world around you.

The future as it is

Sometimes there are great shifts in society and what once was, is no longer. Sometimes there are great changes and then we are completely different people as a result. Will this happen to us again? Yes it must happen. It has always happened with the advent of new technologies that are so striking that they change everything. Of course new technologies and new methods will change us and inspire us. Of course they will change the very fabric of our environment, the very way we live our lives. But will they change us at our core? This depends. This depends on how much we are willing to change and how much we need to change. What does your life look like now, and what would you change about it? We keep coming back to this question. The future won't be the same as what is going on now, either in your life or in the life of the world. The structures and contexts might change. The beliefs might change. What is accepted and not accepted might change. Find a way to know what your own core values are. Find a way to be aware of the truth of yourself. The truth of yourself, and your alignment with this is what will see you through. The truth of yourself, your core being, has been the same and has always been the same. It may be overshadowed sometimes by the environment you are living in. It may be affected by the beliefs of the society you live in, and the beliefs of the people around you. But these are all layers. The core of you is the same and has been for centuries. It has been the same since the dawn of time, and since God fashioned you from one of the strands of Divine essence. You are at this core. The real you – immaterial of gender, background, race, society, culture. You will always be safe in the future. Because you have always been safe. Find the real you. Find the real you within yourself and you will be at peace and this peace will never be taken from you.

The future now

When you consider the future, you need to do this with the greatest of optimism and hope. The future can be a really good thing. It can be filled with light and love and wonderful things. It can be filled with fulfilment and joy. Whatever your present looks like right now, the future doesn't have to resemble it. The future can be quite different from what you are currently experiencing. In this current moment, you are sowing the seeds of your future. In this current moment, you are imagining your future and the way it will be created. You shape your future just by considering it and thinking about it. You don't see everything yet. You don't see the exact shape of the road. You don't see all the twists and turns. And you can't know how things will change in society and how these changes will affect you. You can't know this. You have to put your best efforts into creating a wonderful future. You need to summon your enthusiasm for it. Think about what would make you happy and joyful. Think about what would give you peace. If there are ways that you are constrained, ask for these to be released. If there are ways that you are not happy find ways to make improvement. It is wrong thinking to believe that things are bad and things are always going to be bad. It is wrong thinking to believe that things are good now and so in the future they must take a turn for the worse. Believe in yourself. Believe in your future. And believe that your future is wonderful. And take steps to make sure that this is true. Take steps from today, and this very moment to create a wonderful trajectory and experience for your life.

The future as it should be

We might have ideas about the future. We might have ideas for the path our life should take. Perhaps these ideas originated in our childhood. Perhaps we had people around us who had certain ideas about life. Perhaps the society we live in has certain ideas about life. Perhaps this is true. But we have the ability to develop new mindsets. We have the ability to travel in new directions and to allow our ideas to have a new form and a life of their own. The future doesn't have to abide by some idea you developed when you were a child. It doesn't have to dictate the agenda of your society, of your environment in any way. You need to think about how you want the future to be. You need to think about what you are comfortable with, what you are seeking, and what would be a good way of life for you. Your autonomy is very important. You cannot be true to yourself if you are always following the ideas of someone else, or of anyone or anything other than yourself. Listen to what your heart and spirit are telling you. They may not always communicate how you will achieve the future you need, but they will always tell you what you like and don't like and what is important for you to do in this moment. Trust yourself and chart your own future. Trust yourself to determine a good future for you.

Don't completely discount the ideas and beliefs of others. But weigh and measure them against what you know to be true, against what is right for you. Once you learn how to do this, the path forward is easy. There is no more difficulty.

Contain the future

Plans for the future can overtake the present. We might get caught up for a future event that is really important to us. This is understandable but don't neglect the present. Contain the future as best you can. Contain it so it doesn't rush out and capture all your time and attention right now. How can you make the present more interesting to you now? Resist the urge to completely fill the present so that it contributes to the future. You need to build in time to do nothing. You need to build in time to think and sit quietly. Have faith that the future is evolving at its proper pace. Can you be at peace about this? It's important to be at peace and let the future unfold. Just as the past has come and gone, so too will the future. The future is on its way to you. You don't need to hurry it along. You need to prepare. But you also need to enjoy what is happening right now.

Future, intricate future

The future is made up of so many things we don't know, and can't understand. The future is made up of forward movement, new ways of doing things, new solutions to old issues. The future might revisit the past for inspiration, ideas, and nostalgia. Sometimes the future looks only to the new, to the latest. We are caught up in all of this. We are caught up in now, and in the past, and in the future already. We live in all three times at once. And so we inform the future and it informs us even before it has occurred (at least in our perception). And what will we bring to the future? What will we bring to now? And what do we bring to the past? For even now and in the future, we will still be judging and evaluating our past. We will still be participating in it. The future is so beautiful. It is embellished like needlework upon cloth. What will we write in the future? How will we add our own embroidery and work upon the future? The texture and the cloth of time are already woven. They are woven and we put our mark on all of it all the time. The creativity we have inside of all of us pushes us to do this. We are pushed to live our lives as artists, writing upon time. Some of us are aware of this. Some of us are not. Even if you are not aware of this you are still writing upon time. You need to write the right things. You need to write and create the things that are right for you. Do not do something because you should or because it is the thing to do right now. Do things because they spring from deep inside you and they are asking you to do them. This is not an invitation to neglect your obligations. You must always fulfill them. Instead it is a request to live more deeply, from a place of spirit and to acknowledge the value and the voice of your own heart and spirit.

Simplifying the past for the sake of the future

We might remember the past in tremendous detail. We might remember the past vaguely or not at all. The Angels want to caution us about the past and the way we remember it. They say that we never remember it quite right, we don't get all the details right, we mix up events and timelines and things become foggy in our memory. The Angels want us to simplify our relationship with the past. They say we can remember it as we do, in whichever way we remember it. But they say it is good to reflect on the past and to ask ourselves what we learned from it and what we still might learn from it. We can't change the past. But we can use the tools of the past as resources for the present. We can use what we have learned from the past to feed us now and to feed our future. So simplify your thoughts about the past. Don't seek to remember all of it or any of it necessarily. Seek instead that the lessons be revealed to you. Think too about how the events that transpired would be different today. How have things changed, for you and for the world? And what different choices would be made today. Do not harp on the memory of what is done. Do not try to relive it over and over again. Instead welcome the present, welcome the future. And welcome all that it may bring.

The future: to now, and again

When we think about the future from our vantage point of the present, it doesn't seem entirely that it will ever get here. We can't picture it and we don't know what it will look like or how things will change from now. The future, in a sense, revolves around now. The future is born in now. The things you do today may bear fruit in the future. We can think long term. We can think about how our current actions create our future reality. We can think about the forces that are shaping our present. We might think that we are subject to all kinds of forces, but that is not so. We are more the arbiters of our own destiny than we know. Go forward first with goodwill. That is the first requirement. Go forward first and always with goodwill so that your motives are not questioned, so that your intent remains clear and pure. When you sow goodwill in the now, you reap vast rewards beginning today. You will not even have to wait for the future. The future returns to now. The future returns to now because the future references it. The future is born from now and so it will always contain now in its story. Are you cognizant of the now? Are you aware of the now you live in? It is good to be very aware of your situation, of your environment, of your world and what you think your place in it is. It is good to be aware of all of these things. When you cannot define yourself, when you cannot articulate to yourself who and what you are, then you give yourself more difficulty in determining the future. Start from within and know yourself and develop yourself truly. And then the future will arrived beautifully for you. What you plan out well, you will receive. What you conceive of imaginatively and with your own inner power, this will be created and your creations will in turn make their own wonderful new things. Set your future in motion by being very aware of yourself and of what you want and need to do.

The future, the future

Some people wring their hands at the future. Some people are very worried about what could go wrong and what has gone wrong already and imagine all kinds of negative possible outcomes. This kind of negative thinking will do you no good. This kind of negative thinking will only give you stress. Some people like to keep very busy. Some people cannot think about anything beyond what they have to do today. This suits them. They don't want to think beyond this moment, this day or this week. They want to keep busy so that they don't have to consider the future, so that they don't have to consider their future or the future in general. It is an intimidating thought. Instead of all this fear about the future, we are asked to dream instead. We are asked to dream of wonderful futures for ourselves, for those around us, and for the whole world. We are asked to dream of a future where happiness and good health and prosperity abound, where no one is left behind, and where everyone is able to follow their dreams and to even have dreams. The future is a powerful concept. The future is a wonderful thing. We can make many plans for the future and watch them unfold, and make them occur. What will you do with your future? This is for you to decide. But begin with a dream. Begin with a wonderful dream and bring all your powers of imagination to bear on this dream. You don't have to feel that you are engaging in some kind of escapist fantasy. You can consider that you are imagining a new reality for yourself, one that maybe you can't even imagine. You can think about this and then you can consider how this might happen, how this might come to occur. Leave yourself some room for the unexpected and for synchronicity and serendipity. Leave yourself some room for magic and for miracles and divine intervention. Your future is waiting to be written. Your future is wonderful and waiting to appear before you. The future, your future, is calling upon you to create it. See what kind of creative forces you have at your disposal. See how creative you are and how powerful you are. When you recognize your own power you are halfway to creating the future you want and need.

Incantation to the future

I summon the future for you.

I summon a future that is bright and wonderful, full of magic and mystery.

I summon a future that is good in every way. I summon a future that lacks for nothing, where all your dreams are fulfilled, and where all your longings are answered.

I summon a future that is right for you, that is made for you, that is comfortable for you.

I summon a future that calls you to be your best self in a way that is easy for you, in a way that is natural and has no cost.

I summon a future that you will love, even if you cannot see it, even if you cannot imagine it.

I summon a future where you feel loved and will love in return. I summon a future where you have joy.

I summon a future where there is no hate, only peace. I summon a future where there is no war, only happiness. I summon a future where there is no poverty or hunger or strife, only prosperity, abundance and ease.

I summon this future for you and for everyone. I summon this future because the power that is within you, and me, and all of us is too strong to be vanquished, and too strong not to summon all of these things

I summon a future where you feel safe and protected and where all feel safe and protected.

I summon a future where you are free to plan and dream and think and grow. I summon a future where the full expression of yourself is never a problem for you or anyone else.

I summon a future where we are all free, all equal, all at peace, and all complete.

Let the future be everything good, and let it inspire you and your life. Amen.

Appendix D/Dare

Dare to the future

Dare to the future we tell you. Dare to the future because the future is your destiny and it needs to be a good destiny. Plan for the bravest future you can. Plan for the best and most beautiful future you can. And then let us add magic to this. Let the angels add magic and momentum to all your dreams for the future. Do not be concerned that your future will be difficult, that it will not be good or even harsh. Plan instead for the boldest thing you can imagine. Plan to be audacious. Plan to be able to have what you need to have and want to have. Dare to the future. Take risks but only the ones that make sense. Take risks but only the ones that are safe for you. Dare to create the future of your dreams. Dare to create the future that is beyond your dreams. Dare all of this and we will help you.

Dare to the present

The present also requires its own daring action. The present requires you to dare. Dare to be brave. Dare to be present in the present. Dare to be who you really are. Dare to be in alignment with your true self. Do you dare be anything else but this? It is important to reach down into the true meaning of yourself and bring this out to the world. No falsehoods. No pretences. Be that which you are. Dare it to be enough. Dare yourself to be enough and wonderful the way you are. Do you want to change yourself? Do you want to change your present? Make these changes in the way that best befits you. Make these changes in a way that is the most peaceful for you. Dare to the present. It is waiting for you to do all that you can with it. It is waiting for you to participate in it fully, and whole-heartedly. Do not leave your spirit behind in this. Do not leave your heart or any part of you behind in this. Dare to be fully you and fully alive and aware right in this moment and always. Your presence, your energy will carve a path for you more precisely, more abundantly than you could possibly know.

Dare to the past

The past is its own thing, its own container of joys and sorrows. The past is memory, faulty memory. The past is instruction and learning. The past is pain and remorse. The past can be everything. We challenge you to not make it everything. Dare to the past that it feed you and nourish you only. Dare to the past to let it inform you and create the future that you want. Dare to the past that it bend and twist to become something that is soothing to you, something that is real and right for you. Dare to the past that it become the past you need and want and not a past that plagues you. Dare yourself to accept the past and then consider it no longer. Dare yourself to learn the lessons of the past and then integrate them into your life now. Dare to be a part of the past but not contained by it. Dare to not let it hold you to an environment that doesn't exist any longer. Dare it to not shape your attitudes or colour your perspective. Dare to let it guide you but only to the point where it should. Dare to let the present take over and to release the hand of the past. Dare to leave it behind. Dare to make the past small in your mind and face boldly forward. Dare to let the events of the past recede and to give these events only the significance they deserve and not more. Dare to not live in the past and to not let the past live in you. Dare to be a product of your time and of your future time. Dare to not be relegated to something that is over with and complete. Dare to be finished with the past and to tell it that it can no longer own you or rule you. Dare all these things and then you will dare to be free.

Dare to be whole

Dare to be whole in all ways. Dare to be whole, body, mind and spirit. Dare that your intellect be as bold and as brave as it can. Dare that your knowledge be as complete as possible. Dare that your understanding be wide and vast and open to learning more. Dare that your awareness and your compassion are unrestricted. Dare to be kind and to look upon the world with open eyes. Dare to be whole and not piecemeal. Dare to not compartmentalize yourself or your life in any way. Dare to look upon all of it, all at once. Dare to fix what is broken and to not accept what is imperfect. Dare to admit that not everything suits you right now, and that not everything is right. Dare to make the improvements that you want. Dare to evaluate yourself and the world around you. Dare to be the best you can be. Dare to define this for yourself. Dare to listen to the voices of others. Dare to trust your own voice always. Dare to be true to your spirit, to your one true spirit. Dare to listen and to recognize your own way of thinking. It is unique and it will not fail you. Dare to not follow. Dare to lead. Dare to not lead also. Dare to be the inner voice for those around you. Dare to be the spokesperson for your environment, physical or otherwise. Dare to be perfectly you and perfectly whole. Dare to be abundant and at peace with yourself. Dare to dare.

Dare to be at peace

Dare to have peace in your life and to live free of drama and
pettiness. Dare to live with integrity and with alignment to yourself.
Dare to feel free and to be whole. Dare to not have any problems.
Dare to be perfectly happy in all ways. Dare to be okay in all ways.
Dare to improve your life in the ways that matter to you. Dare to
have peace now and always. Dare to not have conflict in your life.
Dare to be okay with everything. Dare to be okay that things are not
the way you want them to be. Dare to be at peace no matter what
your situation is. Dare to be an example of peace in the world. Dare
to be a shining example of peace.

Dare to be free

Dare to have freedom in your world and in your life. Dare to feel
free and to be free right now. Dare to be free of the shackles that
have bound you. Dare to be free of any pain you have had. Dare to
be free of all of it. Dare to say to yourself, 'I am worth more than
this.' Dare to say that you are free and you will not accept any
treatment that renders you less than free. Dare to not be bound.
Dare to not be imprisoned, constrained, or shut down. Dare to
speak your mind. Dare to speak your mind even if it makes you
different and not popular. Dare to be free enough to create the kind
of world that you need to live in. Dare to be free enough to create
your own reality. Dare to be free to have your own separate
identity. Dare to depend on others and dare to have them depend
on you. Choose freedom always. Dare all things. Dare freedom.

Dare to be serene

Dare to be serene and calm though the storms rage around you. Dare to find peace wherever you are and accept no disturbance of your equanimity. Dare to construct your world in such a way so that peace reigns in it and all non-peaceful elements are forced to flee. Dare to enforce serenity. Dare to be serene and to spread serenity within your world. Dare to make peace your mantra and to accept nothing but this. Let no drama unfold before you. Let no politics create a maelstrom of anything. Let there instead be only perfect days and perfect sunshine in your heart and your world. Create your world so that you can breathe in it. Create your world so that it is the right size for you and so that it belongs to no one else. Create your world so that it suits your system perfectly and in all ways. Dare your way to serenity. Claim back the territory you have lost to chaos and strife and struggle. Claim it back for you, for your peace of mind and for the flourishing of your spirit, your heart, and your soul. Dare to be serene and dare to have this serenity embrace you and to nourish you. Dare to be rooted in this nourishing place. It will do you well.

Dare to have what you need

Dare to put in place the things that you need. Dare to have your life filled with things and people that contribute to you. Dare to have only what you need and want. Dare to exclude the things that detract, the people that distract or cause damage. Dare to be whole and to evaluate what it is you truly need. Dare all of this. Do not shirk your responsibility to yourself. Maybe you have always looked at the needs of others. Maybe you have done this. It is time, if this is so, to look inside and see what you have been neglecting for yourself. Your needs are many and varied. Your needs must be accounted for and tended to. Dare to do this and to tend your own self as if it were a garden that you depended upon. The garden that you are asks that you pay attention to it. The garden that you are asks that you take some time to look at yourself, to look at the things that you need for yourself. Do you have the right people in your life? Are there some people that encroach upon you? Are there some people that do not serve you well? What do you need to change in these relationships? What do you need to do to feel that you are in a better place? Take care of the things that you need to do. Take care of these things and then you will feel better in your world, you will feel more at ease in your heart and in your spirit. Take care that you are tending the garden of you. For no one else will tend it. No one else will know all the things you need.

What do you need?

What you need is different for each person. Some need hope. Others need bread. Some need peace. Others need a new way of thinking about something. It is good to be introspective about what you need and to really think about this. It is good to think about the different categories in your life and to see what you need in each of these. At the most basic, we need to consider food, shelter, and safety. These are paramount. You have to take care of these before you look at anything else. And then after that you need to consider the other things that are important – relationships, health, education and any other thing you want to think about. Take some time to think about these things. Take some time to honour yourself and to consider what you need. What you need is important. What you need drives and fuels your life. It is no good saying to yourself that you might want something but can't have it. If you define it as a need, if your system defines it as a need, then you are compelled to seek it out. These needs must be healthy. If you discover needs within yourself that you know are not appropriate, or if others tell you they are not appropriate, then you must seek out help for these. You cannot become uncontrolled and unfettered in the world. You cannot just do whatever you want. There are consequences to all your actions. And you seeking out the fulfillment of your needs must be in harmony with what is right and true and what is good. If you do not know if your needs fall into this category, you must reflect on this and seek out help.

Dare with all of you

In all the things you do, in all the things you endeavor to do, you must dare with all of you. You must dare with every part of you. You must construct your dream with all parts of you. You must dare and you must dare to dream. Do not let part of you stand away from the dream. Do not hold a part of you back. Dare with all of you. Bring all of what you have and what you are to this dream. Bring all of what you have – mind, heart and spirit. Bring all of you so that your dream may be energized, and so that your dream may take flight. It is in the dreaming that we awaken our deepest imaginings. It is in the dreaming and the daring that we awaken our spirit and our soul. Dare with all of you so that no part of you will feel that you did not do the thing you ought to have done. Dare with all of you so that nothing will remain unfinished, so that no part of the great thing you are doing is incomplete. Dare with all of you so that you will be the most complete and whole person that you can be. Dare with all of you because this is the chance you are taking now and this opportunity presents itself right now to you. Dare with all of you because you have to light a fire under your dreams to propel them forward. Dare with all of you because this is yours to do and I and the Angels have the utmost faith in you and in your dreams. Dare with all of you because you must dare, because something deep inside you dares to dare and will not be silenced, and will not be refused. Dare with all of you because the Divine part of you knows that this is what you can do and what you must do too.

Be who you truly are

Be who you truly are and you will not be silenced. Be who you truly are and you will not be ignored. You will not be turned away and all doors will open for you. Do not think that there is no power in who you are. There is great power. There is the greatest power in who you are and all that you are. Be who you truly are so that the world will come to know you quickly. Be who you truly are so that you can express your perspective and your potential to the world. When you are not truly who you are, when you are busy being another, then the world does not know the true shape of you. The universe does not know the true shape of you. They do not know the clay you are made of. They do not know what you will become or what you can do. Much simpler to be who you truly are from the beginning and then you will be shaped and stretched and pulled by the forces that be, by the universe, by the external events. And you will be shaped and stretched by these and you will take form and your form will be an expression of yourself and of the world at the same time. And then your actions, thoughts, and words will represent your full potential, and you will be able to act, you will be able to do and to change and shape things. Be who you truly are because the world and all of humanity needs the trueness of you. We need the trueness of you to help move the world forward, to help with the progress of all things. Be who you truly are so that you may contribute your light in the best possible way to your own life and to the world too.

Be free

Be free to be who you are. Do not shy away from yourself and from the right and full expression of yourself. Be free to do what you have to do in the world. If you think that things are holding you back, you need to think about this and see what you can do. Be free to be the most ideal you that you can be. Be free and be aligned with yourself, with your true self. There is a self deep within you that is waiting to be known by you. There is a self deep within you that is your Universal self, that is your Divine self. How can you get to know this self? You must listen to the depths within you. You must listen to the inner voice within you, the one that tells you what is good for you and what is not good for you. It is not only your conscience that you must listen to. You must listen to your conscience of course. But you need to listen further, to the other parts of your internal world that are speaking to you. You have a vast internal world. You have a vast connection to God, the Divine, and to the Universe. Whether this is part of your reality, whether this is part of your awareness, is a different story. You might not be aware. You might not be fully alive with this knowledge. But trust me when I say this to you. You have a vast storehouse within you. You have a vast storehouse of all that has ever been, and all that is now, and all that will be. All of this resides within you. This enormous repository of knowledge and of spirit and of energy. All of it is there. And it may not be that you can access all of it. You may not be aware of all your possibilities and all your actualities past, present, and future. It may be that this is too overwhelming to consider and maybe you don't believe it anyway. But listen, all the same, to the voice within you. Because it can tell you everything you need to know and will ever need to know. It can tell you everything about yourself and the things you believe and the reasons that you believe these things. It can tell you about the people in your life and why they say and do the things that they do. All of this is freely available to you. Look inside to that vast storehouse and to that truth-speaking voice that you have. Look inside and listen and be free enough to open yourself up to this knowledge and to everything it can tell you and give you. Be free. You only have to be free.

Be happy

The Angels wish for you to be happy. The Angels and God and I wish for you to be happy. It is important for you to have happiness. It is important for you to be happy and to do the things that make you happy and that happiness is a part of your life now and always. Do not wait to be happy. Do not wait for a particular event to come about or a particular thing to come to pass before you can be happy. You can be happy now, and you can be happy regardless of your circumstances. Commit to being happy now and watch the world open around you. Commit to being happy now and see how that makes you feel. Joy can reside within you. Happiness can reside within you. You can be as happy as you dare to be. And you must be happy. You must be happy, for that needs to be your default state. Happiness does not have to be available to you in scattered moments and only upon certain occasions. Happiness can be present for you right now and it can be present for you always. All the happiness in the world is available to you and to everyone. All of this is available. You might have to dare to be happy. We encourage you to do this. It might be that happiness is not accepted in your environment. It might be that happiness is frowned upon, and that joy is viewed with suspicion. Pray that this will change. Pray that the state of happiness will spread in your environment and be happy anyway. Be happy if the weather is not good. Be happy if circumstances are not perfect. Be happy even if some things go wrong. If happy is your default then life will be brighter and easier for you. Commit to a life of happiness and peace.

Be content

Be content. Wherever and however you find yourself be content. If things are not perfect with you and where and how you are then search for that little thing that is okay and grab hold of it. If you do not feel at peace in your environment or situation then reach inside yourself and discover how much inner peace you have. If you want to change things, you will find it within yourself to change things. If you want things to improve, set your intention and put your energy into this. But be content also. Be content with who you are and where you are and see how you can rise from it. Be content with how things are and then you will see the good in things. And if there truly is no good in where you are be content in your strength and your stamina and have faith that things will change for you. The Angels are reaching out to help you and you must ask them for assistance. The Angels request that you ask. And the Angels request that you put faith in yourself, more faith perhaps than you have. They have perfect faith in you. And when you start from a point of contentment, from a place of equanimity then you will have a vantage point, then you will have a place to stand. You will be able to go forward and do a lot of things. And these will lead to your success and happiness and they will lead to a life of peace too.

Be at peace

The Angels would like to say to you that peace is the most important thing. Peace is the most important way of being. You have to be at peace before you can do anything else. You have to be at peace before you can be content and happy, with yourself and others. You have to be at peace so that you can stop worrying and being anxious about your life and the things that are going on. If you are at peace, if you can put yourself in a state of peace, then life is much easier. If nothing can rattle you then you will see always how best to deal with the things that you are going through. Be at peace, the Angels urge. Be at peace because this is the strongest position you can take. You make yourself strong when you are at peace. You make yourself strong and you will be able to live your life in a way that is more suited to you, that is good for you. When you are at peace, then the world will be at peace with you too. The world will be at peace with you and with everyone who is similarly at peace. Perhaps this peace will take hold and spread beyond you and enter into the consciousness of the world. Perhaps this peace within yourself is more valuable than you know. Make an effort to be at peace. Make an effort to be imbued with peace and communicate it outwards to the world. Dare to be at peace. It is the most important thing you can do.

Float freely

Float freely in your life. Float freely and be happy to experience life the way that it comes to you. You may think that your life is too slow, too mundane and that you need adventure. You may think that your life is too chaotic or filled with difficult things. Whatever the case it is good to let go. Let go of your feelings about your life right now and float freely in it. Float freely and allow yourself to go where you are led, where you are meant to be. Listen to the things that are calling you – from outside and from within. Listen to the signs and signals around you that tell you where you should be or what you should be working on. Maybe some of the things you are doing right now feel forced to you. Maybe some of the things you are involved with do not feel right to you. Let go of them. Let go of them and go instead to things and people that are more appealing to you. Maybe you feel obligated in your life. Maybe you feel obligated by commitments or by people around you. Let go of these too. See how you can lighten your obligations. See how you can let go of the things that are hemming you in. Seek instead to be more free and more at peace. Seek instead to be freer. When you learn how to float more freely then you will more easily be taken towards the things that are important and the people that matter. False obligations and false ties will hem you in no longer. Trust that you will be free this way. Trust that you can live this easily. Dare to live this easily. Dare to float freely.

Be free

Be free in all that you do and all that you are. Be free in your
thoughts and in your considerations. Take the time to know
yourself completely and thoroughly. Be free in your estimations of
what is important to you. Be free in your evaluation of your worth
and of what aligns truly with you. Be free and honest with yourself
because your life is being guided by your thoughts. Your life is
improved by the honesty you bring to bear upon it. If you are
honest with your ideas, if you are honest with yourself about what
you think about things, then you will know yourself. You will know
what it is that suits you and what you need to turn away from.
Consider your own self in this. Consider your own self and your
own counsel before the counsel of others. Consider your own self
and be free within yourself. Be free to develop yourself. Be free to
develop your inner world and your connection to the outer world.
Be free to experience the way the world is and do not filter it
through expectations or false understandings. Be free to know too
what you are and what you bring to the world and how you
connect to it. You must be strong in your self-definition and in your
sense of yourself. You must be strong in your awareness and in
your ability to communicate yourself. This is how you can be free –
by being fully self-articulated, by being fully self-aware. When you
do this, when you develop yourself to this degree, then you will be
stronger and freer than you have been. Then you will be better able
to interact with the world and to know who you are within it.

Attain happiness

It is important to attain happiness, to actually achieve this state. We
can spend a long time in trying to be happy, in trying to find this

state. We must decide, however, that we will find this state and that we have found this state. It is better to live in a state of happiness than to not live in this state. It is better too to say that we have attained it and to say that we have arrived at it already. We may want to argue about certain details. We may want to say this is not right or that is not right. But even if there remain things that need improving, even if things are not completely picture perfect, we must let it lie where it is. We must accept this picture of happiness. We are not asking you to accept something less than what you need and what you want. We are asking you to recognize that there might be a tolerance range that you could accept, that could enter into your definition of what happiness is. If you live from the state of happiness, from the conviction and the certainty that you are happy, then you will see these minor things as nothing to much be worried about. If you live from the certain state of happiness then you will find easier ways to deal with these things and even alter and change them. Do not tell yourself that happiness is just a few minutes or days or changes away. Tell yourself that it is here now. Look around and observe the happiness that you have and that is possible for you. Look at it and let it inform you and fill you. Let yourself be cognizant of your happiness. Let it be inspiring and sustaining and rejuvenating. This happiness can enter your body and rejuvenate your cells. This happiness can enter your mind and spirit and refresh it, taking away all that is old and tired. The state of happiness is a fuel that sustains you. The state of happiness is a way of being so that you can be at peace and fulfilled. Attain it now and live from within this state. This state does not need to wait for perfection. This state only requires that you accept happiness from where you are right now.

Dare to dream

Dare to dream because you can and because within you, and within your mind and spirit, all things are possible. Dare to dream because you can afford, always, to let your imagination soar. Dare to dream because your heart needs to be happy and all of you needs to have joy. Dare to dream so that you can release your voice to the world and express the trueness of all that is you. The world needs your ideas and your spirit and your imagination. The world needs your dreams and your courage and your perfection. The world needs all that is uniquely you. When you shut down your dreams, when you do not dream your dreams, then the world becomes a little lost, the world then tries to seek out what is missing. But the world cannot find you if you choose to hide. The universe cannot help you if you refuse all assistance. Dare to dream and dare to tell others and the world your dream. Dare to dream, and dare to let your imagination and your capability take over in the dreaming and the doing. Dare to dream and be bold in your aspirations and in your ideas. Do not hide your light. Do not hide and conceal your Divine source. Release it to the world. Show the world the beauty of your dreams. Show this to the world so that we may all create the most wondrous future together. Your dreams, and all of our dreams are the linchpin for the future. Your dreams, and all of our dreams are the recipe for the happiness and the conscious self-realization of the planet. Dream little dreams and dream big dreams. Dream that all of us may profit. Dream that all of us may reap the rewards of your unique expression, of your voice and of your imagination. Your spirit and your soul do not need to be confined any longer. Dream your dreams and dare to unfold them and to create them. Dare to make them real.

Dare to have

Dare to have and to make having a good thing. Dare to release any ideas you have that having is not good and that you should remain as you are. Dare to shed all the vestiges of the old world where success is not always valued, and doing well is sometimes disparaged. Dare to erase all that from your subconscious. Dare to release all of that. We need you to be pure in heart and in spirit. We need you to have so that you may give to the world. We need you to have so that you may truly be who you are. We need you to have so that you may be comfortable and happy. What do you need to have? Think about this and think about it in a contemplative spirit. You may need a little or a lot. You may need a particular kind of thing. What you need doesn't matter. What you need is not important. But needing is important. It needs to be acknowledged. It needs to be fulfilled. Be happy with having. Be happy with the idea of prosperity. Don't shut yourself off from it. Don't push it away or fail to reach out and have what presents itself to you. Having is important for your peace of mind and for your creativity and spirit. You may have problems with having. You may think that it makes you not a good person. You may think that you should not have, or that you should only have enough. These are old ideas. These are outdated ideas. But they are within us. They are within us individually, in our consciousness and in the consciousness of the world. When we are faced with the idea that not everyone in the world is abundant, we may then deny ourselves the right to have. But in denying ourselves this, then we contribute to the lack of abundance in the world. We become part of the problem. Better to have abundance. Better to develop our own path to abundance and then to show others that path too, or to share our abundance with others. Do not deny yourself having. Do not deny yourself this. Dare to have. Dare to have always.

Dare to want

Dare to want and to let your desires have expression. Dare to want and to acknowledge that there are things that would add to your life. Dare to want and to feel the sense of wanting. Dare to be aware of it and to let it shape you. The wants that arise from within us sometimes seem to come from somewhere else. Are we compelled without knowing why? Can we channel these feelings? Can we suppress them even? The nature of want is that it demands acknowledgement and awareness. The nature of want is that it will be heard. So approach it in this way. Listen to what you are being told by your own self. Listen to what those wants and desires are. Listen to them and acknowledge them. And then you can see if you should pursue them. Then you can see if they are in your best interest to do something about. Then you can see if they point to something else. You can honour your wants and desires but you must make sure that they are healthy and right for you first. You must make sure that they are things that will contribute to your life and not hurt others. You must make sure that they are sustaining. Look at this freely without judgement. Look at this clearly with your whole heart. Then you will know what kind of action to take or whether to take any action. Then you will know what to do. Dare to want. And dare to be honest about this and then see how it will impact you and how it will shape you.

Dare to claim

Dare to claim the things that you want and need. Dare to claim them if they are right for you and if they are healthy and do not hurt or harm others. Dare to claim them if they are ethical and responsible. After your evaluation, after you have decided that they are right and healthy and sustaining, then dare to claim them. Do not shy away from claiming what you need. Do not say to yourself, there will be another time. Do not say to yourself that you do not need this now or that you do not really need this. Think always about what you need and the repercussions of those needs and desires. And if you have decided that they are positive, then dare to make them real. Dare to step out of the confines of your imaginings, and to make them real. Dare to see if the real fulfillment of these needs matches what you thought it would. Dare to see if the reality fulfills the dream. When you dare this way, then you will grow. When you dare this way, then you will complete a part of yourself. You will be more fulfilled. You will be expanded. In your expansion you will understand more things, you will have more awareness. Perhaps more dreams will emerge. Perhaps other needs and desires will emerge. Dare to see if the reality is important to you. You will shape your mind and your intellect and your feelings this way. You will shape your interactions with the world. You will change and this change will affect you positively and negatively. This is part of your personal journey. Dare to claim because until you do you will never be fully whole, you will never be fully realized and you will miss a side of yourself that you did not know was there.

Dare

Dare with all your heart and mind and spirit. Dare with your soul too. Dare because it is the thing you must do in order to be realized in your life. Dare because it is the thing you must do in order to fully express yourself and to be fully present in the world. If you hide in the shadows or the corners then you will have a great knowledge of shadows and corners but of little else. If you feel too afraid to venture out and to be in the world, or to dare at all, then you will only be intimately acquainted with your own fears, with your own thoughts. Dare because this is how you bring yourself to the world. Dare because this is how you present yourself in the world and to the world. Dare because you need to be a fully articulated being, a fully realized being. Dare because you need to be strong, and your endurance will not develop by hanging back and hiding. Dare because you are strong and because the world needs you. Dare because this is the fulfilment of your destiny. Dare because you are everything that you can be and you do not know it yet. Dare because your true self and your universal self needs you to do this, needs you to fully express yourself to the world and to yourself. Dare because your inner self needs to be truly aligned and you cannot be aligned if you are not fully you. Dare because you don't know all the colours and textures that you are. Dare because you are special and important and because you are significant in the world. Dare because when you do you demonstrate your capabilities and you demonstrate your towering presence. Dare because then your creativity will know no bounds. Dare because you can and because it will fill your heart with joy and with everything. Dare in all ways and in all manner of being. Dare and everything will be created for you and for the best things that you need. Dare and be whole in your daring. Dare and be whole in all ways.

Dare always and dare anyway

In life, daring is not necessary but required somehow. It is required if you are to have the best life that you can. It is required if you are to have an ideal life. It is required when you need to stand up for who and what you are. It is required when you need to find out who you are and declare it to the world. Somehow daring is required. Even if you want to hide and not reveal yourself truly, and even if you want to not be fully present, daring will still be required of you. Daring will still come to you to do. So do not wait. Do not wait to take your life into your own hands and to shape it how you want to. Do not wait for someone else to tell you who you are and what to do and who to be. Do not wait. Dare instead as you can. Dare always and dare anyway. Dare because daring will always bring you closer to your goal. Dare because daring will tell you who you are in a way that nothing else will. Dare because daring is important to your sense of self and self-definition. Dare because it is in your identity that you find your power. Dare because your identity is yours and if you do not dare, your knowledge of this might be clouded and hidden from you. Dare because you are important to the world and until you dare, you will not know this. Dare because your significance is as yet unmeasured and untapped. Dare because you are needed and dare because you need to do this. When you dare, the pieces will fall into place. When you dare, the steps you take will lead to other steps and actions and to things that you have not imagined. Dare that your dreams be realized and dare that you live freely in the world. Dare that your hopes always overshadow your fears. Dare that you can stand tall and be proud of who you are and what you can do. Dare too so that you can help others and teach them how to dare also. Dare so that you may be free. And dare so that you can display and model the kinds of actions that take root in the world. The world will see your efforts. The world will see all that you do. Dare so that everything you had hoped for will be realized and so that your false fears will finally fall away. Dare always, dare anyway. May you always be at peace and have happiness, joy, and hope in your heart. Namaste

The Closing of the Realm

Once, a long time ago, many eons ago, the Realm was shut tight. The Realm was shuttered and no one could enter or leave. That was not perhaps strictly true. B could enter and leave. Her supporters could enter and leave. But the true residents and rulers of the Realm could not. The true rulers had been banished, or had left, depending on your understanding of the story. And now B was in charge. And she set many things in motion. So many things that your head would spin. So many things that were not good and that were the epitome of all that was not good. She had many supporters. Most of them had been coerced into their roles. Some found their roles appealing though. They liked the power they had and they did not mind the evil that went along with it. Somehow this kind of behaviour led to many things in the Realm, and in our world too, that were not appropriate, that were misguided. We had wars and we had strife. We had poverty and we had dictators. The brutalization of humanity had begun. B was responsible but she was not alone. She had many followers.

The rulers of the Realm looked upon this in shock. They did not quite understand, when they left, the point to which things would get. But at the same time they had an inkling. They had an inkling about this and really most of this was allowed to happen. It was allowed to happen because certain things had to be understood and seen for what they were. Certain things had to be known. And we could not have known it just by imagining. We could not have known it just by thinking things through. We had to put a plan together and see what the agents of change would do, we had to see what they were capable of. They always had free will – B and her followers always had free will. But they mostly chose to do the wrong thing. They mostly chose to advance their purpose and goals in the worst way possible. Why was this so? They did not see the end game obviously. They also did not think through their results. They did not think about where this all would get them and why they would want it. What was the use of all the power in the world? What was the use of all that? They didn't know necessarily but it was a hunger in them and so they chased it. They abandoned the good and the good abandoned them too. After a while they seemed to grow tired. After a while they seemed to lose their appetite for evil action. After a while, even evil seemed banal to them.

B knew after a while that things had to change. She knew too, after a while, that this had been a really long game and that she was the protagonist. She knew too that she was not really getting much in the way of what she wanted. She had gotten everything she wanted but after a while she realized how empty this was. Eternity is a long time to spend being empty. And B was eternal, just like all of us. But she knew this to be true. And in her eternal emptiness she had created her own damnation, the Realm notwithstanding. That is to say, it did not matter that she had appointed herself the ruler of the Realm, no one else would talk to her, except for a few mindless followers. And so after a point in time she relaxed her grip and allowed things to slip. She relaxed her grip and admitted that this was all rather pointless.

At this point it wasn't as if things became magically better in our world. The dictators didn't all die off to be replaced by healthy democracies. Corruption and abuse didn't suddenly cease to exist. But still some kind of tide had turned. We all realized, all 8 billion of us, that we were free. We all realized, every last one of us, that we were not owned and that we could make our own decisions. We all rose up, in some big ways and some little ways. And more injustices were redressed. More wrongs were righted. And people began to see a way to heal themselves and each other. People began to see a way to not live in fear anymore. Somehow the tide had turned.

The real rulers of the Realm came back or were coming back and all was well. B requested just a small garden for herself to live in and the rulers said that they did not think that would be fitting given all the hurt that had been done. The verdict on B is still out. Maybe it will always be out. But the verdict on all of us is not out. We are free to live our lives in the best way possible. We are free to live our lives without evil and without evil or less than good choices on our part. We are free and this is the thing we must celebrate. Live your life in the best way possible, for you and for the people around you. Live your life from the place of most good and in the most Divine way possible. The realm was closed. But it is closed no longer. The Realm was closed and now that it has opened, we can have a lot more peace than we could have ever imagined. So live in Peace. Live in Peace. Namaste

(Other Tales We Could Not Tell)

There are other tales we could not tell up to now. There have been other tales that perhaps we can now somewhat release to the world.

Tales of being constrained in society, economically, in order to truly experience the gravity of nothing.

Tales of not being believed and of being thought dreamers and non-realists because certain words and experiences were far beyond the understanding of the mainstream.

Tales of being held back from bringing powerful new techniques to the world because too many other factors were still in play.

Tales of doubt and belief and repeated redemption and confirmation that all we were doing and seeing and feeling was real.

Tales of how the Angelic realm crosses over to touch us and work with us each and every day.

The Angels want me to say that you cannot fully know our journey and that many parts of it would not make sense to you.

And that they also want you to know that you have your own mystical and wonderful journey that you are living and that you need to open your eyes a bit wider and then you will see all that you need to see in all ways.

The Laws of Wonder

Introduction

The Angels have given me some information about our world, about the way it works and about how we can interact with it to have a better experience for our lives.

They sometimes give me information about interesting ideas and ways of looking at things that are beyond the normal subjects that we tend to preoccupy ourselves with as humans.

From their Angelic perspective and understanding, they can see things in new contexts, and clearly they are not restricted by our particular frames of reference.

The Angels want me to introduce you to something called the *Laws of Wonder*.

They are natural laws that govern our world and do not have any negative impact on us. Only a positive one if we choose to follow them.

Of course the obvious reminder is to the Laws of Attraction. The Laws of Wonder are different than these. The Angels are not disputing the Laws of Attraction. But, they are saying, the Laws of Wonder are so much better. And indeed they are.

So what are the Laws of Wonder?

These are ways of living that can enrich our human experience in every way.

They can open us to abundance, to love, to energy, to friendship, to connection. They are about our ability to interact with the world, with each other, with the Divine in ways that can make us feel completely at peace and completely at One with All.

There are nine Laws in all. Here is what the Angels say about how they can help you in your life, how you can implement these laws to bring you wonder and abundance, happiness and joy.

These are Laws that can help you welcome peace in your heart.

The Law of Enchantment

The first Law of Wonder is the *Law of Enchantment*.

The Law of Enchantment is the blessing of being able to be enchanted in big ways and small; the ability in yourself to enchant also - and to bring more of this wonder into the world.

Enchantment is not a thing that is reserved just for children. Enchantment is wonder at its most precious and distilled level.

Can you allow yourself to be enchanted? Are you too grown-up to be charmed?

Try to bring the wonder of enchantment into your life. Allow yourself to be pleased just a little. Allow yourself to be very pleased. And then allow yourself to be enthusiastic about the whole experience.

You have just experienced the first step of enchantment.

One thing to note – enchantment doesn't quite work with sarcasm, anger, or bad feelings. Suspend any negative emotions that are running through you. And allow yourself to feel delighted, at peace, in bliss, contented. Allow yourself to feel the wonder of life and of the space you inhabit in it.

Simple rules for bringing more enchantment (and wonder) into your life:

1. Pause to experience the moment that you're in. Don't just live in the moment though, or even fully engage. Pause to look at what aspects of that moment bring you wonder and joy. Are the surroundings beautiful? Does someone give you a beautiful smile? Do you observe that things are working in synchronicity at this moment. Pause and dwell in that. Allow yourself the luxury of registering a moment of enchantment in yourself.

2. Think about the small things that you can do to enrich a particular experience for yourself. Is there something that you can add? Is there something that you can take away? What small thing can you do to make it more meaningful or more vibrant for you. Take the time to make something more right for you in this moment, or in an experience that you are having. Small things can multiply to bring more wonder to your life. Try some of these ideas and see how the beauty of small improvements to your life can bring enchantment to you.

3. Think about how you can add enchantment to your interactions with others. Consider how in your dealings with people you might make them feel better. Consider how your interactions might be more pleasant. Consider how you do your work too and how you could make that more appealing to those who receive the things that you make and create in the world. Do this from an honest place. Do

this without compromising yourself. Take the time to add some wonder to the world.

These are simple steps, deceptively simple. But they are valuable because they have not been paid attention to. There has been such a rough and tumble quality often to life here on earth. Some of the magic is gone. This concept of enchantment, the first Law of Wonder, is about bringing some of that magic back. Could you, perhaps use, a little more magic in your life? Even the attempt at enchantment can bring you joy. Try out these ideas and see if they bring your life into a more harmonious and delightful space. Enjoy the process of adding wonder and enchantment to your life. It will be richly fulfilling to you and enhance your life in many ways.

The Law of Liberty

The second Law of Wonder is the *Law of Liberty.*

The Law of Liberty is the law that upholds liberty as one of the most perfect aspects of our existence.

Where there is liberty, there is life. Where there is liberty, the soul and spirit can soar beautifully and freely and magnificently. Where liberty is diminished or absent, life itself suffers. The curtailing of liberty is the ultimate curtailing of wonder in the world.

The importance of freedom cannot be underestimated in terms of adding or taking away value from life, from a society and from the world.

In discussing liberty in the world, it is important to discuss this in terms of how you can add more liberty to your life. It is important to start with that. But it is also then important to look at how you might bring more liberty and freedom into your environment – to people you know, to your society and to your world.

Make it a practice that you will gently resist intolerances related to liberty.

Begin by articulating the lack of liberty in a situation. Whether your focus is the disempowerment of a whole group or assisting a family member that is having trouble with power dynamics in their own family, there is much you can do.

Add your voice to bring more liberty to the world. You will naturally add wonder to it. You will naturally add wonder to your own.

It is important to stand for things and principles and to stand up for other people too. Isn't that what the best stories are about?

Take small steps today and every day to add wonder and liberty to the world and see how you can contribute to the epic tale of man and womankind that is unfolding all around you.

Here are some steps that the Angels say would be helpful to you in bringing more liberty to your life and to the world.

1. Take measures always and everywhere to note the amount of liberty in a situation. Just in taking the step of noticing what the level of liberty is, you will effect a change in the situation and the energy of it. You will also feel more likely to articulate your views and do something about any lack of liberty if you make it a practice to always notice this.

2. Adopt a zero tolerance attitude against any kind of infringement of liberty in your very person. Carry this with you in your presence and people will understand that they cannot act a certain way around you. Maybe you have not intrinsically changed the person by doing this. But you will have increased the amount of liberty in the world. This is because acts that are counter to liberty will not be able to be

done in your presence. You will have raised the bar and that helps everyone. Every time we raise the bar, that bar is raised not just in your life and your sphere of influence but everywhere else too.

3. Question the structures for the defense of liberty wherever you are and wherever you have influence. Is liberty adequately defended? Are there any changes that can be made to the rules or structures that can increase the amount of liberty available? Do not discount small steps. Many small steps together can achieve a lot of liberty in the world. Look for gaps in the structures that protect liberty and improve them. If there are flagrant holes in these structures, or if they are a sham or non-existent, see what work you can do to ameliorate these conditions too.

These are some steps that the Angels say would be helpful to add liberty to the world and wonder to it as well. See how this makes sense in your life. See what truth and liberty you can create today in the world.

The Law of Aliveness

The Law of Aliveness is the third Law of Wonder.

The Law of Aliveness - the ability and blessing to be fully alive in the world, to be at play with all the energies around you - not to be susceptible or to dominate but to be at play - to be in perfect enjoyment of the beingness of being alive

The Law of Aliveness is about the moreness of life. The frisson of energy that you can see on the drop of water on the leaf. The earth in the springtime. The smell after the rain.

It is the whipped cream on your sundae, the feeling of joy you have as you sit by a fire or drink some tea. The sweetness of a new baby. The affections and loyalty of a favourite pet.

It is the pleasure of good company, the pleasure of good food. The feeling of your soul spreading and soaring. The feeling of your soul resting easily where it needs to be.

It is the feeling of certainty. The surge of confidence. The feeling of success, of a job well done, of an obstacle surmounted.

Can you feel these things? Can these joys be yours. Can the aliveness you see around you, can you feel this in you?

This Law of aliveness will enrich your life in all ways. It is the way to be in the world. Always in harmony with the energies of life. Always the sense of being in play.

In this joy, in this aliveness, in this flow of life you will feel more bliss than you thought could exist, more joy will surge through your veins, more laughter will erupt from you, more magnitudes of happiness will be available to you.

How can you make Aliveness more of a practice for you in your life? The Angels have some suggestions about how you can be more present and more alive in all aspects of your life.

1. Begin always with the present moment. Embrace it fully in all ways. Breathe into it and experience it. Look at what you like about it and look at what you do not.
2. Allow for aliveness to be present in your life. Do not turn it away thinking that it is not supposed to be a part of your existence, that it is not something that you are supposed to have. Do not feel that you have to live only on the surface. Allow yourself to have the depth of experience available to you. Allow yourself to have the space, the experiential range

to experience Aliveness. Do not discount it's presence. Do not discount it's value to you.

3. Acknowledge aliveness and articulate aliveness to others. Comment on how beautiful things are on the scent of the rain, on the happiness of a child, on the beauty of a smile. Seek to encourage more aliveness in others. Smile when they do not. Lighten the mood. Allow others to recognize that aliveness and the beauty of existence are their birthright. You do this by your conscious experience of aliveness and all the ways that you bring it to others.

Do not forsake aliveness. Do not think that this very simple thing is not important. It is a magnificent thing and it will add wonder to your life and to the world too.

The Law of Kindness

The law of kindness is the fourth law of wonder. It speaks about compassion and the good treatment of all others. When you have kindness, you have civility in the world. When you have kindness you have a practice of non aggression, you have a practice of doing good that inspires others to do good in turn.

The presence of kindness in the world naturally adds more wonder to the world. The presence of kindness adds more self-worth to all things, gives all who are treated with kindness more dignity, and increases the dignity of the person who acts kindly to others.

Whenever you find kindness or practice kindness you create more beauty in the world, you create more beauty, nurturing and love. You ease the tensions in the world created by ugliness and hate. You erase these things and make the world new.

It is up to you to practice the law of kindness in your own life, towards others and towards yourself. This is the way that you add to the value of the whole world. With a kind thought, a kind word, a kind gesture, you may open up possibility where there was despair. You may give someone the very tool that they needed at that precise moment of their lives. What a wonderful part you can play, just by being kind.

The law of kindness means that wonder can flourish in the world. Wonder will grow in an atmosphere of goodness and hope. Wonder will grow when there is a helping hand when the world seems kind in itself too.

This law of wonder is in many ways the law of civic responsibility. What it is that you can do to make the world a kinder place? Each time you add to the kindness quotient of the world, you add to your own well-being in the world too and most importantly you increase the goodness of the world too. When you add kindness and wonder to the world then beautiful things can happen for all and wonder can occur.

The Law of Awareness

The law of awareness speaks to the use of the senses in all ways to help you in your life. These senses are all the senses that you know and includes the sense of intuition or connection to the divine.

Your senses and your awareness are what help you to plug in to your world. They are what help you to realize the wonder of everything around you from the smallest detail to the largest experience that you can have.

Your awareness is what enables you to look outside of yourself, to experience your world outside the bounds of your prescribed experience, outside the general description of your life. You can see, touch, feel, smell and know a variety and panoply of experiences just by tuning into your senses and allowing them to guide you in your life. This can give you a richness and an extra dimension to your life and increase your sense of wonder in the world.

Everything around you can become magical when you do this, when you explore with your senses and with your energy even the world around you. Your inner world too becomes a more fertile place too. Awareness and your senses can let your imagination take hold.

Awareness can also have meaning to do with the sageness of action, the wisdom of right action. And this is also very true in terms of the law of wonder.

When you act with sensitivity with discernment, you are respecting the natural flow of things. The natural expression of energy. The acknowledgement of equality between people.

In the law of wonder, this law of awareness speaks to the personal joy and experience of an individual in the world, and it speaks to how they can treat others and affect their joy and experience of life in the world too.

The law of awareness means to be aware in all things, in your actions, in your knowledge of yourself in the world and in all the ways that you interact with it. Govern your actions and use awareness to act in concert with all things. In experiencing this togetherness with all you will experience wonder and bring it to others too.

The Law of Love

The Laws of Wonder are about how to have more wonder and more of everything good in your life and in the world as a whole. The presence of Love in the world, the existence of love in the world is a key component of this in so many ways.

The ability to love fully and the ability to receive love fully is both the expression and experience of wonder at the same time - by the giving and receiving of love you are delighted in both ways.

The presence of love in the world eases the difficulties of the world, eases the difficulty of so many factions, so many people, so many different groups contained within the same vehicle, contained within the same container called Earth.

How is it that you can all strive to have something? How is it that you can all fight to have your portion of something? How can this be done without tearing things apart? Without creating a rift and a rent in the whole of everything?

The presence of Love is the joining force – it is the glue that binds when things are difficult – it is the joy that is yours to have at all times. The weaving force of love to weave through many disparate interests, many disparate aspects of this entire world. Can you not marvel at that? Is that not in itself a source of wonder?

The existence and creation of love in your world is what strengthens you and it strengthens the world too. The more love that you have, the more that you can express, creates a better source, a better foundation of love in the world. The world, and all its peoples, feed from this source, feed from the source of love that you yourself are emanating.

If the world could not love, then it would be a cold sunless place. If you cannot love right now. If you do not feel love from anyone or anything, seek to engender it in all ways that you can. Seek to see love in the world. Seek to acknowledge the presence of love in whatever way you see it occurring, even if it is not personally occurring for you.

Forgive others their lack of love, and forgive yourself too where you have found it difficult to love. But above all, try again. Try to love so that you can create this force of goodness in the world. And as the world becomes more and more blessed, and more and more filled with love, you and all others will feel the wonder of that. You will feel the wonder and the love breathing from the very soul of the earth. And this too will emanate forth to all peoples of the earth and bathe them with this sense that nothing is wrong, that everything is right and that all is well and that love is strengthening them in every way possible.

The Law of Magnificence

The Law of Magnificence - the magnificence and majesty of who you are, of who you are at the core of you, when you let it shine out you bring wonder to the world - you express your Divine nature and shine a Divine beam upon the world

The Laws of Wonder have to do with Wonder in the world and this sense of wonder, this sense that everything can be wonder-ful extends even to yourself, personally.

We see this in the Law of Wonder known as the Law of Magnificence.

The Law of Magnificence is about the magnificence and majesty of who you are, of who you are at the core of you.

If this light at the core of you is dimmed, or finds it difficult to burn brightly, then your magnificence is dimmed too and you are bringing less wonder to the world and to yourself than you could be doing.

If you let your light shine out to the world, you express your Divine nature and you shine a Divine beam upon the world.

You are a part of the Divine. And your magnificence, through the light that comes through you, brings light, magnificence and Divinity to the world.

You are a source of Divine for yourself and for all that is around you. You yourself bring wonder to the world.

This law of magnificence extends to all things and all people. All things and all people have an innate spirit, an innate essence that is capable of shining brightly and of bringing wonder and indeed more peace and harmony to the world.

How can we increase the amount of magnificence in the world? How can we increase the amount of wonder in the world?

It is by allowing your spirit to shine and to not be clouded. It is by allowing the spirit of everyone else to do the same. It is by allowing the expression of Divine nature that is inherent in all people and things to freely be, and to freely be expressed.

You cannot be magnificent if you are afraid or worried that you are not good enough. You are magnificent in and of yourself. You need to be at peace with that. You need to be at peace that you were created as a magnificent creature, a magnificent expression of the Divine, and Divine yourself.

Here are some ideas and exercises for you to reattune yourself to this idea, and to gain a new perspective on yourself, and yes to begin to reclaim your magnificence and to augment it in all ways that you can.

The Law of Grace

Grace is forgiveness and love in action. Grace is patience, waiting for things to materialize, certain that they will in their best form, in all the good that they are capable of being.

Grace is the attitude that says that all people and things deserve respect and deserve the respect of allowance, of the assumption that they are acting in good faith, that they are acting the best way they know how.

Grace takes the high way always. Grace does not look at pettiness, does not acknowledge it. Rather Grace allows for everyone's best selves to emerge, for everyone's highest self to take their role, to play their part.

Grace does not say you did this to me and therefore I must do this to you.

Grace does not say you have taken from me and so then I must take from you.

Grace instead says you have done what you have done and it matters no longer.

You have taken what you have taken and pray that it serve you.

Grace is not about the excusing of bad things, nor is it a way of making room for evil acts to be allowed. Rather it comes from a place of strength, and says if these things have transpired how are we to understand them? What do we need to change and heal in ourselves and in each other so that we can surmount this, so that we can find a better way to exist? How can we turn to the Divine too and let all of this be washed away? How can we be made whole, after all of this, and because of all of this?

Grace is important to turn inwards too. Grace is important in alleviating your anger towards yourself, towards others. This is not about taking what has happened. It is about rising above it and going on gracefully and magnificently and wholly in every way.

The Law of Angels

The Laws of Wonder invite us to consider how we can bring more Wonder into our lives and into the world around us. They invite us to bring more magic into our lives.

The Law of Angels or of Angelic Involvement takes this one step further. This law is about how we can extend this magic and sense of wonder and multiply it exponentially through the help of the Angels. This is the new and surprising Law – the idea and the blessing that Angels can help us in our lives.

All these Laws of Wonder culminate with this one. These Laws show how Wonder adds beauty and Grace to life on earth and in the physical plane of existence.

The Law of Angels is the law that states that Angels not only can help us in our lives but also bring the perfect wonder of the Divine to all that we do and all that we are. They bestow wonder and gifts upon us just by their presence.

If there is Kindness, and Awareness, and Aliveness, and Grace, and Enchantment and Liberty and Magnificence and Love in the world and in your life, be assured that the Angels are there also. How can they not be present in the presence of these various expressions of Divinity?

And so you are encouraged to enhance your life further, enhance your experience of this earthly plane further to all that it can be, simply by including them in your life in all ways that you can.

The Angels can be in communication with you to bestow these gifts upon you.

The Angels can help you in many ways.

This Law of Angels is not something to be forced upon you. It is simply there for your enjoyment, for the enhancement of your life in all ways.

If your life is grey, if it is in need of some wonder, in need of some kind of new awakening, consider that the Angels can help you in this in all ways.

Some of you have fear about Angels or about things that are Divine. The Angels want to let you know that they have no wish to scare you, they have no wish to frighten you. Perhaps you could suspend for a little while, your fear of the unknown. Perhaps you could consider that you will live eternally and that they are here to be your friends, to help you to an extent that you cannot comprehend. If you start in little ways to allow them in your life, you may find it is not so difficult to accept the beneficence that they bring to you and your life.

How can you involve them in your life? Here are some ideas and exercises to get you started.

1. Let the Angels know that you want them to be part of your life. Simply talk to them inside yourself and let them know that you would like their assistance and guidance in all things. If you want to do this in a more formal way you can speak this aloud. If you don't know what to say here is what you can use – *Archangels Michael, Uriel, Raphael and Gabriel please assist me in my life in all ways from here on and help me in all the ways that are possible whether I ask directly for assistance or not. Please provide me with guidance and signs that I may easily recognize and follow and take care of me always and everywhere that I go and in all ways needed.* By speaking this out loud, or to yourself quietly even, you will let the Angels know that they can help you, and that they have a standing invitation to help you always.

2. Begin to listen and to watch for indications of Angelic guidance in your life. Listen to your inner voice – that is where the Angels will often communicate with you. Look at the pictures or images that you receive in your mind. Some of you will also hear words or even music lyrics in your head. Pay attention when you suddenly feel that you know

something. This is often the way that knowledge or information from the Angels will come to you. Begin with the understanding that you are connected to the Divine. You have this connection and there is nothing you have to do to improve it. You just have to recognize the connection and open yourself up to it in all the ways that you can. Listen for guidance. Look for signs, they will come to you. Ask the Angels to give you concrete signs about things. Ask them to show you proof about something in a certain way. When you do this you will build your confidence in terms of your communication with them and then you will be more able to recognize other signs as they are given to you.

3. Begin a practice too of journaling. Journal daily or however often you would like and write down things you might like to ask the Angels. Then see if you can get an answer. Journaling is very positive in many regards. It can help you sort out your thoughts and feelings about your life and what's going on in it. It is a good way to communicate with the Angels also. When you are journaling with the idea of communicating with Angels ask them about things that matter to you and see what answers you get. But you can also ask them about things that you don't matter so much to you because in those cases, at least at first, the answers may be easier for you to receive. It is a simple matter of training yourself to receive this guidance. And it also involves suspending your disbelief. This is not to say that you should not have any skepticism about messages that you receive. But instead it is to say that once you have tested this out and grown in the confidence of it, then you can trust these messages more and more. The Angels would also like to tell

you before you even begin any kind of exercise or practice of asking them for information, that they will never tell you to do anything negative or harmful against yourself or anyone else. Angels are only here to help and to assist you in the highest possible way and they only have your highest interest in mind when they are helping you. So pay attention as best as you can and see what kinds of interesting messages and guidance they have for you. Very often they will take you in an entirely different direction than you might go on your own and the results can be quite amazing and wonderful.

Communicating with the Angels is very rewarding and will add a great deal to your life. Their guidance and direction is also beneficial to you and will give you an additional perspective to base your decisions on. They do not want to take away from your own ideas about how to do things or how to live your life. They simply want to add an additional voice of counsel that is always true to what you need at that very moment. Take some simple steps and try these ideas and add the Angels to your life in whichever way feels right to you. This is a guaranteed way to add more wonder and more ease to your life in all ways.

Conclusion

The end was here. The ending time was here. The end time of stress and sorrow. The end time of difficulty and hardship. The end time of war and strife. The end time was here. The Angels had returned to the earth. The Angels have returned and they can help you now. Ask them for help in all ways that you need. Ask them for help and be blessed in all ways. Ask them for help and feel the blessings of the Divine upon you and upon your life.

The Angels request that you allow this book to nourish and complete you. Simply ask for this. Ask to be complete in and of yourself and in your person.

The end time of all that is wrong is here. Go then and celebrate. Go then and live your life in the best way you know how. The end time is here. Be at peace. Finally, be at peace.

About the Author

Anita Colussi-Zanon is an Angelic Intuitive and an Inner Influencing Master Practitioner. She helps people by targeting the issues that are affecting them and releasing energy blocks from their systems and self-conscious. She works with the Angels and uses the tool of Inner Influencing to remove old belief systems from the subconscious.

Anita's Angelic guidance comes to her mainly in the form of images and information that she receives about the person she is working with. The Angels tell her information about what the person is experiencing and feeling and also give her guidance on how best to use energy techniques to clear away these issues for her clients.

She is available for sessions over the phone and Skype. Please contact her at anita@angelsandinsights.com if you would like a session. More information is available on her website at www.AngelsandInsights.com.

You can also visit her website to sign up for free weekly emails which provide insights from the Angels, coaching, and other information. Please sign up today and receive a free bonus audio of this book as a thank you. Please go to http://www.angelsandinsights.com/books-of-light.php and sign up!

Notes Regarding the Website

The following is a sample of the 'Angelic Insights' on the website www.AngelsandInsights.com and what you will receive each week for free for signing up for her emails.

Angelic Insight on Love

"Love is a many-splendoured thing," says the famous poem. This is true, dear ones, but only if you can find the right one, the one that is right for you. Love does not live where abuse dwells, where cruelty abides. Love lives where freedom does. Love thrives where kindness flourishes.

To say otherwise is to deny yourself, to deny your humanity and the humanity of the one that you love.

Your intended, your beloved, who are they? Do you hold them up to a too high standard? Do you not hold them up to any standard at all?

Perhaps this is not about standards, but there should always be some kind of match in love. Is this not what you have talked about throughout your history? Match-making, always this concept of going together with another – one fitting with the other, the search for the true partner.

What if you never find your true partner? Does this mean you cannot find love? Perhaps you should not spend your whole life searching.

Sometimes you search for something but it is this thing that you should be finding in yourself. Before you seek out love in another, make sure you have found it in yourself. Make sure you are at peace with who you are and know who you are too. Make sure you like who you are so that you can attract someone who is likeable too.

Like attracts like. Be at your most complete before you seek out love. Otherwise you will only be seeking out healing. And being incomplete as you are, you may instead find pain.

It need not take a lifetime to get to a place of healing, a place where you can seek out love. It takes only intention and awareness and a willingness to heal and to know yourself. Begin by caring for yourself.

Give yourself this gift. Love yourself, and then all other loves are possible. We wish you well in your quest for love. It is the essence of the Universe and the most complete expression of God here on earth. Open your heart to love and love will find its way to you.

And we will help you to find it.

81881280R00201

Made in the USA
Middletown, DE
29 July 2018